MYTHATYPES

Signatures and Signs of African/ Diaspora and Black Goddesses

Alexis Brooks DeVita

Foreword by Ralph J. Hexter

Contributions in Afro-American and African Studies, Number 198

GREENWOOD PRESS
Westport, Connecticut • London

Library of Congress Cataloging-in-Publication Data

Brooks De Vita, Alexis.
  Mythatypes : signatures and signs of African/diaspora and Black goddesses / Alexis Brooks De Vita ; foreword by Ralph J. Hexter.
     p.   cm.—(Contributions in Afro-American and African studies, ISSN 0069–9624 ; no. 198)
  Includes bibliographical references and index.
  ISBN 0–313–31068–8 (alk. paper)
  1. African literature—Women authors—History and criticism.   2. Black literature—Women authors—History and criticism.   3. Myth in literature.   4. Women in literature.   5. Africa—In literature.   I. Title.   II. Series.
PL8010.B76   2000
809'.89287'096—dc21   99–056463

British Library Cataloguing in Publication Data is available.

Library of Congress Catalog Card Number: 99–056463
ISBN: 0–313–31068–8
ISSN: 0069–9624

First published in 2000

Greenwood Press, 88 Post Road West, Westport, CT 06881
An imprint of Greenwood Publishing Group, Inc.
www.greenwood.com

Printed in the United States of America

The paper used in this book complies with the Permanent Paper Standard issued by the National Information Standards Organization (Z39.48–1984).

10 9 8 7 6 5 4 3 2 1

With loving gratitude to my father, Wilbur Perry Brooks, for his love and faith in me, to my children, Johnea, Novella, Ceschino, and Joseph Brooks De Vita, and to my husband, Joseph Michael De Vita, for endowing academia with intimate and infinite significance.

Contents

Foreword

Mythatypes: Signatures and Signs of African/Diaspora and Black Goddesses is a work of incantation and invocation, of binding spells and ghostly presences. I use the vocabulary of bewitchment advisedly. This enchantment is not casual delight but discomfiting danger. Brooks De Vita summons a pantheon of African deities, goddesses predominantly, to illuminate a broad range of women's texts, both African American and Continental African, the latter in several languages. Wielding her potent concept of the "mythatype," she uncovers deep structures within these fictions and gives voice to the inner sympathies that exist between works written at times hundreds of years and thousands of miles apart. While some of the links recede into a distant ancestral past, Brooks De Vita's own position is self-consciously present and political. She fearlessly takes on current theoretical shibboleths and sacred cows, refusing to call a power imbalance that is nowhere near being righted "post colonial," choosing instead the more activist "decolonialist." For all its theoretical and scholarly underpinnings, *Mythatypes: Signatures and Signs of African/Diaspora and Black Goddesses* is more than theory or scholarship. Brooks De Vita herself "cuts the border" between analysis—with a very sharp knife—and mythopoiesis. Like the Sibyl, she makes of her interleaved texts oracles and words of power.

Ralph J. Hexter
Professor of Classics and Comparative Literature
Dean of Arts and Humanities
University of California at Berkeley

Acknowledgments

Thanks to the Ford Foundation of the National Research Council and its warm-hearted administrative staff for the Predoctoral Fellowship Grant and all attendant acts of support and encouragement. Thanks to Dr. Ralph J. Hexter, dean of Humanities and Professor of Comparative Literature and Classics at the University of California at Berkeley, Dr. Christopher Braider, chair of the Department of French and Italian at the University of Colorado at Boulder, and Dr. Michael duPlessis, director of Graduate Studies and assistant professor of Comparative Literature and Humanities at the University of Colorado at Boulder, for their selfless support of my studies, goals, and independent undertakings. Thanks to the Graduate School of the University of Colorado at Boulder for graduate fellowships that made it possible to conduct extensive comparative research which would have been, otherwise, impossible. Very sincere thanks to former President John Buechner for his unflinching faith in the worth of my studies at the University of Colorado at Boulder. Heartfelt thanks, much too deep for adequate expression, to Dr. Karla F. C. Holloway, dean of Humanities and William R. Kenan Professor of English at Duke University, Dr. Maude Southwell Wahlman, director of World Studies and Dale and Dorothy Thompson Professor of Art at the University of Missouri at Kansas City, and Dr. Sheila Walker, chair of the Department of African and Afro-American Studies and professor of Anthropology at the University of Texas at Austin, for their interest in and sometimes sacrificial support of an analytical project of this scope. Blessings upon Myriam Warner-Vieyra, Dr. Holloway, and Cynthia Banks-Glover for their receptivity to me and to Dr. Holloway and Myriam Warner-Vieyra for their patient and generous reception of my analyses of their works, an encouragement which made the present volume possible. Finally, sincerest thanks to my editor, Dr. James T. Sabin, director of Academic Research and Development at Greenwood Publishing Group, Inc., for his unfailingly encouraging faith in the worth of this book.

1

Introduction: Reading African/ Diaspora Women's Mythatypes

> Verily the faces of these are as the pupil of the eye; although the pupil is created black, yet it is the source of light.
> — 'Abdu'l-Baha'
> *Lights of Guidance: A Baha'i Reference File*

> Sometimes I feel like a motherless child, a long way from home.
> — Traditional Spiritual Song

The following work is an analytical survey of Pan-African women's literatures written predominantly in English, French, and Italian, including poetry and essay excerpts in Spanish. The goal of these analyses is the exploration of historical, legendary, and mythical culturally relevant female figures as they appear in, and interact with, the protagonists and creators of Pan-African women's literatures. The inclusive term "literatures" is intended to diffuse the importance of genre identity in these creative writings, which include works of fiction, poetry, essays, and autobiographies.

This study is based on the seminal work *Moorings and Metaphors: Figures of Culture and Gender in Black Women's Literatures* by Karla F. C. Holloway, in which is established the interpretive validity and approach for applying mythatypical analytical models to writings by women of African descent in the United States and West Africa. Holloway argues on behalf of the interpretive relevance of African-descent women's community antecedents, specifically ancestresses, historical figures, and goddesses. For ease of reference, rather than repeatedly attempting to differentiate or identify ancestresses-becoming-historical-figures-

becoming-legends-becoming-deities, I have termed these shifting female
identity models "mythatypes." This term is meant to clarify an ancestress's or goddess's fluid passage from life to death to spiritual interaction with living communities, which is often present in womanist literatures and philosophies. A second fundamental theoretical work that
has inspired and guided my own is Nobel Prize Winner Wole Soyinka's
Myth, Literature, and the African World. In this work, Soyinka explains the
complex Yoruba theology of "epiphanous deities" that European colonialist ambition unwittingly spread worldwide and which has become an
influential basis of thought and literature not only in the African Diaspora (see Booker Prize Winner Ben Okri's *The Famished Road*), but on the
Continent as well (in such works as Ayi Kwei Armah's *Two Thousand
Seasons*). The entirety of my work is also based on Henry Louis Gates
Jr.'s position statement as he prepares his arguments for *The Signifying
Monkey*, analyzing the interwoven patterns of language, institution,
metaphysics, and form which have emerged as a new and truly unique
Pan-African culture. Beyond the need for culture-specific, literary analytical tools is my further agreement with Holloway's convincing eluci-
dation of the historical understanding and analytical considerations—no,
demands—that gender poses. In the following essays, the Pan-African
applicability of woman-centered critical tools, which Holloway's *Moorings and Metaphors* defines and establishes, is demonstrated.

The goal of this work is to analyze some of the most frequently recurrent symbols in the creative writing of women in the African Diaspora and on the Continent. In this work, to analyze means to isolate,
compare, and attempt to decipher or read the possible meanings of patterns. The purpose of such analysis is twofold: it may contribute to the
growing sphere of alternative and ever broader readings of these
women's literatures, and it may enhance and add to the profundity of
interpretations of the literatures of Pan-African men and of women and
men of European descent.

The analytical approach used in this work is best termed womanist.
The term "womanist" most safely avoids risking misleading interpretations of the term "black feminist." The most obvious misinterpretation
of my own analytical framework that I wish to avoid concerns my position on the traditional Euro-American feminist stance, which views sexist persecution as predominant in severity, the most fundamental of all
forms of oppression, and the one needing the most urgent attention
among the world's histories of inhumane traditions and practices.

It is not my position that sexist oppression outweighs or has ever
needed more urgent rectification than do the oppressive results of racist
and colonialist practices. Therefore, I wish to avoid the term "feminist"

for this work to avoid a misreading of my analytical findings or a misapprehension of my analytical position.

That analytical position is best summarized in Rosalyn Terborg-Penn's "Discrimination in the Woman's Movement, 1830-1920" in the anthology *The Black Woman Cross-Culturally*:

The black feminist movement in the United States during the mid-1970s is a continuation of a trend that began over 150 years ago.   Institutionalized discrimination against black women by white women has traditionally led to the development of racially separate groups that address themselves to race-determined problems as well as to the common plight of women in America.   At the same time, Afro-American women, motivated by [a] sense of racial solidarity and a special identity arising out of the uniqueness of the black experience, have tended to identify in their own way with the larger social movements in American society.[1]

Terborg-Penn does not identify her views as womanist but as black feminist. I take the liberty of agreeing with and quoting Terborg-Penn's black feminist stance while choosing to identify such views with Alice Walker's definition of "womanist," which is the following:

Usually referring to outrageous, audacious, courageous or *willful* behavior. Wanting to know more and in greater depth than is considered "good" for one. . . . Responsible. In charge. *Serious*. . . . A woman who loves other women, sexually and/or nonsexually. Committed to survival and wholeness of entire people, male *and* female. Traditionally universalist. . . . Traditionally capable.[2]

Walker further elucidates the qualities she apprehends in the writings of some African American women, qualities I take to be motive and dynamic among women writers both on the Continent and in the African Diaspora:

Creative, moving, thoughtful, and evolving human beings, not to mention human beings who have the added possibilities that come from being black women.[3]

Above, Walker delineates qualities that she may assume to be operative in most professional creative writers. Additionally, she suggests that a person's ethnicity, race, cultural experience, and gender may contribute unique perceptions that in turn lend distinctive traits to that person's creative writing.

The theory that the writings of women of African descent may have specific qualities generated by cultural and gendered experiences is not unique to Walker. In her essay, "Words Whipped Over Voids: A Context for Black Women's Rebellious Voices in the Novel of the African Diaspora," Abena Busia rejects the doubly negative description of African Diaspora women writers as being neither of European descent nor male gender. Instead, Busia doubly affirms these women writers as both black and female, presenting these combined positives as the generating force of transformational narratives.

In *Moorings and Metaphors*, Holloway posits that there is "a textual place where language and voice are reconstructed by black women writers as categories of cultural and gendered essence," going on to explain that the writings of these women have "inversive, recursive and sometimes even subversive structures that . . . give it a dimension only accessible when its cultural context is acknowledged."[4]   Holloway further argues that "it is through the ancient spirituality of this literature that the unity of soul and gender" is finally "recovered and celebrated" through the "metaphor of the goddess/ancestor."[5] It is through identification of a protagonist with a perceived ancestor and in the conflation of the deceased ancestor with spiritual forces or female deities that the work transcends a narrow or individualistic space and enters a realm that Holloway terms "spiritual." The interactive relations among protagonist, ancestor, and deity, Holloway concludes, animate African American and West African women's literatures concurrently on three levels of time, experience, and existence: the individual (which may or may not be contemporary), the historical, and the mythical. These three concurrent levels of story, she argues, give the writings of African-descent women an evocative, magical, or surrealistic quality. As Michelle Cliff has her heroine explain, "'For some, this is fantasy; for others, history.'"[6]

Whether or not the symbol systems in Pan-African women's works may ever be exhaustively excavated in an academically accepted archaeology of ancient African religious systems and their predominant female figures is questionable and possibly immaterial to early efforts at mythatypical literary analysis. Holloway convincingly postulates that "recovery [of lost cultural antecedents] means an act of spiritual memory." She argues that literary criticism must concern itself with "the elements of myth—metaphor, spirituality, and memory—as they appear in the systems of literature" rather than in "individual myths of West Africa."[7]

Holloway ends this argument by noting that "mythologies are the reconstructions of memory," recovering a historical voice that is "at once sensual, visceral, and real" and in whose reconstruction remembrance is "a restoration of fluidity, translucence, and movement."[8]

In agreement with these arguments, I have found that it is most productive to isolate recurrent symbols and analyze them in context for their

possible mythical relevance. I call both these symbols and the historically distanced female deities to which they may refer "mythatypes."
The construction of the term "mythatypes" will be further explained below. At this point, it is necessary to explain that its use here is intended
to obviate the loss of my overall argument because of shifting, blended,
nuanced, or obliterated cultural and theological details. For example,
even the fact that many religious similarities were shared between dis-
crete indigenous ethnic groups on the continent of Africa and, eventually, among its forced emigrants in the Diaspora is a most reasonable
evolutionary hypothesis, and yet some literary critics may see this as de-
batable. On this point, because I am in complete agreement with Gates'
carefully worded opening arguments to *The Signifying Monkey*, I quote
him at length:

Common sense, in retrospect, argues that these retained elements of culture
should have survived, that their complete annihilation would have been far more
remarkable than their preservation. . . . There can be little doubt that certain fundamental terms for order that the black enslaved brought with them from Africa
and maintained through the mnemonic devices peculiar to oral literature continued to function both as meaningful units of New World belief systems and as
traces of their origins. We lack written documents to answer the historical questions of how this occurred, questions about the means of transmission, translation, and recuperation of the ensuing difference. Nevertheless, this topos functions as a sign of the disrupted wholeness of an African system of meaning and
belief that black slaves recreated from memory, preserved by oral narration, im-
provised upon in ritual—especially in the rituals of the repeated oral narrative—
and willed to their own subsequent generations, as hermetically sealed and en-
coded charts of cultural descent.[9]

The consistent quality of metaphorical presence and their choice of
unique mythatypical tools isolates, defines, and distinguishes Diaspora
and Continental African women's literatures. Because of its interpretive
centrality, the reading of culturally inherited mythatypes should be considered a basis for analysis of these women's writings.

Attempting to identify ancient goddesses who shared specific traits
and were worshipped by peoples exported to European plantations, and
are still invoked by African and Diaspora women writers is an undenia-
bly challenging task. Traditional African and Diaspora attitudes about
deities seem to have been fluid; as heroines become ancestresses and ancestresses become deities, their defining characteristics and names may
change. As well, deities' powers redefined themselves to answer the
exigencies of their oppressed worshippers; for example, the riverain
goddess Yemoja of *Ifa* gained dominion over the sea and immense protective power as she became Yemayah of Macomble and Santeria. This

fluidity of definition and the as-yet unanswerable questions about suppressed Continental African and Diaspora cultures present a challenge to the bookbound academic in a procolonialist university environment. My goals in this work are to gesture toward, to indicate, and to suggest as convincingly as I may. Beyond the problems of the cross-cultural translation of relevancy, and the issue of referring to lost, demonized, or renamed deities in the interpretive language of a culture whose deities are traceable in writing, is the problem of unexcavated African religious influences. For instance, the apparently vanished culture of ancient Meroe is preserved in hieroglyphics that historically receive little or no funding for their study and interpretation.[10] These problems of cultural suppression and erasure make the pinpointing of goddesses' names and traits across dispersed cultures a nebulous pursuit. I acknowledge my own limited facility in this absorbing pursuit of African deities. Perhaps a procolonialist literary education such as mine leaves a critical reader insufficiently prepared for the analysis of Diaspora and Continental African mythatypes; I have attempted to support my thesis with research developed in other disciplines, such as comparative theology, anthropology, archaeology, art history, and sociology. It is to be hoped that other analysts who wish to depart from procolonialist theories may benefit from these insights, painstakingly gained during what has been for me a challenging process of critical study and substantiation.

Despite these difficulties in cross-cultural scholarship, the fact that Pan-African women writers regularly invoke certain symbols such as trees, rain, and wind in the metaphorical depiction of their protagonists' dilemmas and decisions becomes abundantly clear as one reads these women's writings from a variety of cultures and in multiple languages. It is, therefore, this detailed and yet floating referential aspect of mythatypical analysis that I wish to emphasize, relying upon the premise that myth is both "traditional story" and "fictitious story," and that type may mean "a pattern."[11] With these definitions in mind, the term "mythatype" should serve as a signifying reminder that the following study traces patterns of Diaspora and African women's traditionally inherited or legendary figures in dynamic interface with their fictitious or fictionalized literary heroines. Mythatypical analysis as a working description is also intended to avoid conflation with universalist Jungian arguments about the "primitive" mind[12] and the assumed positive or negative cross-cultural value of multiculturally held symbols, which are implied in the use of the term "archetype." Further, "mythatype" is meant to avoid implication or entanglement in psycho/socio/theological arguments about the comparative merits of faith, pluritheism, animism,[13] monotheism, and atheism. My only aim in this work is to contribute to the development of culturally relevant literary analyses of African and Diaspora women's literatures, not to argue relative theological positions. "Mythatype" should serve as a constant delineator of the limits and aspirations of that aim.

A love of literature, exploration, and discovery generated this study. It is rewarding to discover mythatypes that appear to exhibit traits that deepen, clarify, or offer alternative interpretations to any particular story. Therefore, when linkage between elements, acts, arguments, and outcome seems to indicate the sympathetic intervention of an ancestress or goddess, I have developed the analysis to explore the legendary figure's embracing of the heroine and the heroine's community. The added dimension of reading a goddess's influence or intervention in a protagonist's story often rescues the heroine, and her author, from possibly dismissive readings of apparent frustration and defeat by delineating the heroine's successful completion of a quest that took place in a less tangible — but no less real and dynamic — realm.

A third necessary working definition for these analyses is that of the term "decolonialist." Chinweizu, Onwuchekwa Jemie, and Ihechukwu Madubuike have well described the decolonialist literary aim as an awareness that

To insist on judging African literature by European criteria, or by criteria allegedly universal which, on closer scrutiny turn out to be European, is indeed to define African literature as an appendage of European literature and to deny its separateness and autonomy.[14]

Further, the decolonialist analyst must privilege "continuities" with "pre-colonialist culture," welcome "vitalizing contributions from other cultures," and synthesize the two by the use of "inventive genius," thereby evolving a culturally relevant system of criticism that "should expand and renew the tradition . . . rather than leave it unchanged and in moribund stasis."[15]

Use of the term "decolonialist" in defining the analytical basis for the following work is not intended to reflect sympathy or interchangeability with postcolonialist theories. First, postcolonialist theorists retain an analytical focus upon the values, tools, and central self-positioning of procolonialist cultures. Postcolonialist theory and approach do not necessarily negate or frustrate Eurocentricity in analysis. For example, in *Culture and Imperialism*, Edward Said pictures people of colonized world cultures "voyaging in" to the "metropolitan heartland" and analyzing previously inviolable colonizers' spaces "now invaded and re-examined critically by a dissenting native [sic] . . . using the techniques, discourse, [and] weapons of scholarship and criticism once reserved exclusively for the European."[16] Decolonialist theory, on the other hand, cautions that the colonized subject's appropriation of the colonizers' tools in postcolonialist essays risks repeatedly reinscribing the silencing and erasure of people low in various sexist, racist, and classist hegemonic hierarchies. For example, in the collection of essays on the Hill/Thomas sexual harassment hearings entitled *Race-ing Justice/Engender-ing Power*, postcolonialist theorist Homi K. Bhabha employs Freudian totem and taboo analysis of Clarence Thomas' interaction with the men on Capitol Hill to effectively discount Anita Hill's agency in bringing about those hearings in the first place. But Audre Lorde has already warned that "the master's tools will never dismantle the master's house."[17]

Mythatypical analysis attempts to turn again toward a culturally inherited (though as the result of the cultural imperialism that made the African holocaust possible, occluded) basis of analytical perspective. This reinscription of African deities as the basis of literary analysis was convincingly introduced by Soyinka, the Yoruba Nobel laureate. The obvious presence of deities or their story patterns is maintained in Continental African literature, which is not always accepted in a procolonialist literary canon. I am referring to the durability and popularity (on the Continent) of such works as Thomas Mofolo's *Chaka*, Fagunwa's *Forest of a Thousand Daemons*, Amos Tutuola's *Palm Wine Drinkard*, and, consummately bridging Pan-African traditions and procolonialist literary vehicles, Chinua Achebe's *Arrow of God*.

Secondly, postcolonialist theory inadvertently signals the end of an era that has merely passed to a secondary—and less transitory—stage, from occupation to economic stranglehold; "post" remains misleadingly synonymous with "after."[18] "Post" as a descriptor compromises and confuses *de*colonialist vision and aims. It is not my premise that African-descent women are writing in a world in which colonialism is a phenomenon of the past. Rather, many Pan-African womanists and feminists argue that colonialism's economic and sociological legacies are a worldwide imperialist force with which most Pan-African women must contend. Such contention must of necessity remain an ever present component of the interpretive approaches used in analyzing these women's literatures. Filomina Chioma Steady has written that "liberation from colonialism and racism has been an equally important dimension of African feminism on the continent, as well as in the diaspora."[19] Though Steady is thoughtful and well advised in her use of the term "African feminism" to describe what she further calls "humanistic" feminism, I remain wary of historically racist, specialized, or exclusive appropriations of the term "feminism" and am concerned that African and Diaspora or black women's movements may have a human rights history that is ignored.[20] In pairing the terms "womanist" and "decolonialist" as descriptive of what may clearly be seen as a single operative critical philosophy, I am risking redundance in an effort to obviate such confusion and rectify potential ignorance.

Further, where Holloway's analyses move toward language in her demonstration that Pan-African women have tended to "speak out" rather than produce writings that "act out" (an attribute more typical of African American men's literature, according to Holloway), Steady emphasizes instead a broad range of Pan-African women's operative concerns and goals:

Human totality, parallel autonomy, cooperation, self-reliance, adaptation, survival, and liberation have developed as important aspects of African feminism. These are important concepts in developing a framework for the study of women in Africa and in the diaspora. [21]

This is not to suggest that literatures written by Pan-African men have no traits in common with those of women who share those cultures. Indeed, in his sharply defined analysis of Yoruba theology and cosmogony, *Myth, Literature and the African World*, Soyinka describes the interactive universe as "a proverb of human continuity which is not unidirectional," but in which the "paradigm of this experience of dissolution and re-integration . . . in the ritual of archetypes" continues as an "existing consciousness of cosmic entanglement in the community," demanding "an intelligent communication of what is, indeed, pure essence."[22] The cosmos of Pan-African men and women seems the same; Holloway agrees, stating that "the literate owes its ideology to the mythic" in a scheme where "events that link memories . . . also connect history to the idea of ancestry."[23]

Given the cosmic scope of Pan-African men's and women's writings, then, how do their literatures differ? In *Black Womanist Ethics*, Katie G. Cannon posits that "male writers tend to focus . . . on the confrontation between the white and Black worlds."[24] Trudier Harris develops this argument by adding that "economic and social restrictions on black males are centered upon the actual bodies of the characters," asserting that "male writers who perpetuate this tradition of ritualized violence are more directly tied to realistic fiction."[25] Some theorists, such as Phillipa Kafka, seem to dispute the tone, if not the substance, of Harris's argument. Kafka argues that "flogging a man's body" (a statement that begins with the assumption that whippings and lynchings have been the predominant forms of physical degradation suffered by men of the African Diaspora), "and gaining access to and entry into a woman's body" (based on the assumption that rape and its resultant abortions, infanticides, and pain-filled births of hated or feared offspring have been the most recurrent physical degradations of African-descent women), are "tantamount humiliations."[26] Hazel Carby qualifies Cannon's argument that race relations have been almost exclusively treated by African American men in literature when she finds that Pauline Hopkins "was a black intellectual" who thought her writing should "stimulate political resistance."   Carby points out that Hopkins used her "easily accessible narrative forms to question the morality of, rather than restore faith in, the social formation."[27] Cannon goes on to argue that "Black women writers concentrate more intensely on the Black community and [its] human relationships,"[28] a position that Kafka restates emphatically by wondering about some male writers' "glaring omissions . . . their silences, their seeming blindness to family and domestic matters."[29] Finally, while Barbara Christian asserts that "people of color have always theorized," she credits women in particular as having "continuously speculated about the nature of life through pithy language that unmasked the power relations of their world,"[30] what Holloway calls the female trait of speaking out rather than acting out.[31]

Holloway credits the gender specificity of this mode of writing with women's inheritance of ancestresses and goddesses, female protagonists of the historical and mythatypical roles that have descended to modern and contemporary writers, what she refers to as the "metaphorical presence of ancestors and feminine deities."[32] Cannon views "Black female protagonists" as being "forced to see through shallowness, hypocrisy and phoniness in their continual struggle for survival."[33] The grasp of women's tales of autonomy wrested from penury and helplessness, survival in the face of defeat, and adaptation in environments that are assaultive or destructive is made clearer through the interpretation of mythatypical symbols that are peculiar to these women's writings. Cannon argues that

The triple jeopardy of Black women's lives and the lack of ability to control the ongoing dynamics of oppression mean that the mystical ground of dignity and the need for love and community in struggle really must be made explicit.[34]

This is my own aim and hope. My goal is to enable readers of Pan-African women's literatures to see how these women "who celebrate Black life" have "transform[ed] the tradition" in the most ideal application of decolonialist principles "to make a reaffirmation of their spiritual roots."[35] Perhaps mythatypical analysis is ideally suited for decolonialist criticism in that it provides perspective distance from interpretations of history. Overlaying a mythatypical prototype onto an historical event or lifestyle frees the critical reader from both responsibility for, and guilt caused by, ethical evaluation because the text is distanced to the point that it reflects an autonomous and ongoing story of the individual's relationship to her society and its cosmic scheme.

For example, mythatypical distance allows the analyst to posit that the lynch/burning sacrifice and sexual usage roles of enslaved Africans and their descendents by colonizers in a so-called New World reflected the European colonizers' faith in the fertilizing effects of their pre-Christian, pagan rites.

Acknowledging that "the lynching of Southern Negroes . . . routinely" involved "the emasculation of males and the burning of both sexes,"[36] Harris summarizes the findings of anthropologist James George Frazer on sacrificial ritual in undeveloped societies (such as the procolonialist Euro-American):

Human scapegoats, who took upon themselves the sins of the group and the disfavor of the gods, were sacrificed only when the survival of the society was in question. . . . Death was deemed necessary for the health or re-fertilization of the world and for the lives of the people.[37]

Harris's recounting of the castration and trophy-taking American rituals harks back to ancient Mediterranean rites in which it is "castration or dismembering that is the harvest . . . so that new life can spring forth."[38] Harris's analysis emphasizes the differences between the English colonists' rituals of human sacrifice and those of the English colonizers' claimed and reconstructed prototypes, the ancient Greeks. However, Harris's argument about a difference in attitude is weakened by her assumption that "the alleged threats of survival to the society were not grounded in the immediate context of life and death" and her position that "the expulsion of evil for American whites had none of the cosmic consequences"[39] ascertained in European antiquity. Surely, this point is arguable. For fear of uprising by the "New World's" original inhabitants or divine wrath for the genocide, kidnapping, and inhumanity that assured America's prosperity were surely adequate causes for the dominant society's desire to ensure its fertility and scapegoat its evils. In the "early multinational corporation . . . called America," Paula Giddings explains that "profit had to be wrung out of an erotic wilderness." Here, it was inexorable that enslaved Africans would come to represent both "the means of wealth and the 'dark,' sensuous side of the English soul." Particularly, "Black women . . . would be impaled on the cutting edges" of the resulting "race/sex dialectic" that would shape "the law of the land,"[40] brilliantly harmonizing European America's apparently contradictory drives of lust, "racism, sexism, greed, and piety."[41]

In the colonized world where African-descent women, assigned the first two of what Giddings summarizes as Plato's three female categories of "whore, mistress, and wife,"[42] must write, mythatypical analysis offers a critical alternative system of literary interpretation. By isolating the ways in which, as Jacqueline Bobo writes, "the original voice of black women" recounts "the specific details of black women's history," these women's writings can be shown to "demonstrate the ways in which black women cope, survive, and most important, triumph despite centuries of abuse."[43]

In the following analyses, it is my goal to isolate and define possible culturally relevant mythical types reflected in cited literary works. Perhaps it is better to avoid interpreting these mythatypes' arguable moral significance in contemporary colonized societies to highlight the self-affirmative outcomes such mythatypes indicate for these heroines, which may not be immediately clear to the reader.

The next chapter, "Trees as Spiritual Mothers," analyzes the role of trees in the metaphorical calibration of a woman's development in such works as Toni Morrison's *Beloved*, Harriet Jacobs' *Incidents in the Life of a Slave Girl*, and Ken Bugul's *Le baobab fou (The Crazy Baobab)* as analyzed by Irene D'Almeida in *Francophone African Women Writers*.

The third chapter, "She Who Nurtures and Devours," focuses on "la diablesse" (the devil woman) and the Hathor/Sekhmet dichotomy evident in Jamaica Kincaid's *The Autobiography of My Mother*, Shirin Ramzanali Fazel's *Lontano da Mogadiscio (Far from Mogadishu)*, and Mariama Ba's *Une si longue lettre (So Long a Letter)*. All describe a powerful mythatypical figure who seems to signal the advent of both self-actualization and doom.

The fourth chapter, "Child Sacrifice and Salvation," analyzes the giving of life to assure survival in Bessie Head's "Looking for a Rain God" in her collection of short stories entitled *The Collector of Treasures and other Botswana Village Tales* and devorah major's *An Open Weave*. The introduction of this loving, lethal figure leads to an important aspect of her relationship with heroines who are "black" and colonized.

In the fifth chapter, "Rape and Rage," Gayatri Chakhravorty Spivak's translation of Bengali Mahasweta Devi's "Draupadi" in Spivak's collection of essays entitled *In Other Worlds: Essays in Cultural Politics* supports Kathleen Cleaver's categories of "colonized and colonizer" while retaining the equation of "colonized" and "black." This work joins Cliff's *Free Enterprise* and Nafissatou Niang Diallo's *Le fort maudit (The Cursed Fort)* in analysis for evidence of black goddesses' revolutionary consequences, specifically when a woman suffers rape on behalf of her colonized people.

The sixth chapter, "Air and Fire, Bringing Rain," analyzes these natural elements as objects of Oya's divine intervention and empathy. The chapter examines their roles in Zora Neale Hurston's *Their Eyes Were Watching God* and Myriam Warner-Vieyra's *Juletane*.

The seventh chapter, "Cruelty, Castration, and Claiming," analyzes Gayl Jones' *Eva's Man*, Bessie Head's "The Collector of Treasures," the title story in Head's book of the same name, and Myriam Warner-Vieyra's "Sidonie" in her collection of short stories entitled *Femmes echouees (Beached Women)*, exploring Pan-African women's literary phenomenon of castrating abusive, abandoning lovers and husbands.

The eighth chapter, "The River and the Wall," examines the self-destructive frustration of Pan-African heroines who lack spiritually, psycho-emotionally satisfying role models and social aspirations. The chapter analyzes Tsitsi Dangarembga's *Nervous Conditions* and Diane McKinney-Whetstone's *Tumbling*.

Finally, the concluding chapter, "This Moment of Epiphany," explores the loss of self that is exemplified in Eufemia Mallegui's "*Dimmi chi sono*" ("Tell Me Who I Am") and Anty Grah's "*Cronaca di un amicizia*" ("Chronicle of a Friendhsip"), both in the short story collection *Mosaici d'inchiostro (Ink Mosaics)*. This chapter looks at women of African descent in negating or masking environments. The alembic community-creating symbols of Marlene Nourbese Philip's "Burn Sugar" in the collection of writings entitled *Daughters of Africa: An International Anthology of Words and Writings by Women of African Descent from the Ancient Egyptian to the Present* concludes these essays, questioning the implications that aggressive self-affirmation by African-descent women holds for readers in a colonized world.

I have read each of the analyzed works in the original language, except Devi's "Draupadi" and Bugul's *Le baobab fou*. Spivak and D'Almeida's interpretative criticisms of these works figure considerably, therefore, in my analyses.

Translation remains a challenging point of Pan-African literary analysis. Translators who wish to capture the sense of an original text exercise great interpretive license. They function as critics in the act of translation. Where I have translated for the reader, I have translated less creatively and more literally, hoping that this sacrifice of poetic facility assures the reader of a chance to judge the work independently of my analysis. Where translation has been at all necessary (mine or anyone else's), it has seemed best to avoid extremely close readings of the *words* of the text in order to focus on the text's *images*. This analytical preference presupposes that the translations I have offered the reader have left the original images intact.

To clarify the methodology of mythatypical analysis, I have chosen to analyze a broad spectrum of works. It is my hope to demonstrate the Pan-African applicability of the reading of mythatypes. That is, I have chosen to analyze one mythatype per chapter as it operates in multiple texts, for the most part, rather than analyze all of the mythatypes in multilayered reciprocity in only a few exhaustively studied texts. Mythatypes usually interact in a text. Several mythatypes will appear together in one text, interactively building a symbolic storyline that underscores and enhances the literal and obvious story. For example, a cursory reading of *Beloved* leads the reader to suspect that the mythatypes of the sacrificial child and the goddess triplicity are at work in this text; and yet, I have chosen to analyze *Beloved*'s use of the maternal tree mythatype, one the reader might not have thought to search out and analyze. It is my hope that the analytical reader will become invested enough in her or his understanding of mythatypical analysis to supply the additional interacting analyses that would enhance perception of a single text. For example, a thorough analysis of the operative mythatypes in *Beloved* should include a dynamic apprehension of the multiple female triplicities, three child sacrifices, nurturing/devouring mothers, and mother-as-tree symbols that thrust themselves upon the reader. I have chosen, for demonstrative brevity and impact, to analyze texts for the least obvious but most dramatically operative mythatypes to dramatize for the reader the epiphany that the mythatypical method of analysis allows. I have found the illumination of elusive goddess traits striking, and I hope to share this experience of sudden, clear insight with the reader.

This is not to suggest that only the following vividly imaged, emotionally striking, rather surrealistic works offer themselves to the search for African and Diaspora deities and ancestresses in Pan-African women's literatures. I have found that even the most socio/historic, realistic autobiographies can be read for goddess intervention or signatures at key transition points in the heroines' lives. For example, from the earliest African American woman's published autobiography, Harriet Wilson's *Our Nig; or, Sketches from the Life of a Free Black*, to one of the most recent, "Ruthie Bolton's" *gal*, one remains struck by the fact that goddess symbols periodically interrupt the narratives to signal that some force greater than these heroines has suddenly shaped or defined their experiences of life.

Naming in these works is significant. Wilson names her heroine and entitles her life story after the derogatory nickname her pseudo enslavers gave her, one hundred years before Ruthie Bolton (a pseudonym) was born. And still, patterns of sociological neglect intact, *gal* is a new African American woman's autobiography, aching with the search for love

and the desire to be wanted, titled with the derogatory epithet her abusers used to denigrate her standing as a member of the household.

Naming oneself and being named by others is a crucial act of claiming self and community, as has been humorously depicted in *The Salt
Eaters*. In this novel, Toni Cade Bambara describes the naming struggle
in a women's dance class:

She'd started out with "bitches," then "witches," which was just too much, too
much. Sometimes to puff them up on rainy days she'd say "goddesses" or
"queens." . . . The women had finally sat Miss Geula down and exercised their
democratic rights. There were eight votes for "ladies" and six for "goddesses."
Five held out for "sisters" and were lobbying all the time.[44]

What Miss Geula is offering her students is a positive reclaiming of
all their female aspects, through naming as well as dance. "Bitches"
gives permission to embrace the fullness of the women's emotional and
sexual make up, reclaiming themselves through a constant reminder of
self-affirmation. Perhaps one need think of the negative uses and associations of the word. Bitches are spiteful, angry, lacking in docility and
demonstrations of willing domestication. They are also well known for
sexual allure and promiscuity. Being named "bitches" by their dance
instructor is meant to force the women to call their most assertive, sexual, powerful emotions to mind and draw upon them as a source for release of inhibitions and creative abandon. Miss Geula even wants the
women to "breathe like you mean it."

But beyond all this, "witches" are suspected of exercising not only
bitchy traits but the additional one of (perhaps unwitting) magical
power. Conrad E. Mauge explains the Yoruba conception of witches:

The power is often referred to as "Mother's Wrath." . . . She has an inherent malevolent psychic power. . . . The witch may not even be conscious of her action
since she exercises her power automatically.[45]

When Miss Geula names her students witches, she is offering them a
seizing of their peculiar gendered magical capacity for power and
autonomy on a scale beyond what they may have conceived when they
joined her class.

But a woman has the right and responsibility to self-name. Gates explains as he introduces *Our Nig*:

Harriet E. Wilson allows these racist characters to name her heroine, only to *in-
vert* such racism by employing the name, in inverted commas, as her pseudonym
of authorship . . . its inverted commas underscore the use as an ironic one, one

intended to reverse the power relation implicit in renaming-rituals. . . . Transformed into an object of abuse and scorn by her enemies, the "object," the heroine of *Our Nig*, reverses this relationship by *renaming herself* not Our Nig but "Our Nig," thereby transforming herself into a *subject . . . she* transforms her tormentors into objects.[46]

Miss Geula's students refuse the reclaiming power of "bitches" and "witches," not recognizing many (if not all) of the same traits in the loftier titles of "goddesses" and "queens" and the politically assertive title of "sisters." The teacher concedes less to democracy than to the "democratic" prerogatives of the renaming ritual, agreeing to call the women by the patriarchal approbation of "ladies," which she delivers "with a tincture of iodine." For Miss Geula wants the women to claim the spiritual freedom she offers them; their refusal of her renaming signals their preference to experience and enjoy the sensuous power in themselves without renaming themselves to claim it: "The classes were fun, and Geula was a welcome madness." The women identify the madness as belonging to their teacher but available to them as transient sensation. Far from altering their own identities to embrace the self-assertion Miss Geula offers, the women respond to her fun "madness" by reaffirming their own desire for patriarchal approval when they choose to rename themselves "ladies." They serve as an early contrast to the novel's heroine, Velma, who will make the cataclysmic acceptance of her own magical, sensual, healing power that will draw the novel to its close.

Wilson and Bolton have similar self-naming decisions to make. If Wilson frees herself of object status by seizing her derogatory nickname of "Our Nig," Ruthie Bolton instead embraces object status as a sign of tenuous belonging, recognition, and possibly even distinction if not acceptance. By her autobiography's close, Bolton is still struggling to hold on to the abandoned house and near-sister status in the family of her stepgrandfather and abuser, going so far as to brag that she has preserved, tattered but intact, the mementos of her tortured childhood:

And all those things are precious to me. Especially that blue chair. I don't let nobody sit in it. That's the chair that he [stepgrandfather] threw me in and my head went through the window. . . . I don't want that to be touched. . . . I want it to stay as it was.
    Still there.[47]

If Wilson seized subject status by putting her derogatory nickname in inverted commas, Bolton claims her denigration by spelling her derogatory gendered nickname, "Gal," with a lower case "g" in the book's title, emphasizing that it is to her a common noun, not a proper one. To

Bolton, "gal" is neither a name nor nickname but a description of what she is. In insisting upon this lower case spelling even in the title, Bolton exonerates her stepgrandfather by agreeing that she essentially was, and is, what he and his family considered her to be: a girl less deserving of respect than his daughters with proper and capitalized names, because she is not one of them by blood yet is dependent upon them for survival. Bolton agrees to be a "gal," explaining the life she has lived as a girl child held in contempt by the family that kept her and treasuring the tangible objects that will not let her stop reliving her life's most violent events.

In keeping with the cues of their renaming rituals, Wilson and Bolton also supply the reader with goddess clues as to how to see the turning points in their lives. Bolton explains the advent of her stuttering, which led her to prefer writing, as the trauma suffered when she was beaten for her inability to read well. Shortly before this decisive trauma, Ruthie watches her stepgrandfather beat his favorite daughter for her inability to learn to drive, lessons he had initiated with the gift to his daughter of a pair of cat-eye glasses: "And they were *cat*, now, cat to the max. We called her Cat Woman."[48] The driving lessons fail, however, despite the glasses, and the favorite daughter is badly beaten. Throughout this beating, the daughter speaks up for herself and forces her abuser to see himself through her eyes: "Florence said, 'That's right. Go ahead kill me. Kill me like you killed my mama.'"[49] Bolton, always fearing rejection, is incapable of this kind of forthrightness. When she is beaten into stammering helplessness for her poor reading, she asks for glasses like those she has coveted. She explains that

I told them I couldn't see, but I was lying. I wanted the cat-eye glasses. Somehow, I thought if I had those cat-eye glasses, I would be able to talk right.[50]

Bolton implies that she linked the cat-eye glasses not with a need to see in order to read better, but with the ability to speak. This recalls the incident of watching her aunt speak up as she was beaten, not only on her own behalf but on behalf of the mother/grandmother whose beating death the houseful of girls all witnessed. Florence is beaten but speaks up against her father's vicious injustice. Bolton is beaten and internalizes the criticisms unfairly leveled against her: "They told me that I was a stuttering jackass. A stuttering fool. . . . I was scared to open my mouth."[51]

The Cat Woman recalls both Bast/Pasht, the ancient Egyptian black cat goddess of healing and happiness, as well as Sekhmet, the lioness manifestation of the lifegiver Isis and her benevolent nurturing aspect, Hathor. Sekhmet was given the sun god's eye to see the mortal men who plotted against him. She became so enraged that she went on a bloody rampage of harsh justice, killing not only the plotters but their community.

Bolton clearly could use some harsh justice in her own defense. Yet by the autobiography's close, she is still vindicating her stepfamily's misuse of herself, her children, and her husband, excusing acts of betrayal and abandonment even as she reveals them. She is still a stutterer, unable to speak. Her writing has not freed her fearful tongue. Nor has it freed her from her fruitless pursuit of her stepfamily's acceptance. Bolton closes with the self-limiting hope that someday she may make enough money to buy her stepgrandfather's house, still reeking with the stench of bodily wastes and tragic memories, from the daughter who inherited it.

Wilson, on the other hand, routinely exposes and criticizes her racist oppressors to the reader: "'Saucy, impudent nigger, you! is this the way you answer me?' and taking a large carving knife from the table, she hurled it, in her rage, at the defenceless girl."[52] Wilson even brags about having shoved the daughter of the family that misuses her into a river one day and, with understandable glee, reminds the reader of this incident on the occasion of that daughter's death, joking that

"She got into the river again, Aunt Abby, did n't she; the Jordan is a big one to tumble into, any how.   S'posen she goes to hell, she'll be as black as I am. Would n't mistress be mad to see her a nigger!" and others of a similar stamp.[53]

The river symbolism is significant.   Art historian Robert Farris Thompson explains that

The coolness of the riverain goddesses is problematic. Vengeance, doom, and danger also lurk within the holy depths (ibu) of the rivers. . . . For Yemoja and all the other riverain goddesses . . . are supreme in the arts of mystic retribution and protection against all evil.[54]

Wilson's triumphant celebration of her co-abuser's death, who dies by as her having fallen into a spiritual river in whose depths she will be burned truly black, harks to the balance of cooling and retributive powers feared and called upon among African goddesses of rivers. Thompson philosophizes that "the cool, dark depths of the river may shield mankind from the full blast of the fiery powers of witchcraft harnessed by the river goddesses."[55] It is significant that just as Wilson's heroine despairs of life and wishes to be whipped, at last, to death, her chief abuser's daughter dies instead, and "Our Nig" is granted a time of reprieve: "There was, indeed, a season of quiet grief; it was the lull of the

fiery elements."[56] The river goddesses' penchant for protective vengeance or witchcraft, Thompson explains, "militates against not only total
male dominance but the threat of class formation and drastically unequal
distribution of wealth"[57] and social power. For Thompson adds that a
river goddess's "darker side is ultimately protective of her people."[58]
Ironically, it is the mistress and her daughter who have prevented "Our
Nig" from becoming fully Christianized. Her joyous announcement of
her tormentor's riverain descent into fire signals that her racist exclusion
from Christianity has, in fact, returned her to the protective purview of
her father's inherited African spiritual forces. In fact, Wilson's feisty and
tragic heroine does not crave the acceptance of the family that whips and
overworks her. She only loves those who are kind and help her to survive. Her turning the tables on their misnaming of her is amplified in
her acts of rebellion:

"Stop!" shouted Frado, "strike me, and I'll never work a mite more for you" . . .
Frado walked towards the house, her mistress following with the wood she herself was sent after.[59]

Though her end is tragic, Wilson, unlike Bolton, preserves her human dignity because she makes no excuses for her abusers. Perhaps this
is why her autobiography still serves as eye-opening historical commentary, despite what is described as its "sentimental novel"[60] trap-
pings. Even as she dies, writing, Wilson is emotionally and psychologi-
cally independent enough to expose the fraudulent slavery tales, by
which her husband has made a living, and the racism of Northern aboli-
tionists "who did n't want slaves at the South, nor niggers in their own
houses, North."[61] This independence of spirit, available to women of
African descent through the protection of their riverain goddesses, inspires a traveling European's fearful account of a man snatched by a
river crocodile from his raft and into a river. The man's companions assume that his wife had prayed to Nimm for vengeance, and they continue their journey.[62] Wilson's falling back in loneliness upon her
scorned ethnic heritage adds her voice to a stream of empowering
mythatypical traditions and tales.

Is this empowering reading of three concurrent levels of story, the
personal/historical/mythical, a womanist exercise? Is it necessarily
limited in its application solely to the literatures of Diaspora and Continental African women? I think not. Rather, this critical tool, which is
apparently developing in response to the need for in-depth readings of
the mythapoeic in African-descent women's literatures, transcends ethnic, cultural, and gender boundaries, firstly in a gesture of self-defense.
For as Holloway has noted, when it comes to Diaspora and Continental

African women's writings, "both object and subject are politically enmeshed and victimized by the divisive dialectic about race, class, culture,
and gender,"[63] and both object and subject are forced in the pursuit of
academic survival to forge multi perspective bridges. Or as Hortense
Spillers has said, "There are days when her household cuts the border."[64]
To cut the border is to tend to the affairs that fall between definitional
cracks, to claim and tend to no one's land that, conversely, in a problematic state, becomes everyone's morass. To cut the border is to bridge
points of incommunicability, stasis, and interactive abandonment. It is
to redefine. After asking, "by what finalities of various historico-cultural
situations are we frozen forever in precisely defined portions of culture
content?" Spillers proceeds to interpret VeVe Clark as having answered
that the "New World culture always 'dances' between the stationary
points in absolute abeyance of closure,"[65] a movement similar to the re-
ligionist's ecstatic dance "along the knife-edge" that religious compara-
tist Bahiyyih Nakhjavani describes.[66]

Clark calls for the development of a "marasa" consciousness for the
reading of Diaspora literatures; that is, for the development of a third-
dimensional perception that rises above and describes a meeting point
for apparent polar opposites. "Marasa" means twins, but Clark expands
this definition to draw attention to the importance of the child born after
the twins, meaning the possibilities announced by the birth of twins:
"Marasa denotes movement and change . . . movement beyond the bi-
nary nightmare."[67] This movement is the means by which African and
Diaspora women writers produce a literature that "reconstructs the
schismatic pair," a feat that Clark sees as "a clear challenge to the Western [Hegelian] notion of their polarity," restoring "an oracular and primal text — myth."[68]

Below will follow two mythatypical analyses of European literatures.
This cross-cultural application of mythatypical analysis highlights the
multicultural, border-bridging potential of this system of analysis that
calls for "the interaction of opposites."[69]

This border-bridging of cultural, gendered, and colonialist opposites
takes place in literary worlds where spirit, body, dream, vision, and
waking reality not only interact but constantly call each other to account.
Many Diaspora and Continental African women's writings have been
called "gothic" in tone; this may be because of the transcendent quality
they share with the European and Euro-American Gothic genre. Jung
calls this transcendent grasping at spiritual realities from within the material world "the exclusively vertical perspective of the Gothic Age."[70]
Gothic analyst Devendra P. Varma has explained the Gothic vision as the
search for the numinous. This is the spiritual or metaphysical search for

the regulating, decrypting worlds beyond realism in which the writer

In an ecstasy of communion . . . makes humble obeisance before the great Unknown: fear becomes acceptance, and senseless existence fraught with a dark,
unfathomable, sacred purpose.[71]

Varma is here privileging literary defamiliarization in its Russian
Formalist sense. Such defamiliarization is, above all, what the woman
writer of African descent must accomplish to break through the habitu-
ated emotional and psychological anesthesia of her readers—of any ethnicity, on occasion—in order to communicate the psychosocial horror
and tenuous hopefulness of Diaspora and Continental African women's
experiences and perspectives. The writer must replicate enslavement,
racial viciousness, joblessness, the loss of children, and the conscienceless
sexual assault of women of African descent in such a way that "perception is impeded and the greatest possible effect is produced through the
slowness of perception."[72]   Varma is not, in fact, attempting to analyze
Continental African and Diaspora women's literatures. He is simply
offering a broader dimension of understanding of European Gothics and
their heroines. Yet Varma's description of Gothics provides a perfect
articulation of the defamiliarization that must take place when a writer
seeks to communicate the experiences of the colonized in the worlds and
words of her colonizers:

Uprooted from her proper society with . . . emotional and intellectual pattern
intact, thrust into a barbarous and primitive age, subjected to . . . various men-
aces . . . she serves . . . as a sensitive barometer of emotional reaction to horrors . .
. an impression of the grotesque.[73]

Varma argues that Gothic literature seeks to feel out the nebulous
possibilities beyond the limits of literary realism: "to touch the still center of intersection of the timeless with time."[74] An overwhelming body
of literature by African and Diaspora women also asserts the multiple
intersections of human lives with history and mythatype, less seeking
than illustrating that these points indicate not intersections, but an interface of existence and mutually informed experience. Kimberly Rae Connor concludes that writings by African American women "affirm the
sacrality of being and describe the experience of encountering 'That
Which Is Beyond Understanding But Not Beyond Loving.'"[75] In essence
this is a body of literature that may be read as indicating that the woman
lives with the myth, calls upon it, and interacts with it in her own life,
sometimes to explain her suffering but more often to effect change.
Nagueyalti Warren explains this change in terms of re-creation: "Instead

of embracing that which inhibits us, our task is to reconstruct images until they reflect our presence." Part of the reconstruction needed here is perceptive, that of shifting the gaze to perceive the mythatype beyond and animating the heroine.[76] Holloway explains in *Moorings and Metaphors* that for women writers of African descent, linear progression is a delusion displacing perception of a universe which is actually recursive. This analysis establishes the validity of the story that envelops and develops beyond the world of the physical senses, privileging myth as personal history. Womanist literature, then, does not so much privilege Jung's perception of the "purely vertical perspective" as it asserts what Joy James calls "the nonduality of time and space." James writes that

In traditional African cosmology, as expressed in Kongo philosophy, living thinkers are initiates in a philosophical system in which they channel between the metaphysical and the physical. . . . Philosophers travel full circle to realize metaphysical ideals.[77]

The Pan-African women philosophers that James describes as living thinkers "think and act in service to the community," which is "not bound by physical or temporal limits." In this circular relationship with community including ancestors, historical heroines, goddesses, and future children, James writes that

The women participate in collectively realizing potential and actual, archetypal, African, female, living thinkers. . . . [These archetypes] present not only models for theorizing and organizing but also a conduit. As a passage for reflection and development, archetypes can organize our thoughts and direct or channel our theorizing into transformation or revolutionary praxis.[78]

Holloway explains that "mythology, as an instant of memory . . . is a moment when a metaphysical disturbance substantiates the physical."[79] This reciprocal experience of the numinous community in African and Diaspora women's literatures lends itself as an analytical tool for approaching other literatures, as well. Reading the transcendent in the mundane is the common factor, or border being cut. In an analytical structure paralleling that of Holloway, religious theorist Nakhjavani delineates:

The first reversal is that the reader finds the solid ground of authority and convention swept away. . . . The second reversal confounds our sense of measured time. . . . In a single event we can discover a poignant historic moment, an event that can recur throughout our lives . . . as well as the spiritual archetype.[80]

In order to illustrate the efficacy of mythatypical analysis when applied to spiritual or metaphysical literatures not written by women of African descent, a brief analysis of two European works follows. The mythatypes employed in both the following analyses are ancient Egyptian. The choice of ancient Egyptian mythatypes serves two purposes. First, it queries procolonialist Enlightenment theories about racial superiority based upon a separatist assumption of the development of Christian religious feeling and thought by pointing to a trans-Mediterranean spread of African influence. Second, it allows an early opportunity to introduce my assumption that Egyptian and other Nilotic religions reflected more widespread African animist belief systems, which have been less thoroughly documented in the European and Euro-American academic communities in which many women of African descent pursue college degrees:

The greater number of the gods of Egypt worshipped in dynastic times are of Nilotic origin. . . . The animistic or religious views of the peoples of . . . Lower and Upper Nubia and the Egyptian Sudun [sic] influenced greatly the inhabitants of Upper Egypt and the Delta.[81]

Mythatypical influences of African origin beyond Egypt, in African and Diaspora women's literatures and European and Euro-American literatures must often be discerned by traces of these mythatypes' signs rather than by their signatures. All deities and ancestors from the Continent and in the Diaspora are not as well known to the Europeanized academic as they are to those from Egypt. But Egypt's thoroughly documented Africanist theological base provides an excellent testing point for the general mythatypical theory.

The first European work to be mythatypically analyzed is a section of Angela of Foligno's *Memorial*. Angela of Foligno was a mystic woman who lived in the valley of Umbria, in what is now Italy, from 1248-1309. Angela narrated "with precision and shuddering immediacy" the tale of her conversion and personal relations with Christ to her confessor, Franciscan Brother Arnaldo. Considered the most "excessive and volcanic" of Christian mystical texts, Angela's *Book*, including the *Memorial*, recounts her "passionate love affair with the 'suffering God-man,'"[82] including a passage in which Angela and Christ embrace in the sepulcher. Finding herself in the sepulcher, Angela first kisses Christ's breast and then his fragrant mouth. She places her cheek to his, and he places his hand on her cheek to bring her closer, saying, "'Before I was laid in the sepulcher, I held you this tightly to me.'"[83] Angela concludes this vision by explaining that it left her with an immense and indescribable joy. Regularly, following these ecstasies, Angela found that the intensity of her feeling "generated in her a hunger so unspeakably great that all her members dislocated."[84]

There is a question of precedent. Angela's vision of herself in the tomb with Christ might well be read as blasphemous, compromising as it does all acknowledged doctrine about his unassisted resurrection. However, Angela's account is unflinchingly devoted to Christ and his church's teachings; she clearly intends no sacrilege. On the contrary, she recounts that Christ has assured her that he loves her "so much more than any other woman in the valley of Spoleto" and has found a place to rest in her.[85] Because Angela's mother, husband, and sons stood between her and the life she wished to devote to Christ, she has prayed for and received what she calls the "favor" of their deaths.[86] Though the Christ of her visions assures Angela repeatedly throughout the *Memorial* that she, personally and intimately, is his daughter, temple, delight, and even his chosen spouse, Angela opens the lessons of her suffering to teach whomever may read her story how to be devout, to make the sign of the cross, and to take communion with love and deep feeling. She even uses the visions of anguish (remarkably similar to those recounted by Head in *A Question of Power*), into which she is regularly flung, as lessons in humility and longsuffering:

She found consolation in her awareness that she had been handed over to many demons and they were responsible for the reawakening of these past dead vices as well as the addition of unknown ones. . . . She desired that all her afflictions and ills be doubled. [87]

How is Angela, called devout and chosen, and her adoration of Christ in the tomb to be reconciled with her obvious desire to serve and suffer for his cause, not compromise it?

Angela of Foligno has a mythatypical predecessor who also joined her martyred husband and religious head in his coffin. As the only religion originating on the African continent that has been thoroughly academically documented, the ancient Egyptian worship of Isis and Osiris may serve here to overlay the interaction of Angela and her envisioned Christ.

Murdered by his jealous brother Set, Osiris also lay awaiting resurrection. Explanations of Isis's involvement with Osiris's dismembered remains vary and are not mutually exclusive. Jungian analyst Sylvia Brenton Perera states simply that "Isis fertilizes herself with Osiris's member when he is dead,"[88] a rather abrupt and utilitarian view of what is surely a complex relational act. Fellow Jungian analyst and theorist Clarissa Pinkola Estes further develops the implications of Isis's presence in Osiris's tomb to the point that "Isis works from dusk to dawn each night to piece her brother back together again before morning, else the sun will not rise."[89] Perhaps the most well-rounded coalescing of myth and meaning is offered by feminist theologian Asphodel P. Long:

She [Isis] is able to breathe the breath of life into the nostrils of Osiris' corpse which she has re-assembled to revive him, thus bringing immortality into the practical sphere. . . . Adored as a means of the soul's salvation, Isis is also very much of this earth.[90]

This seems our best set of clues in deciphering the very moving spiritual messages of her station and purpose, which Angela of Foligno intended to convey when she shared this vision. Perhaps the sepulcher scene was meant to impress upon her religious witnesses, as had been impressed upon Angela herself, that studying and following the mystic woman's teachings was, far from an act of sacrilege, a means of Christian salvation available to those less rapt than she. In fact, Angela's *Book* was still being translated and discussed as late as the mid-nineteenth century, long after accusations of heresy and witchcraft had silenced women reporting such visions as hers, in which the mystic's "physicality is explored and embraced . . . freed and transfigured."[91]

The second example of the boundary-breaking potential usage of mythatypical reading will be an abbreviated womanist/decolonialist interpretation of the outcome of John Dryden's *All for Love*, a fictionalized account of the joint suicides of Cleopatra of Egypt and Mark Antony, her lover and would-be conqueror. I would like to emphasize Cleopatra's Macedonian background, though she was the female ruler of Egypt, as one indicator of the route ancient Egyptian mythical influence took in its cross-cultural spread. What is crucial in this reading, however, is the intact interpretation, as far as may be done, of the relevance of Cleopatra and Antony's deaths *to Egypt*.

Popular Restoration theory continues to argue that Antony's death, in particular, be read exclusively as one of three types of unfortunate conclusions: tragedy, crisis of confidence, or the portrayal of ideological vacuum.[92] These exclusive categorical options are perfectly satisfactory for the Anglocentric theorist once the procolonialist assumptions motivating these limited choices have been acknowledged.

However, as women and men of colonized cultures continue to pursue graduate degrees in Western universities, it seems an act of academic censure and constriction to force them to adopt procolonialist views that may be anathema to their own ideologies. As an example of alternative thinking, the following abridged reading of *All for Love* may gesture toward the space needed for critical dialogue about European literatures which are required reading for theorists whose views are neither Eurocentric nor procolonialist.

To state that Mark Antony's death was tragic is to presume as universal the procolonialist view that the would-be conqueror's death was not desirable or fortunate. The following reading has as one of its goals the illumination of the possibility that for Egypt, as one of the play's Egyptian characters states, Antony's death is, from a mythical standpoint, fortunate indeed.

The play opens as Octavius's troops descend upon a dying Egypt. Serapion, a priest of Isis, mourns that "'Egypt is no more!'"[93] The remainder of the play is taken up with Cleopatra's efforts to bring about a reconciliation with her ambivalent and suspicious lover, Mark Antony. After many misadventures, they reconcile, and Antony announces to Cleopatra:

> And now to die each other's; and so dying . . .
> Whole troops of lovers' ghosts shall flock about us,
> And all the train be ours.[94]

Cleopatra explains that she is dying as Antony's wife. It only remains for Serapion to clarify that the "train" flocking about the dead queen and her consort-king signifies their sitting "in state together" as if ruling "half mankind."[95] Indeed, they now rule the dead half, and Antony's descension to this throne, alongside the queen of Egypt, is the key to understanding Egypt's triumph in the face of conquest. Jung goes so far as to credit the Osiris-Horus myth with predominant influence upon Christian symbolism:

The Christian era itself owes its name and significance to the antique mystery of the god-man, which has its roots in the archetypal Osiris-Horus myth of ancient Egypt.[96]

By meeting his death as Cleopatra's spouse, Antony fulfills the mythotypical pharaonic role of Osiris. Cleopatra, then, represents Isis, Osiris's sister, wife, and queen who "overcome[s] Destiny." Her "sister goddess, often identified with her," is Ma'at, "goddess of truth, right and order."[97] Signifying "cosmic energy and power," Ma'at "tends to be more a concept . . . who *was* existence."[98]

Ma'at was cosmic harmony "through whose power the kings governed." Due to this empowerment, Egypt's pharaohs "called themselves 'beloved of Ma'at'"[99] and wished her to be pleased with them at their deaths, as Serapion announces that Cleopatra is "pleased,"[100] at the last, with Antony. The pharaoh in death continues to embody Ma'at's ability to keep "at bay an omnipresent chaos." For what did Ma'at mean to the Egyptians "when their cities were plundered and their young men murdered?"[101] It meant that Pharaoh as Osiris would descend to death only to rise again as Horus, his own son, eternally reborn through the revitalizing agency of Isis, "Queen of the Tomb, Mother of the gods, whose myth and mysteries . . . persevered into Roman and early Christian times."[102] Faithful followers of the cults of Isis and Osiris could look forward to "their own resurrection from death and eternal life in the realm of Osiris."[103] Egypt itself would live on, in and through Antony as pharaonic symbol of Osiris, "the god who dies and is ever reborn,"[104] escaping annihilation in Octavius's chaos because "the universe was good."[105] Egypt will rise because Antony has re-enacted the sacrificial death of Osiris, elevating Cleopatra to the revitalizing position of Isis and restoring the known order of existence: "At the ends of the universe is a blood red cord that ties life to death, man to woman, will to destiny. . . . I am water and dust walking."[106]

Mythatypical analysis enables the reader to perceive what Soyinka calls "epiphanous deities" as they move into and through the realm of "that which can be tangibly metamorphosed."[107] It is my hope that in the following essays the reader will increasingly experience, as have I, the truth of poet Micere Githae Mugo's vision that

> our wombs
> > issued forth
> > > one populous
> > > > global family
> > > > > of women
> > > > > > combatants.[108]

Their literature describes a healing and humanizing cultural evolution.

NOTES

1. Rosalyn Terborg-Penn, "Discrimination in the Woman's Movement, 1830-1920," in Filomina Chioma Steady, Editor, *The Black Woman Cross-Culturally* (Cambridge, MA: Schenkman Publishing Company, Inc., 1981), p. 313.

2. Alice Walker, *In Search of Our Mothers' Gardens* (New York: Harcourt, Brace & Company, 1983), p. xi.

3. Ibid., p. 323

4. Karla Holloway, *Moorings and Metaphors: Figures of Culture and Gender in Black Women's Literature* (New Brunswick: Rutgers University Press, 1992), pp. 1-2 and 11.

5. Ibid., p. 2.

6. Michelle Cliff, *Free Enterprise* (New York: Dutton, 1993), p. 29.

7. Holloway, pp. 21 and 89.

8. Ibid., pp. 69 and 107.

9. Henry Louis Gates, Jr., *The Signifying Monkey: A Theory of African-American Literary Criticism* (New York and Oxford: Oxford University Press, 1988), pp. 4-5.

10. David Sweetman, *Women Leaders in African History* (Portsmouth, NH: Heinemann Educational Publishers International, 1984), p. 11, referring simply to the history of Meroe, to say nothing of its theologies: "In fact the little of what we know about this amazing civilization comes from outside sources or from what can be dated from buildings."

11. *Webster's Deluxe Unabridged Dictionary*, Jean L. McKechnie, Editor, (New York: Simon and Schuster, 1979), pp. 1190 and 1979.

12. C. G. Jung, "Archaic Man," in C. G. Jung, *Modern Man in Search of a Soul*, W. S. Dell and Cary F. Barnes, Translators (New York: Harcourt, Brace & World, Inc., 1933), pp. 125-151.

13. When employed in this work, the term "animism" is always in sympathy with the positive "reclaiming" of psycho/theological antecedents as defined by anthropologist Sheila Walker: the belief that "everything has energy." (Private interview on December 21, 1997.)

14. Chinweizu, Onwuchekwa Jemie, Ihechukwu Madubuike, *Toward the Decolonization of African Literature, Volume 1: African Fiction and Poetry and Their Critics* (Washington, DC: Howard University Press, 1983), p. 10.

15. Ibid., p. 239.

16. Edward Said, "The Voyage In and the Emergence of Opposition" in Edward Said, *Culture and Imperialism* (New York: Alfred A. Knopf, 1993), pp. 237-261.

17. Audre Lorde, *Sister Outsider: Essays and Speeches by Audre Lorde* (Freedom, CA: The Crossing Press, 1984), pp. 110-113.

18. "post . . . (a) *after in time, later, following,*" in Jean L. McKechnie, Editor, *Webster's Deluxe Unabridged Dictionary*, p. 1406.

19. Filomina Chioma Steady, "African Feminism: A Worldwide Perspective," in Rosalyn Terborg-Penn, Sharon Harley, and Andrea Benton-Rushing, Editors, *Women in Africa and the African Diaspora* (Washington, DC: Howard University Press, 1987), p. 13.

20. Paula Giddings, *When and Where I Enter: The Impact of Black Women on Race and Sex in America* (New York: Bantam, 1988) is an exceptional documentary of African American women's humanitarian suffrage and feminism.

21. Steady in Terborg-Penn, Harley, and Benton-Rushing, p. 20.

22. Wole Soyinka, *Myth, Literature and the African World* (Cambridge, UK: Cambridge University Press, 1976, reprinted by Cambridge, UK: Canto, 1992), pp. 7, 10, 30, and 54.

23. Holloway, pp. 104-105.

24. Katie G. Cannon, *Black Womanist Ethics* (Atlanta: Scholars Press, American Academy of Religion, 1988), p. 88.

25. Trudier Harris, *Exorcising Blackness: Historical and Literary Lynching and Burning Rituals* (Bloomington: Indiana University Press, 1984), pp. 192-193.

26. Phillipa Kafka, *The Great White Way: African-American Women Writers and American Success Mythologies* (New York: Garland Publishing, Inc., 1993), p.

150. For thought-provoking arguments that challenge the enthusiastic reception of Frederick Douglass's autobiography, in glaring contrast to the continuing resistance to Linda Brent's (Harriet Jacobs's) *Incidents in the Life of a Slave Girl*, see Kafka's "Harriet Jacobs's Use of Self-Image" chapter in *The Great White Way*, particularly pp. 148-151.

27. Hazel V. Carby, Introduction to *The Magazine Novels of Pauline Hopkins* by Pauline Hopkins (New York: Oxford University Press, 1988) pp. xli and xlviii.

28. Cannon, p. 89.

29. Kafka, p. 139.

30. Barbara Christian, "The Race for Theory," quoted in Holloway, p. 63.

31. Holloway, p. 11.

32. Ibid., p. 75.

33. Cannon, p. 89.

34. Ibid., p. 174.

35. Ibid.

36. Richard Maxwell Brown, "Legal and Behavioral Perspectives on American Vigilantism," quoted in Harris, p. 7.

37. Harris, p. 12.

38. David Leeming and Jake Page, *Goddess: Myths of the Female Divine* (New York & Oxford: Oxford University Press, 1994), p. 78.

39. Harris, p. 12.

40. Giddings, p. 35.

41. Ibid. , p. 37.

42. Ibid. p. 34 as it introduces p. 43 of the same book: "The White wife was hoisted on a pedestal . . . beyond the sensual reach of her own husband. Black women were consigned to the other end of the scale, as mistresses, whores, or breeders."

43. Jacqueline Bobo, *Black Women as Cultural Readers* (New York: Columbia University Press, 1995), p. 159.

44. Toni Cade Bambara, *The Salt Eaters* (New York: Vintage Contemporaries, 1992), p. 167.

45. Conrad E. Mauge, "Warriors Against Man," in Conrad E. Mauge, *The Yoruba World of Good and Evil* (Mount Vernon, New York: House of Providence, 1994), pp. 108-109.

46. Henry Louis Gates, Jr., Introduction to Harriet E. Wilson, *Our Nig; or, Sketches from the Life of a Free Black* (New York: Vintage Books, 1983), p. li.

47. Ruthie Bolton (pseudonym), *gal: a true life* (New York: Onyx, imprint of Dutton Signet, 1994), p. 331.

48. Ibid., p. 65.

49. Ibid., p. 66.

50. Ibid., p. 68.

51. Ibid., p. 67.

52. Harriet E. Wilson, *Our Nig; or, Sketches from the Life of a Free Black* (New York: Vintage Books, 1983), p. 64.

53. Ibid., p. 107.

54. Robert Farris Thompson, *Flash of the Spirit: African and Afro-American Art*

and Philosophy (New York: Vintage Books, 1984) pp. 73-74.

55. Ibid.

56. Wilson, p. 107.

57. Thompson, p. 74.

58. Wilson, p. 80.

59. Ibid., p. 105.

60. Gates in Wilson, p. li.

61. Wilson, p. 129.

62. "Nimm the Terrible," an excerpt from P. Amaury Talbot, "Through the Land of Witchcraft: Part 1," *Wide World Magazine* Volume 31 (1913), pp. 428-437, in Terri Hardin, Editor, *Supernatural Tales from Around the World* (New York: Barnes & Noble, 1995), p. 211.

63. Holloway, p. 5.

64. Hortense Spillers, "Introduction: Who Cuts the Border? Some Readings on 'America'" in Hortense Spillers, Editor, *Comparative American Identities: Race, Sex, and Nationality in the Modern Text, Essays from the English Institute* (New York: Routledge, 1991), p. 16.

65. Ibid., pp. 12-13.

66. Bahiyyih Nakhjavani, "Artist, Seeker and Seer" in *Baha'i Studies/Etudes baha'ies,* Volume 10 (Wilmette: Baha'i Publishing Trust, 1982), p. 5.

67. VeVe Clark, "Developing Diaspora Literacy and *Marasa* Consciousness," in Spillers , pp. 44-45.

68. Holloway, p. 31.

69. Clark, p. 54.

70. C.G. Jung, "Analytical Psychology," in C.G. Jung, *Modern Man in Search of a Soul*, p. 177.

71. Devendra P. Varma, *The Gothic Flame* (New York: Russell & Russell, 1966), pp. 15-16.

72. For an excellent and perfectly applicable explanation of defamiliarization in literature, see Victor Shklovsky, "Art as Technique," in Lee T. Lemon and Marion J. Reis, *Russian Formalist Criticism: Four Essays* (Lincoln and London: University of Nebraska Press, 1965), p. 22.

73. Varma, p. 70.

74. Ibid., p. 16.

75. Kimberly Rae Connor, *Conversions and Visions in the Writings of African-American Women* (Knoxville: The University of Tennessee Press, 1994), p. 274.

76. Nagueyalti Warren, "Deconstructing, Reconstructing, and Focusing our Literary Image" in Joy James and Ruth Farmer, Editors, *Spirit, Space, and Survival: African American Women in (White) Academe* (New York & London: Routledge, 1993), p. 105.

77. Joy James, "African Philosophy, Theory, and 'Living Thinkers'," in James and Farmer, Editors, pp. 32-33.

78. Connor, p. 40.

79. Holloway, p. 88.

80. Nakhjavani, p. 9.

81. E. A. Wallis Budge, *From Fetish to God in Ancient Egypt* (London, 1934, reprinted by New York: Benjamin Blom, 1972), p. 249.

82. Paul Lachance, O. F. M., Introduction to *Angela of Foligno: Complete Works,* Lachance, Translator (Mahwah, NJ: Paulist Press, 1993), p. 1.

83. Angela of Foligno, *Memorial,* in *Angela of Foligno: Complete Works,* Paul Lachance, O.F. M., Translator (Mahwah, NJ: Paulist Press, 1993), p. 182.

84. Ibid., p. 183.

85. Ibid., p. 140.

86. Ibid., p. 126.

87. Ibid., p. 198.

88. Sylvia Brenton Perera, *Descent to the Goddess: A Way of Initiation for Women* (Toronto: Inner City Books, 1981), p. 37.

89. Clarissa Pinkola Estes, *Women Who Run With the Wolves: Myths and Stories of the Wild Woman Archetype* (New York: Ballantine Books, 1995), p. 29.

90. Asphodel P. Long, *In a Chariot Drawn by Lions: The Search for the Female in Deity* (Freedom, CA: The Crossing Press, 1993), pp. 82-83.

91. Caroline Walker Bynum, *Holy Feast and Holy Fast: The Religious Significance of Food to Medieval Women* (Berkeley: University of California Press, 1988), p. 250; for the co-reification and subsequent demonization of Christian mystic women, Bynum is a sympathetic source of detailed information. Guido Ruggiero, *Binding Passions: Tales of Magic, Marriage, and Power at the End of the Renaissance* (New York: Oxford University Press, 1993) may be equally fascinating and certainly gestures toward feminist sympathy; and yet there remains a troubling—if unintentional—implication that demonization and persecution might have been avoided by women whose characters were sufficiently "interesting and masterful," Ruggiero, p. 174. Still, it seems only fair to note that Ruggiero might object to the above reading of Angela of Foligno's sepulcher scene with Christ as reminiscent of Isis's with Osiris on the grounds that such an assumption of a lingering substratum of "pagan" (apparently this means non-Judeo/Christian) belief is dismissive of the possibility that there was an early peculiarity (meaning unique quality) of Christian thought. See Ruggiero, p. 152 for Ruggiero's argument.

92. Susan Staves, *Players' Scepters: Fictions of Authority in the Restoration* (Lincoln: University of Nebraska Press, 1979).

93. John Dryden, *All for Love* (New York: W.W. Norton, 1993), p. 24.

94. Ibid., p. 108.

95. Ibid., p. 113.

96. Carl Gustav Jung, "Approaching the Unconscious" in Jung, Franz, Henderson, Jacobi, and Jaffe, *Man and His Symbols* (New York: Doubleday and Company, Inc., 1971), p. 79.

97. Long, pp. 84-85.

98. Leeming and Page, p. 45.

99. Carolyne Larrington, Editor, *The Feminist Companion to Mythology* (London: Pandora, 1992), p. 24.

100. Dryden, p. 113.

101. Percy Howard Newby, *The Egypt Story: Its Art, Its Monuments, Its People, Its History* (New York: Abbeville Press, Inc., 1978), pp. 65 and 94.

102. Leeming and Page, p. 77.

103. S. G. F. Brandon, *Creation Legends of the Ancient Near East,* in Richard

Cavendish, Editor, *Man, Myth, and Magic* (New York: Michael Cavendish, 1970), p. 99.

104. Edward C. Whitmont, *Return of the Goddess* (New York: Crossroad Publishing Company, 1990), p. 6.

105. Newby, p. 61.

106. Normandi Ellis, Translator, *Awakening Osiris: The Egyptian Book of the Dead* (Grand Rapids: Phanes Press, 1988), p. 180.

107. Soyinka, p. 4.

108. Micere Githae Mugo, "The Woman's Poem" in Micere Githae Mugo, *My Mother's Poem and Other Songs* (Nairobi: East African Educational Publishers, 1994), p. 44.

2

Trees as Spiritual Mothers

One of the most frequently recurrent mythatypes in the literature of women in the African Diaspora and on the Continent is the symbol of the tree. Though this tree symbol is so recurrent, its critical interpretation is remarkably underdeveloped.

For example, in Mae G. Henderson's landmark analysis of Morrison's *Beloved*, Henderson deftly reveals the American sociopolitical climate in which European American men write, European American women voice, and African American men read the signs of African American women's experiences. Henderson interprets these meanings by reading the significance of Teacher's having whipped scars onto Sethe's back, of Amy's reading the scars as a chokecherry tree in full bloom, and Paul D's viewing the scars as simply ugly after he has enjoyed Sethe's sexual vulnerability. By contrast, Henderson's analysis reveals how Baby Suggs's covering her mouth with her hand symbolizes the historical silencing of African American women on the subject of their own and each other's suffering.[1] Significantly, Henderson also fails to interpret for the reader the scars-as-trees whipped onto Sethe's back as she tries to flee with her children from enslavement.

The tree appears in some of Africa's oldest religious systems as a symbol of life, death, and afterlife; it continues its tenacious hold on the Continental and Diaspora African mythical systems with its infiltration into Christian mysteries. Explaining that "blossom and tree are places of mythical birth," Jungian analyst Erich Neumann recounts that Africa's earliest recorded mythatypical tree may be Nut's sycamore: "This sycamore is identical with the goddess of heaven," Nut, eternally pressed above her lover/brother Geb into the sky. Nut "is likewise experienced as a tree," Neumann adds, as well as being, "the coffin goddess of re-birth."[2] Archaeologist and museum curator E. Wallis Budge describes Nut's nurturing of the souls of the dead:

The goddess is seen standing in a tree, out of which she reaches to the deceased with one hand a table covered with bread and other articles of food; with the other she sprinkles water upon him from a libation vase as he kneels at the foot of a tree.[3]

The soul seeking life in the spiritual world prays to this tree, con-flated with its goddess, "Grant thou to me of the water and of the air which dwell in thee."[4] Neumann further explains that the goddess of heaven, Nut, eventually becomes identified with a goddess whose ori-gins seem to be further south along the Nile: Hathor, "the tree goddess who gives birth to the sun."[5] Budge describes Hathor as "a woman standing in a sycamore tree and pouring out water from a vase, for the souls of the dead who come to her."[6] Hathor and Nut combine to be-come the sycamore goddess who offers shelter and nourishment to souls fleeing the wrath of destructive deities and spirits. Archaeologist Don-ald Mackenzie describes the transitional significance of the soul's coming upon the sycamore goddess on the road to eternal life:

If he rejects the hospitality of the tree goddess, he will have to return again to the dark and narrow tomb whence he came, and lead forever there a solitary and joyless existence.
    The soul of him who is faithful eats and drinks as desired, and then proceeds on the journey, facing many perils and enduring great trials.[7]

In imitation of the feasting ritual hopefully being enjoyed by the spirit of the dead in its meeting with the transformative sycamore goddess, pro-longed feasts followed Egyptian funerals, and "food offerings were af-terwards brought at intervals by faithful mourners," a tradition that seems to continue in many Diaspora and Continental African cultures.[8]
    Budge goes on to explain that "the branches of this tree [the goddess' sycamore] became a place of refuge for weary souls." He develops this argument to explain that this tree may well serve as "the archetype of the sycamore tree under which tradition [the apocryphal gospels] asserts that the Virgin Mary sat and rested during her flight to Egypt," and even "once hid herself and her son from their enemies in the trunk of the sycamore."[9] This legend establishes a sympathetic tie between the queen of heaven as defined by the Nilotics and the queen of heaven later intro-duced by (Coptic?) Christians, though superiority of power or rank seems clearly, here, to have been accorded to the older goddess.

Neumann adds that, beyond succoring and ushering the dead into peaceful afterlife, the sycamore or "date palm" goddess also "comprises generation," for in "the top of the tree is the place of the sun's birth, the nest from which the phoenix-heron arises."[10] The birth of the sun is benign Hathor's province; its inclusion in the description of the sycamore goddess further conflates the life-giving Isis with her own mother, Nut, with Hathor, who grants children and presides at their births, and with Mary, feminine symbol of Christianity.

Neumann says that the tree, as crossroads to the afterlife, becomes a coffin symbol, bringing together "the symbolic equations of a Feminine that nourishes, generates, and transforms" as "treetop and nest, crib and cradle." In his summary of the symbolic powers of the tree goddess, Neumann says that her qualities are attributed to the birth of the "Babylonian grain-god . . . lying in his wooden manger" whose story was handed down to Mary's child.[11] (Recall the English lullaby that begins, "Rock-a-bye baby, in the treetop.") Neumann develops this thought to say that wood "as crib and cradle represents the child-bearing maternal significance of the tree" and is "also the mother of death, the 'sarcophagus,' devourer of flesh." He traces this "sheltering of the dead in the belly of the maternal giant tree" south to an East African ethnic group called the Wagogo, who buried their dead in the hollowed trunks of baobab trees. When I lived with my mother among the Bugisu in Uganda, she brought home a regional tale that "the devil" (probably a demonized trickster or chaos deity) had turned a tree upside down to hide its water-filled fruit in the ground and expose its roots to the arid air, causing both the tree and the local populace to both die; this upside-down tree was the baobab. In West Africa, the shrine to the Fon goddess Nana Bukuu is "on a platform by a baobab tree." Like Nut, Hathor, and Mary, Nana Bukuu is the mother of a principal male deity, Obaluaiye. Art historian Thompson explains the Nana Bukuu enjoys such prominence in Dahomey that, there, she is regarded as the "grand ancestress" of all the Yoruba-derived deities of the Fon pantheon, called the Anagonu. Like Isis, Nana Bukuu knows "terrifying secrets" and symbolizes the "courage and accomplishment of women."[12] Her face covered with raffia to hide the ravages of pox, Nana Bukuu in name and appearance may recall Hurston's image of Nanny in *Their Eyes Were Watching God*. Enraged at the prospect of Janie's identity with her mother, Nanny's pitied, feared, antithetic (and significantly named) daughter Leafy, Nanny appears as a wise and angry old tree:

Nanny's head and face looked like the standing roots of some old tree that had been torn away by storm. Foundation of ancient power that no longer mattered. The cooling palma christi leaves that Janie had bound about her grandma's head with a white rag had wilted down and become part and parcel of the woman. Her eyes didn't bore and pierce. They diffused and melted Janie, the room and the world into one comprehension.[13]

Perhaps Nanny's "ancient" power "no longer mattered" because she could not fathom how to seize and use it in her turbulent, postslavery world: "There is a depth of thought untouched by words, and deeper still a gulf of formless feelings untouched by thought. Nanny entered this infinity of conscious pain"[14] and from there, went to her death. Immediately upon Nanny's death, Janie finds herself invested with Nanny's tree identity, beyond Janie's initial sexual blossoming that recalled Leafy to Nanny's mind and made her rush to bury Leafy's daughter, Janie, safely in marriage with farmer Killicks. Suddenly, Janie "knew things that nobody had ever told her. For instance, the words of the trees and the wind. She often spoke to falling seeds and said, 'Ah hope you fall on soft ground.'" Janie herself has fallen on barren ground. Following Nanny's death, Janie leaves her mule-footed farming husband to pursue her dream of love. When this second marriage also results in denigrated and lonely object-status, Janie calls upon the full power of her speech to pronounce death. She points out second husband Jody's "big belly[ing]" around as his demonstration of masculinity. Paradoxically, she contrasts his female pregnancy image with Jody's lack of more masculine anatomical distinctions.[15] The upshot of these pronouncements is Jody's death. Significantly, cursing a man with a swelling belly is how Nana Bukuu's power is invoked to pronounce death.[16] As Jody lies dying, his dwindling belly "huddled before him on the bed like some helpless thing seeking shelter."[17] From Janie? Possibly. Jody and the townspeople are convinced that she has "fixed" Jody to die. Janie is terribly hurt by this accusation, as she would never willingly hurt anyone. However, some traditional African religious systems, such as the Yoruba system of *Ifa*, hold that a woman who inherits her power to do harm may use it unconsciously: "The power is often referred to as 'Mother's Wrath' . . . an inherent psychic malevolent power. . . . The witch may not even be conscious of her action since she exercises her power automatically."[18] Such seems to be Janie's legacy from Nanny, whose "ancient power" was trapped in stasis. Nanny's death, and the passing of her useless power to Janie, seems to have liberated its transformative potential. For example, Nanny laments the world in which women of African descent are the "mule," endlessly laboring so that others may benefit. However, just as Janie's words inflict lethal gender confusion on Jody, the novel's narrative voice manages to conflate Jody with the mule image of Pan-African women's subjugation. The mule's wasting death precedes, parodies, and prepares the reader for Jody's.[19]   Vultures, the symbolic birds of many African death-wielding goddesses such as Isis (in conflation with the vulture goddess Nekhbet[20]) or Oshun and Oya of the Yoruba pantheon,[21] gather to feast on the spoils of the mule, presaging Janie's inheritance of the spoils of Jody's ambitious schemes.

Janie, the possession, gains possession by virtue of the intervention of the goddesses of life, death, and transformation. The vultures' feast begins with the mule's eyes, recalling Walter's warning to Jody as Janie began to curse him: "'You heard her, you ain't blind.'"[22]

These symbols surrounding the reversal of power in the relations between Janie and Jody indicate that Nanny passed on to her granddaughter her "ancient power," symbolized by her oneness with trees, upon her death.

Thompson describes the Pan-African linking of tree imagery with the souls of the deceased:

Kongo elders plant trees on graves, explaining: "This tree is a sign of spirit, on its way to the other world." The mooring of spirit with trees on graves appears in southern Haiti, where the rationale is phrased this way: "Trees live after us, death is not the end." In the continental United States . . . "The evergreen is planted on the grave. These trees are identified with the departed, and if the tree flourishes, all is well with the soul."[23]

Across the Pan-African world, the tree is both the watcher at the gravesite and the visual symbol of the deceased's spirit, for the tree binds and bridges the worlds of living and dead between the reaches of its own roots and branches. Introducing her collection of Haitian folktales, Diane Wolkstein recounts that in Haiti, newborns' discarded umbilical cords may be buried with seeds so that the tree that grows, and its fruit, belong to the child whose cord nurtured it. Though she notes that, "Trees in Haiti are thus thought to protect children and are sometimes referred to as the guardian angel of the child,"[24] Wolkstein seems to miss the specific motif of trees on mothers' gravesites continuing to link them protectively with their living daughters, though such situations recur in her recorded stories. For example, in "The Magic Orange Tree," a girl who is starved by her stepmother steals three oranges and goes to eat them at her mother's gravesite. Her tears water the seeds that have fallen. By morning, a tree has grown and blossomed. It bends to place its luscious fruit in the girl's arms. When the stepmother tries to climb the tree to steal its oranges, the tree grows until it is tall enough to break, and it topples the stepmother to the ground, killing her. The girl revives the tree by planting and singing to one of its own seeds.[25] Clearly, this tale refers to magical protection of a daughter by her dead mother through the medium of a tree planted on her gravesite rather than through the tree as an independent guardian spirit of the child, having been nurtured by the girl's shed umbilicus:

There is a famous Haitian painting which shows a tree, representing life, or the link between the living and ancestral power. The painting also shows a grave-yard to the left and shadow-like souls swimming in the water below the tree, toward live people standing by the edge of the water on the right. They are waiting for these ancestral souls or energies.[26]

This tree symbol that links mother and daughter through death and its resulting empowerment transforms *Beloved* into a tale of child sacrifice. In light of the tree symbol's African ethnology, the chokecherry tree whipped onto Sethe's back as her motherhood is being ravaged develops a mythatypical story that runs concurrently with the obvious story being told in *Beloved*.

Sethe has sent her children ahead to freedom as she doubles back to search for her husband, insisting that no one else should nurse her baby, who will be named in death "Beloved." This nursing injunction establishes for the reader Sethe's intention to own her motherhood of her children, an ownership that is normally the prerogative of free women: "To get to a place where you could love anything you chose—not to need permission for desire—well now, *that* was freedom."[27] Sethe equates the owning of her milk with the owning of her motherhood and her child:

Nobody will ever get my milk no more except my own children. I never had to give it to nobody else—and the one time I did it was took from me—they held me down and took it. Milk that belonged to my baby . . . I know what it is to be without the milk that belongs to you.[28]

The freedom to love and make decisions for her children is a sign of internalized emancipation for which Sethe must learn to speak up, throughout the course of the novel, evolving from her muteness immediately following her sacrificial act of killing Beloved to her angry assertions to Paul D about what her "job" as mother actually is: "'It ain't my job to know what's worse. It's my job to know what is and to keep them away from what I know is terrible. I did that.'"[29] As Sethe explains in her soliloquy, "If I hadn't killed her [Beloved], she would have died and that is something I could not bear to happen to her."[30] The death Sethe feared for her children was evidently a death of the spirit, and thereby the soul, in procolonialist submission. For in attempting to kill them, Sethe explains, she was simply taking them to be with her own dead mother: "My plan was to take us to the other side where my own ma'am

is."[31]   Sethe's sense of daughterhood to the woman with "the sign"
burned beneath her breast is crucial to understanding Sethe's tenacious
grasp of her own motherhood. Sethe is the only child that her enslaved
African mother kept and named: "'She threw them all away but
you...Without names, she threw them away. You she gave the name of
the black man. She put her arms around him. The others she did not put
her arms around.'"[32]   Sethe's puzzle-fitting concept of her mother is tied
up in poignant cameos about the freedom to love: the freedom to love
one's sexual partner, and freedom to nurture one's children, all symbolized for the tiny Sethe by the mark beneath her mother's breast: "'I
didn't understand it then. Not till I had a mark of my own.'"[33] If Sethe's
mother's mark corresponds to Sethe's own, then it was branded onto her
skin as a punishment for trying to escape. However it got there, the
mark is the Kongo Cosmogram, the cross within a circle, representing
the cosmic opposites that make a whole: the worlds of God and the living, the living and the dead, life and rebirth, birth and death, separated
from each other and joined to each other by the lines of the cross at the
circle's center that extend to its parameter.[34] The traditional Yoruba religion of *Ifa* also uses the symbol of a circle within a cross to represent the
worlds of spirit and earthly manifestation, where the past meets destiny.[35] The tree whipped onto Sethe's back will position her, in the cosmic scheme, as the tree at the juncture of the cosmic crossroads, a powerful point of coming together for all the essences of will, intent, and existence. It is Sethe's inheritance of her own mother's cosmographic legacy
that will empower her motherhood with the magic that Beloved draws
upon to return to life.

Though Sethe's mother teaches Sethe to recognize her by this sign,
she concurrently teaches Sethe (with a slap) to refuse the enslavement
that caused her to be branded with it. After wearing the punishing bit (a
mouthpiece inflicted on caught runaways) to the point that she grimaces
in a permanent bitter smile, Sethe's idealized, yearned-for mother is finally hanged.   The only criticism Sethe allows herself about her mother
is the incredulous contemplation of her efforts to escape slavery without
her child: "She was my ma'am and nobody's ma'am would run off and
leave her daughter, would she?" Sethe tempers this speculation with
assurances that, had she been able to get out of the rice fields, her mother
would have nursed and nurtured her.[36] Sethe attempts to grow into a
mother like her own mother, but without the fault of escaping alone.
Sethe claims her motherhood of her children by ensuring their escape
before her own.[37] Sethe's effort to kill her children and take them to join
her fiercely freedom-loving mother fulfills the death and rebirth cyclic
time motif of her mother's Cosmogram. By now, Sethe carries her own

"mark" as a burden on her back, fulfilling the philosophy that "revolutionary African women carry theory whose philosophical core encases the gem of an ancient cosmology."[38] The chokecherry tree flowering on Sethe's back becomes the sign of Sethe's ownership of her motherhood and its cosmographic qualities and prerogatives.

Kaylynn Sullivan TwoTrees is significantly named in common with the two turquoise-colored sycamores of Nut and Hathor that border the dawn as the sun rises from the land of the dead. TwoTrees describes initiating university students into traditional spiritual practices, with chokecherry branches as a threshold between the worlds: "We began this trip into the world of symbols, signs, and feelings, expressing the unseen and unheard," TwoTrees writes, as her students "stepped across the choke cherry branches I had picked and painted to represent the six directions."[39] The chokecherry seems to represent the bridging of spiritual reality; the fully flowering tree indicates that this spiritual reality deals with motherhood.

By embracing the freedom that her own mother sought, Sethe establishes herself as her mother's spiritual daughter and heir: "You are reborn through your blood relatives. . . . Your temporal and spiritual capacities must work together."[40] Sethe claims both her inheritance and her motherhood through the effort to free her children before herself. She claims her motherhood through the cyclic realities of birth, death, life, and rebirth, as bequeathed to her through her own mother's Cosmogram: "Freeing yourself was one thing; claiming ownership of that freed self was another."[41] Freeing herself will never be enough for Sethe; for she has defined true freedom in terms of mother love and seizing this love's totality. Even what Henderson has called the "rape" scene is centered around the violation of Sethe's motherhood through the theft of her milk,[42] Sethe's chosen sign of owned motherhood. For a writer whose goal is "moving aside that veil" of sexual assault and the "interior life" of the enslaved Africans who suffered it,[43] Morrison's neglect of clarifying what constituted Sethe's rape glares. Unless it is, in fact, clear. Sethe's motherhood is ravaged as a punishment for freeing her children. Her autonomous womanhood would have been symbolized by vaginal rape. This scene clarifies *Beloved* as a tale of the theft and reclaiming of motherhood at its cosmic and eternal levels. Presuming that "black women have no voice, no text, and consequently no history," Schoolteacher has tried but failed to inscribe "the master['s] code on Sethe's back."[44] By proceeding to escape, and by preferring to take "and put [her] babies where they'd be safe," Sethe demonstrates that however the colonizing system writes about her or assigns her an unacceptable identity, she has the power to transmute this sign into a reaffirmation of her own autonomy and sense of spiritual community: "Community here is not bound by physical or temporal limits. . . . You determine not whether or not you belong but the nature and the meaning of belonging."[45] Sethe's community, as sensed by Paul D ("Sethe didn't know where the world stopped and she began") and confirmed in her musings ("There is no world outside my door"), consists of her concept of her mother, herself, and her children.[46] When she puts her babies where they will be safe, she secures them in this cyclic community of rebirth. Thereby Sethe, the one child her mother did not kill, learns that a mother can dearly love the one child she does kill.

Schoolteacher's futile punishment only fuels Sethe's determination and marks her indelibly with the multi layered reality of her spiritual quest, as read by Amy (tree), Paul D (scars), and even Baby Suggs, who covered her mouth at the sight of the tree scars and could say nothing. For Baby Suggs, holy, was always overwhelmed by how "me and Beloved outdid ourselves" with the red of blood and Yoruba *Ifa* mysteries, where "sacrifice guarantees success."[47] In a ritual loaded with womanly signs and the signs of mutual pledging, Sethe and Beloved are reunited and reaffirm their mother/daughter bond in the sharing of milk and saliva. Their joy lasts one menstrual cycle—"the travel of one whole moon"—twenty-eight days before the goddess Oshun's hummingbirds take over Sethe's volition and usher her, snatching up all the "life" around her, into the shed (as shrine) where Sethe intends to offer up her children to the safety of the spiritual world where her mother waits. But one "perfect death" is enough. The blood sacrifice of this dearly beloved child ("Denver took her mother's milk right along with the blood of her sister") assures the success of Sethe's quest for her own and her children's freedom.[48] Henderson argues that "Sethe must learn how to link these traces [marks of her passage through slavery] to the construction of a personal and historical discourse."[49] Sethe becomes, in her aggressive claiming of motherhood, a living trace of the mythatypical "she who nourishes, generates, and transforms." Sethe, her mother, and Beloved make up a trilogy that "symbolizes women in both the contemporaneous and historical black communities."[50] It is this discourse which Sethe, Denver, Paul D, and the community that claims them all struggle to comprehend. If "Nan's story of the generational mother enables Sethe to (re)configure her past," and "Morrison's story of the historical m(other) enables the reader to do likewise," how is it finally (re)configured? In terms of "claim and surrender . . . in order to refigure the future," as Henderson suggests?[51]

Jamaican poet Lorna Goodison writes, "her birth waters sang like rivers/my mother is now me."[52] In disjointed images that recreate the

Middle Passage, Beloved insists, "I am not separate from her   the woman with my face is in the sea   I see her face which is mine   I am looking for the join"[53] These associations link her to her mother, her grandmother, who suffered the Middle Passage, and Yemoja, Yoruba goddess of the sea. Beloved's reverie of death and rebirth allows her to transcend linear time and become representative of her theological and historical community.

Perhaps it is the linearity of Henderson's concept of past, present, and future that leaves Beloved surrendered (abandoned?) in what Henderson describes as Sethe's "redemption through the creation of a cohesive psychoanalytical and historical narrative."[54] This narrative lacks the spirituality of an ancestral dimension. A psycho/historical narrative ignores the refiguring that spirals the future back to embrace, fulfill, and incorporate the past and present. Sethe suffers a very understandable doubt about the rightness of her beloved baby's death because that sacrificed child returns angry, needy, condemnatory, a spiritual black hole of want. Sethe cannot prove her good intentions or the ethical superiority of her motherhood to this being. Nor can she understand that it is in the nature of a revivified sacrifice to be abysmally afflicted with negative energy. "She returns demonic . . . selfish, ruthless, willing to be very negative, willing not to care."[55]

Withdrawing from empathy with Sethe's own subjective confusion, it becomes clear that in a circular concept of time, Beloved's "perfect death" unites the lost baby with the grandmother who preceded her in a Middle Passage marked by rape and infanticide, inscribing the signs of chattel enslavement that would begin with the hanged grandmother and end with the last sacrificed child. Beloved has been inscribed in a community whose discourse, to be intelligible, must eschew the linearity of the colonizing narrative and spiral back to its own multiple layers of relevance, as symbolized by the Kongo/*Ifa* cosmogram linking spiritual and material worlds, past and future, through the perfected conduit of Sethe at the crossroads as the cosmic tree of perpetual creation and re-creation through destruction. The pain-filled power of Sethe's inheritance of her mother's cosmogram, leading to her own spiritual (wo)manifestation as the cosmic tree that draws on the powers of all worlds, enables Beloved to circumvent the deceptively lengthy cycle of death and prolonged residence in the spiritual world to demonstrate the traditional animist theosophy that continues to describe the struggle and survival, destruction and reanimation that are the legacy of her Diaspora community. This reading transmutes the sign of double negativity into an act of mythical, ancestral, and personal rememory, becoming Morrison's ideal autobiographical narrative in which Sethe, her mother, and her daughters might each say, "'This is my historical life—my singular special example that is personal, but that also represents the race.'"[56] The sacrifice of Beloved completes the cycle foretold when her grandmother was enslaved and her descendants' bloody destiny was established: freedom or death. Beloved's has been rendered as story to be read, deciphered, and understood in its totality as representative of the lives of those women whose personal revolutions helped bring about the end of the institution (of chattel enslavement). Therefore, this is not a story to "pass on" because its cycle of inheritance is now complete. With Beloved returned to the world of her grandmother, her story becomes one for the rest of her community to witness and keep.

Harriet Jacobs writing as Linda Brent is the type of silenced "interior voice" that *Beloved* is written to amplify. Analyst Kafka theorizes that the perception of traditional African narrative tropes, such as praise-singing and signifying, helps the reader decipher and experience the power of Brent's message.[57] Kafka credits Jacobs with "unusually sanguine expectations that a white female audience would respond favorably to her lurid experiences," especially considering that Jacobs would have to "undergo the suffering of recreating traumatic past 'incidents'"[58] to communicate with this readership. Particularly to gain their sympathy for enslaved African women who suffered sexualized rituals of dehumanization, Jacobs

Chose to signify on her targeted white female audience. She determined to play on them, to disarm them, to manipulate them; to soften them up, only to melt them down.[59]

Even during the meltdown, however, Jacobs' "personal disruptions of the text continually destabilized [her readers'] comfort zones; relentlessly leading them to question themselves" until they arrive at those narrative cruxes where "Jacobs ends by fuming at her readers, daring them to do and be any better [than Jacobs] if they could."[60] Jacobs's narrative implications enlist her readers as her allies in the "psychological warfare" she wages—and wins—against her enslaver, Dr. Flint, creating a "how-to manual for white female readers, not for economic purposes, but for consciousness-raising." Jacobs's employment of traditional African narrative strategies thus accomplishes her "tall order" of inspiring and instructing European American northern women "to actively work for the destruction of the entire economic and political foundations upon which slavery is grounded."[61]

But there is another African narrative strategy at work that strengthens Jacobs's narrative and makes it a voice of and for her enslaved community. Jacobs employs mythatypical images that place her story out-

side the familiar European concept of linear time and give it the feel of
concurrent spiritual/ancestral activity.

Before waging her war of liberation against her enslaver, Jacobs goes
to her parents' graves to vow that her children will be free: "A black
stump, at the head of my mother's grave, was all that remained of a tree
my father had planted." The blasted tree speaks eloquently about the
state of internal and external siege that Brent feels herself to be under at
that time. Attempting to carry out her carefully-developed plans to rescue her children from enslavement looks grievously lonely and daunt-
ing. Worse, Jacobs has, in conceiving these children outside marriage,
willingly become a wealthy slaveowners' mistress and compromised her
ideal image of womanhood in favor of strengthening her aspirations for
her motherhood:

I had received my mother's blessing when she died; and in many an hour of
tribulation I had seemed to hear her voice, sometimes chiding me, sometimes
whispering loving words into my wounded heart. I have shed many and bitter
tears, to think that when I am gone from my children they cannot remember me
with such entire satisfaction as I remembered my mother.[62]

Though Brent feels and expresses that her mother's chastity is a distinguishing trait Brent has failed to fully inherit, the reader is already
aware that the two women's situations were entirely different. Brent's
mother was allowed to marry the man she loved; nobility of character
made it necessary for Brent to send away the freeman that she loved.
Brent's fidelity to one chosen sexual partner is clearly as strong as her
mother's, however, and has the poignant distinction of brutal necessity
to mitigate any condemnation a reader may feel toward the teenage
Brent who had to choose her children's father with such calculation.
Brent's idealization of a mother who was not faced with her own trials
becomes a touching act of simple devotion that, by extension, exonerates
a reader who may have condemned Brent unfairly. Yet Brent clearly
expects her parents to not only pardon her "sins" but to pray for her; she
addresses their God, who is her own and her readers', at her parents'
gravesites:

The idea throughout most of West and Central Africa, is that elders have power,
an energy which does not die when the body dies, but lives on and can be called
upon to help descendants. If you are a good person who takes care of your family and honors your ancestors by remembering them, then you can access this
energy to help you in your life, in times of trouble, or for good luck or protection.[63]

Brent is clearly a good person by the above definitions. As her mother, who is remembered as more chaste and therefore more pure than Brent, is clearly believed to be offering her spiritual capacity for intervention in Brent's favor, so is the reader. These shifts of similar roles allow the reader to experience some safe sense of power over, and superiority to, Brent, vicariously through identity with the idealized image of the deceased mother. Yet even this concession to the need to be seen as morally superior carries with it the assumption of exoneration and prayers on behalf of the success of Brent's strategies:

Trees are important in African American cemeteries, as they are considered images of life and roots, literally, down to the world of ancestral energy. Trees are often planted at the head of a grave and cultivated. A tree can be a symbol of the deceased person and a sign of that person's strength, as it grows.[64]

The "blackened stump" at the head of her mother's grave serves as a poignant visual reminder that Brent has failed to live up to the ideal of womanhood that her mother represents. It also pinpoints Brent's enslavement as the reason for her failures; if she had had free time, she might have attended the gravesites and "cultivated" the tree; if she had had free will, she would have given birth in a state of honorable wedlock and lived up to her idealization of her mother.

The blasted tree and "piece of wood" (dead tree as coffin) that mark her parents' gravesites also emphasize their deaths and subsequent absence from Brent's daily life; yet this enhanced perception of their physical unreachability draws into stronger relief Brent's expectation of mystical powers emanating from their witnessing the prayers she says and the vow she makes. It is this magical power of intervention with which she symbolically credits the sheltered, distant, married northern European American woman reader who has finally seen herself identified in the qualities and idealization accorded to Brent's mother. The reader is gently offered shared status with this tender, spiritualized mother, as well as shared credit for the victory that, at this juncture in the story, is already assured to Brent and her supporters. For Brent's graveside vow is that "I would foil my master and save my children, or I would perish in the attempt."[65] Since Brent has clearly lived to write the tale of how she saved her children, however harrowing the succeeding adventures, the reader who chooses empathic identity with the idealized spiritual mother and prays in her heart for Brent is instantly assured of a share in the power and glory that the spiritualized mother wields. For Brent has already won.

Distancing and its resultant impact on identity are central issues, as well, in Ken Bugul's (a pseudonym) *Le baobab fou*. This work has been translated by Dorothy Blair as *The Abandoned Baobab*, which changes the focus from the original title, which translates literally as "the crazy baobab." Blair's translation focuses on the narrator's actions: Bugul abandons her village, Gouye in Senegal, where the central landmark or point of reference is a baobab tree, and then misses her appointment to return and reconnoiter specifically with that tree. The French title emphasizes the tree's response to the narrator's action of abandonment: the tree goes crazy and dies.

Shifting focus is part of the translator's license in her attempt to capture the sense of the work and render it in English. However, this translation serves to necessitate analytical reorientation, as well.

For it seems crucial to this work to keep the reader's focus on the narrator's animation of the tree. The tree is not an unresponsive recipient of the narrator's actions and fantasies; the tree is a soul-filled ethnic or cultural moor that the narrator searches to identify throughout the course of the autobiographical novel. For it is Bugul's self-acceptance that is the quest at the heart of this work. It is Bugul's identity with the tree that leads her to a level of self-acceptance which will help her survive her internalized colonization.

Literary analyst Irene D'Almeida recognizes "the ambivalence generally felt by African women in relation to feminis." She quotes Ogundipe-Leslie's theory that, "'African women have always been feminists in the sense that they have always been concerned with women's rights in society.'"[66] But D'Almeida does not address the appropriation and subsuming of traditional African pro-woman thoughts and practices into the colonialist rubric of feminism, a relative philosophical latecomer. D'Almeida's literary analyses, therefore, tend to approach, embrace, and expand upon colonialist feminist readings of African women's writings, though D'Almeida cautions against just this type of cultural imperialism. D'Almeida's reading of Bugul's *Le baobab fou* focuses, therefore, on the breaking of silence taboos, rather than the reorientation Bugul must develop toward her own internalized racist self-hatred. D'Almeida's approach is not inappropriate in the case of Bugul's *Baobab* as the writer's background, and presumably many of the taboos she is breaking, are Islamic. However, an analysis that focuses upon Bugul's interaction with a mythatype whose symbolic relevance predates her culture's Islamic conversion may further illuminate this work's complexity and profundity of meaning.

The writer of this work is adept at turning erasure into self affirmation, beginning with her publisher's stipulation that she take on a pseudonym. The writer's name is Marietou M'Baye. She chose the pseudonym Ken Bugul because, in Wolof, it means "nobody wants it." By renaming herself, as an author, "nobody wants it," M'Baye manages to protect her narrative voice, her text, and her authorship from appropriation, attack, and destruction:

When a woman who has had several stillborn babies has a new child, she calls it Ken Bugul to prevent the child from suffering the same fate. It is one of those symbolic names given to children here, in Africa. If you say "nobody wants it," even God will not want it, therefore he will not kill it; the spirits will not want it, therefore they will not steal it; human beings will not want it, therefore they will not harm it. And this will allow the child to live.[67]

M'Baye reverses her publisher's effort at silencing into a self empowering act of protective renaming. Literary analyst D'Almeida asks what is implied as "not wanted" by the author's chosen pseudonym: the narrator/protagonist/events of the story? In light of M'Baye's explanation, it seems immaterial to look for an object of rejection; the name is a final, reaffirmative signature of self-protective self-valuing, the ultimate expression of the quest for self-acceptance that sparked this autobiography.

D'Almeida describes Bugul's story as beginning with separation from her mother, abandonment by her father, and emotional neglect by her extended family. D'Almeida attributes these early and ongoing experiences of deprivation as motive factors in Bugul's turning to French culture with a self-erasing passion. Sent to Belgium on a scholarship, Bugul experiences drugs, prostitution, and abortion. One night she finds herself begging her friend to help her rip her skin off because "its blackness was smothering" her. D'Almeida aptly interprets that

What she wants to destroy is not the *fact* of having a black skin but the *significance* of having a black skin, which so conspicuously marks one's difference in a racist environment.[68]

It is necessary to note that in Bugul's case, the problem was not merely one of "difference in a racist environment." "Difference" minimizes the hostile implications of "racist." "Denigration" might be a more accurate word for describing the subjective experience of being in an environment where one's differentiating signifiers are that one is "'a woman . . . a child without any notion of parents . . . Black . . . colonized.'" For, as D'Almeida notes, Bugul had already accepted—and thrived despite—"the racism that began in her French school texts" back in Gouye, Senegal. It is necessary to reorient the analysis of Bugul's experiences enough to perceive that she may, indeed, have embraced French education and culture specifically because they gave voice to a hatred of her background which was already nascent in the very young, emotionally neglected Bugul. Her shock came when Bugul traveled to Europe and found herself inextricably identified with the culture that, in Gouye, she felt had marginalized and rejected her. In Belgium, Bugul was no longer on the outside of her Muslim African culture, critically looking in at something that had pushed her aside. From her European vantage point, Bugul found herself irrevocably identified with her "blackness," which meant her "roots" back home.

Still rebelling against her earliest experience of those roots and that culture, Bugul internalizes her hatred and directs it against herself, describing her experience of prostitution as desiring "'a moment of attention.'" This is a rather spurious description of soliciting ambassadorial accomplices in her acts of self denigration. These accomplices are possibly unwitting representatives of the racist, colonizing culture that first gave Bugul the imagery and vocabulary for belittling her own ethnicity.

The self-destructive frenzy begins to spend itself as Bugul perceives that hating her culture through the vehicles of her body and her life may lead to more consequences she does not fully wish to suffer. Bugul casts about her for a landmark, a point of reference. She has lost her mother and broken with her grandmother. She remembers the village baobab. D'Almeida explains that "a tree, and a baobab in particular, stands for deep-rootedness, whereas Ken Bugul feels uprooted, alienated socially, culturally, spiritually." D'Almeida theorizes that, had Bugul not had a deep-rooted culture of her own, had she been "a tabula rasa," there would have been "no conflict between Senegal and Europe." D'Almeida perceives Bugul's European ventures into appalling acts of self-destructiveness as her being "in search of recognition and love." The problem is that "Bugul constructs in Belgium an identity that does not allow for the depth and complexity of her own self."

As well, at this point in Bugul's narrative, it is accurate to surmise that Bugul's need to express hatred for the African culture that seemed to have rejected her had run its course in a European environment that insistently identified that African culture with Bugul. The very European racism that empowered Bugul to reject her rejecting culture has also demonstrated that in European eyes, Bugul is inextricably bound to that culture. Bugul awakes to find that in Europe, she is culturally distanced but no longer alienated. In European terms, she has a culture. She has left it back in Gouye.

With no single person to return to, Bugul returns to the tree. It stands in for mother and grandmother. It has missed her: "The tree can speak, sing, laugh, cry, sleep, and dream. It can have facial expressions. It can give comfort."[69]

Not having kept an appointment to return to the tree sooner, Bugul has caused it to grieve, go mad, and die. The dead tree stands "radiantly upright." D'Almeida interprets this beautiful death as a possible sign of hope for Bugul's own future stability. She quotes Mildred Mortimer: "'Bugul is now ready to assume the identity that she first sought to escape. Hence, the protagonist's outer and inner journeys have led to self-knowledge.'"[70]

This analysis is tempered by D'Almeida's opening precautionary statement that

We must recognize that any application of Western theory, however balanced and careful, involves the imposition of a Eurocentric point of view. A writer from an African background must have reservations about the appropriateness of critical methods born of societies that are—if I may generalize—inward-looking and inner-directed, framed in terms of the individual and the abstract.[71]

This caution echoes and restates Morrison's concern, analyzed by Kafka, that modern African American autobiographies are deteriorating into tales of "how I got over." Kafka points out that, "implicit in Morrison's critique is its source: European American valorization of the individual."[72] Giving this analytical trap a slightly wider berth than D'Almeida and Mortimer have already done, I would like to reanalyze Bugul's concluding identity with the dead baobab.

Having accepted the authority of colonizing European perspectives, Bugul has internalized the viewpoint that she is inextricably linked to her African culture whether she feels it has ostracized her or not. In this she shares the identity of abandonment that she assigns, in the end, to the baobab. She has abandoned the baobab, just as her culture, her village, and her mother and grandmother have abandoned her.

The baobab reacts to Bugul's abandonment by going crazy and dying. This is an excellent metaphor for Bugul's behavior in Europe: crazed self-destruction. Bugul acts out with the baobab precisely the acts of contrition and acceptance that she hopes her African community and cultural group will extend to her. By returning to the crazy, abandoned, dead tree, Bugul enacts both her acceptance of it and her grief at having caused it to suffer so fatally. In this act, she is reassuring herself that her cultural community may also be sorry for the suffering it has caused her and be willing to take her back in death. For truly, she has killed that spiritual, idealistic innocence that her culture values in women, not only by her European exploits but by having attended the French school in the first place. In recognizing the beauty of the dead baobab, Bugul recognizes the beauty of her own learned wisdom and her stability in a culture that, even if it abandoned her, will not let her go. Bugul's (pre-

Islamic) culture embraces a theology that links death to rebirth; both Bugul's spiritual and the baobab's physical deaths are not necessarily linear points of finality. They are, instead, indications of an experiential end point whose funeral oratory may mark the beginning of rebirth.

This use of a tree as the sign of, and catalyst for, a woman's spiritual rebirth is also evident in Walker's *The Color Purple*. After a young life-time of physical and sexual abuse at the hands of Pap and Alfred, Celie feels "like wood," the nonliving remnant of a tree that is fit for use, consumption (as in a fire), or a coffin. It is Celie's friend and lover, Shug, who introduces her to a sense of bonding with the cosmos so empathic that she feels it come alive around her, much as Bugul felt her village's baobab to be alive:

Everything want to be loved. Us sing and dance, make faces and give flower bouquets, trying to be loved. You ever notice that trees do everything to git attention we do, except walk?[73]

Shugian theology rejects a racist patriarchal god to return to trees, air, birds, and even people; when it comes full circle to involve her again with trees, Shug feels such empathy that she senses she would bleed if a tree is cut. At this epiphanous moment, Shugian philosophy evolves to her acceptance of being "a part of everything, not separate at all."[74] Sharing this philosophy and its developmental methodology with Celie eventually empowers the younger woman to come back from the coffin-like state of "wood" to the living, tree-like state that allows her to curse and defeat her abuser. The interchange is worth noting:

I say, Until you do right by me, everything you even dream about will crumble.
   He laugh. Who you think you is? he say. You can't curse nobody. Look at you. You black, you pore, you ugly, you a woman. Goddam, he say, you nothing at all.
   Until you do right by me, I say, everything you even dream about will fail. I give it to him straight, just like it come to me. And it seem to come to me from the trees.[75]

Around this time, Celie and Shug have tried to locate Celie's parents' graves, looking for "a piece of wood" or any marker. When this effort fails, Shug announces to Celie that the two of them are "each other people now." Effectively then, as her curses of Albert take place, Celie is technically more vulnerable than the self-destroying Bugul: they were both young orphans and are both African-descent women in actively racist societies. Only, Bugul enjoys obvious advantages of education.

While both will become reoriented to (differing levels of) empowering self-acceptance through their humanized identity with trees, Celie's empowerment obviously activates dormant powers similar to Janie's in *Their Eyes Were Watching God*. Celie's willingness to be a conduit for the power that infuses her from the trees makes her recovery more unequivocal than Bugul's. Her formerly abusive husband weakens and his affairs decline, while Celie's prosper, until he reaches a state where he is ready to make amends, and she is ready to consider accepting them.

Having lost their mothers, all these African-descent women are protagonists of stories in which the reader experiences trees as spiritual mothers and signs of these women's inheritance of a power beyond themselves, beyond death, and beyond social injustice, deprivation, or personal assault.

NOTES

1. Mae G. Henderson, "Toni Morrison's *Beloved*: Re-Membering the Body as Historical Text," in Hortense J. Spillers, Editor, *Comparative American Identities: Race, Sex, and National Identity in the Modern Text, Essays from the English Institute* (New York & London: Routledge, 1991), pp. 68-69.

2. Erich Neumann, *The Great Mother: An Analysis of the Archetype*, Ralph Manheim, Translator, (Princeton: Princeton University Press, 1963), pp. 241-242.

3. E. A. Wallis Budge, *The Gods of the Egyptians or Studies in Egyptian Mythology, Volume II* (London: Methuen and Co., 1904), p. 107.

4. Ibid.

5. Neumann, 241-242.

6. Budge, 107.

7. Donald A. Mackenzie, *Egyptian Myths and Legends* (New York: Gramercy Books, 1980), p. 97.

8. Ibid. The reader may be struck by Mariama Ba's extended description of the feast provided by the grieving widow in *Une si longue lettre (So Long a Letter)*. I would like to add my personal experience of funerals that I have attended or heard described on the East and West Coasts of the United States, as well as the Southern and Midwestern States. Women who are family members of the deceased are expected to provide food, and women who are family and friends bring personally-prepared dishes to the "dinners" provided after family funerals. This surfeit of food can go on for days. As a very young woman, I took this offering of festive, delectable dishes to be a sign of concern that the bereaved family should not succumb to self-neglect, but be reminded that life goes on for those "left behind."

9. Budge, pp. 107-108.

10. Neumann, p. 241.

11. Ibid., p. 243.

12. Robert Farris Thompson, *Flash of the Spirit: African and Afro-American Art and Philosophy* (New York: Vintage Books, 1984), p. 68.

13. Zora Neale Hurston, *Their Eyes Were Watching God* (New York: Harper and Row, 1990), p. 12.

14. Ibid., p. 23.

15. Ibid., p. 75.

16. Thompson, p. 71.

17. Hurston, 80.

18. Conrad E. Mauge, *The Yoruba World of Good and Evil* (Mount Vernon, New York: House of Providence, 1994), pp. 108-109.

19. Hurston, pp. 54-58.

20. Barbara Walker, *The Woman's Dictionary of Symbols and Sacred Objects* (Edison, N J: Castle Books, 1988), pp. 109-110.

21. *Awo* Fa'lokun Fatunmbi, *Oshun*: Ifa *and the Spirit of the River* (Plainview, New York: Original Publications, 1993), pp. 16-17. In *Oya*: Ifa *and the Spirit of the Wind* (New York: Original Publications), Fatunmbi notes Oya's "ability to invoke the assistance of elemental spirits such as deer and birds to assist her in battle. This ability . . . makes *Oya* one of the guardians of issues related to the fair treatment of women" as "it is the deer who teaches the lesson of tolerance, acceptance and compassion," p. 10.

22. Hurston, p. 75.

23. Thompson, pp. 138-139.

24. Diane Wolkstein, Editor and Translator, *The Magic Orange Tree and Other Haitian Folktales* (New York: Schocken Books, 1980), p. 14.

25. Ibid., pp. 13-21.

26. Maude Southwell Wahlman, personal correspondence on January 14, 1998.

27. Toni Morrison, *Beloved* (New York: Plume, 1988), p. 162.

28. Ibid., p. 200.

29. Ibid., p. 165.

30. Ibid., p. 200.

31. Ibid., p. 203.

32. Ibid., p. 62.

33. Ibid., p. 61.

34. Maude Southwell Wahlman, *Signs and Symbols: African Images in African-American Quilts* (New York: Penguin Books, 1993), pp. 80-81.

35. *Awo* Fa'lokun Fatunmbi, *Esu-Elegba*: Ifa *and the Divine Messenger* (Plainview, NY: Original Publications, 1992), p .19.

36. Morrison, p. 203.

37. Ibid., p. 202.

38. Joy James, "African Philosophy, Theory, and 'Living Thinkers'" in Joy James and Ruth Farmer, Editors, *Spirit, Space and Survival: African-American Women In (White) Academe* (New York & London: Routledge, 1993), p. 42.

39. Kaylynn Sullivan TwoTrees, "Mixed Blood, New Voices" in James and Farmer, Editors, p. 20.

40. Mauge, p. 133.

41. Morrison, p. 95.

42. Ibid., p. 70.

43. Toni Morrison, "The Site of Memory" in Ferguson, Russell, Gerer, Trinh,

and West, Editors, *Out There: Marginalization and Contemporary Cultures* (Cambridge: MIT Press, 1990), p. 302.

44. Henderson, pp. 68-69.

45. James, p. 32.

46. Morrison, *Beloved*, pp. 164 and 184.

47. Mauge, p. 133.

48. Morrison, *Beloved*, pp. 95, 99, 152, and 201.

49. Henderson, p. 69.

50. Ibid., p. 75.

51. Ibid., p. 82.

52. Lorna Goodison, "I Am Becoming My Mother," in Margaret Busby, Editor, *Daughters of Africa: An International Anthology of Words and Writings by Women of African Descent, from the Ancient Egyptian to the Present* (New York: Ballantine Books, 1992), p. 722.

53. Morrison, *Beloved*, pp. 210-213.

54. Henderson, p. 69.

55. Sylvia Brenton Perera, "Returning and Its Price: The Scapegoat-Beloved" in Sylvia Brenton Perera, *Descent to the Goddess: A Way of Initiation for Women,* (Toronto: Inner City Books, 1981), p. 78.

56. Morrison, "The Site of Memory," p. 299.

57. Phillipa Kafka, "Harriet Jacobs's Use of Self-Image" in Phillipa Kafka, *The Great White Way: African American Women Writers and American Success Mythologies* (New York & London: Garland Publishing, Inc., 1993), pp. 115 and 120.

58. Ibid., p. 123.

59. Ibid., p. 124.

60. Ibid., p. 130.

61. Ibid., pp. 119, 129, and 131.

62. Linda Brent, *Incidents in the Life of a Slave Girl* (New York: Harcourt Brace Jovanovich, 1973), pp. 92-93.

63. Wahlman, personal correspondence on January 14, 1998.

64. Ibid.

65. Jacobs, p. 86.

66. Irene Assiba D'Almeida, *Francophone African Women Writers: Destroying the Emptiness of Silence* (Gainesville: University Press of Florida, 1994), pp. 13-14.

67. Ibid., p. 45 (D'Almeida's translation).

68. Ibid., p. 51.

69. Ibid., p. 52.

70. Ibid., p. 53-54.

71. Ibid., p. 27.

72. Kafka, p. 120.

73. Alice Walker, *The Color Purple* (New York: Pocket Books, 1985), p. 204.

74. Ibid., p. 203.

75. Ibid., p. 213.

3

She Who Nurtures and Devours

Africa's Pygmy peoples traditionally called their mother goddess "Matu, meaning both 'womb' and 'underworld.'"[1] This combining of a goddess's nourishing and generating powers, in interactive contrast with her deathly qualities, is a widespread mythatypical motif well exemplified in the Igbo goddess, Ala, who "combines the womb-bundle motif with that of Goddess as receiver of the dead . . . the mother that is earth . . . always nearby — with child and sword."[2]

The aspects of life and death have been split for most of the Judeo/Christian colonizing societies that have infiltrated and altered African and Diaspora communities and philosophies. The female figure who combines the power of life and death in her dealings with humanity, often without a blameworthy intermediary, is seen as a particularly frightening paradox in the worldwide human psyche, according to Jungian psychoanalyst Neumann. He struggles to explain her, revealing in the process the depth of his own terror and awe:

Just as world, life, nature, and soul have been experienced as a generative and nourishing, protecting and warming Femininity, so their opposites are also perceived in the image of the Feminine; death and destruction, danger and distress, hunger and nakedness, appear as helplessness in the presence of the Dark and Terrible Mother.

Thus the womb of the earth becomes the deadly devouring maw of the underworld, and beside the fecundated womb and the protecting cave of earth and mountain gapes the abyss of hell, the dark hole of the depths, the devouring womb of the grave and of death, of darkness without light, of nothingness. For this woman who generates life and all living things on earth is the same who takes them back into herself, who pursues her victims and captures them with snare and net. Disease, hunger, hardship, war above all, are her helpers, and among all peoples the goddesses of war and the hunt express man's experience of life as a female exacting blood. The Terrible Mother is the hungry earth, which devours its own children and fattens on their corpses.[3]

The need to demonize a power-wielding female deity is strong in these writings. One wonders about the psychoanalytical healing—to say nothing of archetypal literary insight—available to colonized peoples subjected to such a reversal of historical roles as described by Neumann. Apparently his aim is the description of the archetype he perceives, not an accounting of its origins among the creators of the helpless, subservient mammy and jezebel stereotypes of the "dark woman." (Significantly, both slavery-supporting stereotypes, the mammy and the jezebel, are childless or separated from their children in order to better serve, in contrast to the Terrible Mother "dark woman.") Such value-laden archetypal descriptions illustrate the complex difficulties confronted by the decolonialist analyst of Eurocentric interpretations, in which white is always good and darkness must necessarily represent what is terrifying if not absolutely evil.

There is a tale of a mother goddess who reverses the roles and assigns death to a blameworthy, but initially harmless, intermediary. The Dahomey traditionally believed in a Great Mother called Mawu, who created the world "riding in the mouth of a great snake." The world split and rose in the wake of the snake, and mountains and rivers were made. When their work was done, Mawu threw fire into the sky and breathed life into living beings, finally sending her snake to coil beneath the earth and support the world's weight.

Mawu also created the seed of death and sent it to earth in the body of a bragging upstart who had claimed that he also could create life. In an act of supreme signifying, she made him the carrier of death. "Mawu could breathe the breath of life into people and, lest they value this gift lightly, could suck it out when she chose."[4]

Mawu is one of many goddesses associated with rivers and a benign snake. The Woyo of Zaire have a Great Mother, Mboze, whose incestuous love for her son resulted in the birth of the rain goddess, Bunzi, a rainbow serpent such as Haitian Voudun's Damballah. When he learned who had fathered Bunzi, Mboze's husband killed the Great Mother and left her body to rot where she had formerly presided, bringing rain where the river meets the sea. So the bringing of rain fell to Bunzi of the rainbow.[5]

Goddesses' snakes—and their associations with rivers and seas—are not always benign. In ancient Egypt, Hathor, who shared with Nut and Nut's daughter, Isis, the title of Queen of Heaven, was also known as the nurturing Cow of Heaven. As did Nut, Hathor waited in the sacred sycamore tree to welcome back those wearied by their earthly lives, offering bread and water and a ladder up to heaven. Though Hathor cherished the dead, she particularly acted as a benefactor of living women, granting women the gifts of love, happy marriages, and children. This describes Hathor in her nourishing and generative aspects.

Hathor had a vengeful side. During the time of her great wrath, Hathor set out as the lioness Sekhmet to chastise the men whom she herself had created, for their plots against Ra, supreme aspect of the sun. After killing the guilty, frenzied Sekhmet continued her rampage against humanity. She intended to wash humanity back into the primeval waters on the wave of its own blood.

But Ra heard the people's cries and saw Sekhmet revelling as she drank down their blood. Ra mixed the red clay of Nilotic soil with barley beer and poured this over the land. Thinking this brew was the blood she had caused to flow, Sekhmet lapped it up. She fell into a drunken sleep. As she slept, she recovered the form and placidity of the big-breasted hippo, Hathor. The Nile again ran clear.[6]

Another deadly aspect of Hathor is the cobra goddess Ua Zit or Wedjat. Ua Zit shares with Hathor the title of Eye of the Universe or Eye of the High God. Ua Zit was the third and all-seeing eye, the searing power of the sun spitting out "her venomous and fiery spells of wisdom." She is eternally reborn with each shedding of her skin; she foretells the future as it curves in the spreading of her hood; she is herself a womb arising from a "fiery island of the Nile."[7]

Ean Begg describes Sekhmet as "the time and destiny which devour all things, the wrath of God that is the working of the law of cause and effect." Eschewing Neumann's terror of the regenerative cycle, Begg calls Sekhmet "the merciful" because "like Kali," she "symbolizes the putrefaction without which the spiritual life-force cannot be released at death." But Begg also ties Sekhmet to the child-devouring sphinx, "symbol of Ra's kingship," whose name meant "strangler." Begg believes sphinxes came to be seen as "female or hermaphrodite riddlers [riddling remains a popular Diaspora and Continental pastime] with animal attributes, who carried off boys and youths to satisfy their lust." Still linking the destructive Sekhmet intimately with the procreative gifts of Hathor, Begg reasons that, "Sekhmet is the annihilating power which makes conception possible: one form must die before another can come into being."[8]

This death-that-leads-to-life motif reemerges insistently in Kincaid's *Autobiography of My Mother*. The protagonist, Xuela, has a mother has been dead since the girl's birth. Like Beloved, Xuela yearns to see her mother's face, a face like her own. She begins to dream of her mother as she sits on the bank of a river, where she can see rain falling beyond the lagoon to the sea. River, sea, and rain are strong goddess symbols that repeat themselves as Xuela forms her identity, giving mythatypical clues to the reader as to who Xuela's mother is, and how her mother's story shall become the daughter's autobiography.

Sleeping in the enclosure of river, forest, rain, and sea, Xuela dreams of a ladder, down which her dead mother begins to descend from heaven:

I saw my mother come down a ladder. She wore a long white gown, the hem of it falling just above her heels, and that was all of her that was exposed, just her heels; she came down and down, but no more of her was ever revealed; only her heels, and the hem of her gown. At first I longed to see more, and then I became satisfied just to see her heels coming down toward me. When I awoke, I was not the same child I had been before I fell asleep.[9]

The focus on her mother's heels, and Xuela's eventual contentment with this recurring vision, serves to emphasize the ladder down which the mother descends. The ladder is a symbol of Hathor, Cow of Heaven, heavenly mother. Begg writes that

Hathor was, like Lilith, the ladder on which the righteous could ascend to heaven. She was well-known on the Red Sea coast of Somalia, which may itself be the land of Punt which was originally her home.[10]

The mother's conflation with, or replacement by, Hathor in the child's emotions makes mythatypical sense since, as Begg explains, so much did Hathor "cherish the dead that the person who had died became known as a Hathor." Reinforcing the dangerous aspects of the Heavenly Cow, and conflating them with those of the sphinx and mermaid is Xuela's next significant vision, which takes place when she is on her way to school with a group of children:

I saw it happen. I saw a boy in whose company I would walk to school, swim out naked to meet a woman who was also naked and surrounded by ripe fruit and disappear in the muddy waters where the river met the sea. He disappeared there and was never see again. That woman was not a woman; she was something that took the shape of a woman. It was almost as if the reality of this terror was so overwhelming that it became a myth, as if it had happened a long time ago and to other people, not to us. . . . Belief in that apparition of a naked woman with outstretched arms beckoning a small boy to his death was the belief of the illegitimate, the poor, the low. I believed in that apparition then and I believe in it now.[11]

The aging Xuela, who is recounting this autobiography of herself becoming her mother, says she remembers this boy's face "because it was the male mask of heedlessness and boastfulness that I have come to know."[12] This comment serves as a commentary on why the water spirit might have wanted to lure and kill the child: because of his (unattractive qualities of) maleness. This note adds another dimension to boy-killing sphinxes that Begg describes. He himself quotes Sekhmet as saying, "'When I slay men my heart rejoices.'" Begg also acknowledges "the etymology of Sekhmet . . . as the personification of the chaotic darkness which brings light out of ignorance."[13] This is a power Sekhmet shares with Oya, a Yoruba river goddess who "liked to have lovers."[14]

Following the ladder/mother dream that seems to indicate a metamorphosis of the mother from ancestress into deity, the girl's belief in the beautiful, singing, fruit-carrying woman who lures and drowns the boy also has a Hathor derivation. Anthropologist Sheila Walker describes "la diablesse" (the devil woman), also called "la giablesse," known in the French-speaking Caribbean as a "beautiful, fatal woman with one cow foot" who lures men and boys to their deaths.[15] The retention of a hand or foot from a goddess's animal manifestation often serves as her identifying mark in human form. All of the above might suggest that the goddess appeared in her seductive, nurturing Hathorian aspect, but in Sekhmet mode.

Or the apparition may have been a mermaid. Maude Southwell Wahlman describes "Mamy Wata" as a "West African term for a mermaid-like woman often depicted with snakes,"[16] which are infinity/wisdom symbols also of Isis, Kali, the lioness Sekhmet, and the sometimes lion-headed Ereshkigal. Wahlman mentions Yemoja as "the Yoruba goddess of motherhood . . . associated with the Ogun River in Nigeria and the ocean in the New World."[17] Barbara G. Walker mentions "Yemaya" (Yemoja's Diaspora identity) as "a popular African mermaid Goddess . . . whose hair was said to be long green strands of seaweed and whose jewels were shells."[18]

Fa'lokun Fatunmbi links Yemoja with a male or hermaphroditic force named Olokun in traditional Yoruba theology. He locates worship of Yemoja primarily along the Ogun river and worship of Olokun in Benin and Ile Ife. He believes their worship to have collapsed into the identity of Yemaya in the Diaspora. Fatunmbi lists some "roads" or aspects of Yemoja as "Mother of Fish, the Wise Woman of the Forest . . . the Red Earth Near the Shore [similarity to Hathor/Sekhmet] . . . Crown of the Rainbow [similarity to Bunzi of Zaire's Woyo people]." He credits her with the power of transformation.

Fatunmbi lists one of the "roads" of Olokun, Yemoja's symbiot, as

"Queen of the Ocean (in some regions of West Africa . . . known as either *Mammi Watta* or *Imadese*.)"[19] Thompson explains that

Yemoja and all the other riverain goddesses, especially Oshun and Oya . . . are famed for their 'witchcraft' . . . supreme in the arts of mystic retribution and protection against all evil.

Many riverain goddesses are visualized as women with swords. . . . Witchcraft, in fact, militates against not only total male dominance but the threat of class formation and drastically unequal distribution of wealth.[20]

This last point establishes the importance of Xuela's becoming the daughter of riverain deities. Xuela's autobiography of becoming her mythatypical mother chronicles her development of what Judith Hoch-Smith calls "radical Yoruba female sexuality."[21] For Xuela's story will ultimately be one of her unique triumph over the multiple oppressive social systems remaining as legacies of colonialism in her Caribbean society. Xuela is more than protected; she is empowered. She survives poisoning attempts, sexual ill-usage, abandonment, loneliness, and poverty to become wealthy, respected, and even feared in her old age. Her society's standards of success and prestige measure her as having attained both.

Xuela's power to vanquish social disadvantage begins with a letter that she writes, not to her absent father, "but for the person of whom I could see only her heels . . . coming down to meet me, coming down to meet me forever."[22] The secretive way Xuela goes about writing and hiding the letter, believing in the power of her written symbols, recalls the power attributed to women's African secret societies. Wahlman writes, "The Ejagham people are known for their 400-year-old writing system, called *Nsibidi*. It was most likely invented by women."[23] Thompson refers to *nsibidi* as "signs embodying many powers." He thus explains the mysterious force of *nsibidi*: "*Nsibidi*, in the Ejagham language, means roughly 'cruel letters.'"[24]

Xuela's hidden letter sets in motion events that will bring Xuela's father to claim her. When he does, Xuela will find herself in a home where her stepmother hates her to the point of trying to kill her. As she grows, Xuela is always protected. The poisoned charm kills the stepmother's dog rather than the despised stepchild; the stepmother's engaged daughter falls over a precipice and is horribly maimed; the stepmother's son is struck down by a wasting disease and lies dying, covered with oozing sores. Xuela is as protected as the women who follow and invoke the goddess Nimm with their secret writings.[25]

The young Xuela grows in a state of sensuous adoration of her female self, revelling in an ambience that reads like Matu or Ereshkigal's[26]

(Sumerian for "Lady of the Palace") womb/abyss of pain, death, rot, and regeneration:

And sometimes when the night was completely still and completely black, I could hear, outside, the long sigh of someone on the way to eternity. . . . And if I listened again I could hear the sound of those who crawled on their bellies, the ones who carried poisonous lances, and those who carried a deadly poison in their saliva; I could hear the ones who were hunting, the ones who were hunted, the pitiful cry of the small ones who were about to be devoured, followed by the temporary satisfaction of the ones doing the devouring: all this I heard night after night, again and again. And it ended only after . . . a gasp of pleasure had escaped my lips which I would allow no one to hear.[27]

Here are the sounds of snakes, poisonous things, predatory creatures, and their prey. As Xuela immerses herself in this unreasoning, impartial world where death means regeneration is imminent, she gains strength and gleans self-understanding from her sexual and emotional traumas: "I knew things that you can only know if you have been through what I had just been through. I had carried my own life in my hands."[28] Xuela's most complex, revealing, and complete soliloquy about the process of becoming the incarnation of her mythatypical mother, the beautiful mother who destroys, comes after an abortion forces her to leave school and the foster parents with whom she boarded. The couple sought sexual refuge from each other in the use of Xuela; it is the wife whom Xuela, as she runs away, regrets disappointing:

My life was beyond empty. I had never had a mother, I had just recently re-fused to become one, and I knew then that this refusal would be complete. I would never become a mother, but that would not be the same as never bearing children. I would bear them in abundance . . . but I would destroy them with the carelessness of a god. I would bear children I the morning, I would bathe them at noon in a water that came from myself, and I would eat them at night, swallowing them whole, all at once. They would live, and then they would not live. In their day of life, I would walk them to a precipice. . . . I would cover their bodies with diseases. . . . I would throw them from a great height . . . healing in the way they were broken, healing never at all. I would decorate them when they were only corpses and set each corpse in a polished wooden box, and place the polished wooden box in the earth and forget the part of the earth where I had buried the box. It is in this way that I did not become a mother; it is in this way that I bore my children.[29]

The worlds of souls and bodies overlap, influence, and define each other in Xuela's existence, explaining and enveloping her obsessive desire to be reunited with her dead physical mother. Supremely self-absorbed in her static loneliness, in her torrential abortive bleeding, and in her intense passion for her own sensual allure, Xuela eventually discovers herself to be the essence of a will to survive that needs whatever it wants, takes whatever it needs, and regrets little or nothing. Xuela regularly suffers and despairs, but it is the despair of Ua Zit, of the venomous and farseeing. Xuela eventually poisons the frigid hypochondriac who is married to the doctor Xuela assists. The widower marries Xuela. They age together, contemplating the countryside, ignoring each other and their shared past. Xuela as harsh justice presages a worldwide ascendancy of the colonized over the hearts, lives, and creative imaginations of her colonizers.

The empowering legacy of riverain goddesses who dwell at the mouth of the sea seems to have dissipated throughout the Diaspora into folktales of lonely, gift-giving or trapped mermaids and hags, such as in the Haitian tale "Mother of Waters" and the African American tales "Sukey and the Mermaid" and "The Apothecary and the Mermaid."[30] Kincaid's unflinching exploration of sexuality and suffering as vehicles of magical induction into the empowerment of witchcraft introduces to Europeanized literatures the suppressed concept of African-derived witchcraft as a naturally inherited state, one whose embracing will stabilize a heroine in her colonized and thereby destabilized environment. The reader may well marvel that a life that began with so much pain and passion as Xuela's ends with so much calm and relative peace, an indication of how deeply colonialist societies have ingrained the demonization of African-descent women's "radical power."

That "radical power" is muted and made to serve the protagonist's community in Simone Schwarz-Bart's *Pluie et vent sur Telumee Miracle (Wind and Rain on Telumee Miracle)*. Born after and into multiple family tragedies, Telumee is born on the island of Guadeloupe and raised by her grandmother, Reine Sans Nom (Nameless Queen). The grandmother acts as a reflection of the circular relations between community and the spirit world; tragedy moves her closer to ancestor-as-deity status even while she lives. With the power to curse as well as to heal (Telumee begs the Nameless Queen not to curse her abusive husband because he—by his actions—is cursing himself[31]), the grandmother trains Telumee to become a "femme qui se levait et se couchait avec les esprits" ("woman who rises and goes to bed with the spirits"). The mortal and spiritual worlds that overlap and pressure each other in Xuela's perception of reality are separate but contingent in Telumee's. She is unique not because she lives in a spirit world that increasingly shapes and guides her mortal life, as does Xuela, but because she lives on the threshold and can influence both worlds at once. When her loving, revolutionary second husband is burned to death in a demonstration, he begs Telumee to let him go to the world of the spirits. He points out to her that she is holding him in limbo while dying herself. He supplicates her to "tenir ma position de negresse jusqu'au bout" ("hold on like a black woman until the very end").[32] For her dead husband's sake, Telumee performs the ritual that will separate them.

Selfless Telumee has both prodigious ability and desire to perform good works for others. The greatest miracle of her life, the one that earns her a second name, is the giving of a soul to a man who has seduced Telumee's apprentice/foster daughter and sneaked back in the night to murder Telumee. Telumee Miracle's sole regret, as she ages, is the one occasion on which she declines to forgive, and welcome as a friend, her formerly abusive first husband. Clearly, whichever deity is empowering this woman, Telumee's witchcraft is held in a circle of returning good in exchange for faith, favors, and cruelty alike. Telumee surmises endlessly on the condition of the formerly enslaved inhabitants of her island; but she suppresses—or simply never feels—a drive to release her power as a force for change.

The radical power, the revolutionary rage that, gradually unleashed, allows Xuela to surmount the socio/emotional barriers that threaten her existence, turns inward and implodes, collapsing upon and consuming anorexic Nyasha in Dangarembga's *Nervous Conditions*. It is striking that both Nyasha and Xuela feel themselves to be emotionally estranged from the pro colonialist and (exacerbatingly) sexist values of the societies into which they were born. But Nyasha keeps reaching for human points of contact with her objectionable world; Xuela suffers as mightily as Nyasha does from her sense of isolation but, unlike Nyasha, seeks no human approval. Both young women are bound to pain through their fathers' disapproval; interestingly, Xuela manages to keep making personal sacrifices in an effort to support and please her father, and it seems to be these willing sacrifices that continually draw her closer to an identity with her mythatypical, protective mother.

Fazel presents a convincing set of successive images that demonstrates the power of an aspect of the mythatype which seems to reach out to protect Kincaid's Xuela. In her autobiographical *Lontano da Mogadiscio (Far from Mogadishu)*, Fazel describes life in pre- and postindependence Somalia.

As was previously quoted, the worship of Hathor, and by implication her destructive aspect of Sekhmet, seems to have originated in the region of present-day Somalia. Fazel draws on the implications of this pre-Islamic mythatype in her two most striking pictorial summaries of the state of Somalia as it waited for independence and struggled with the ravages of decolonialist reform. Disrupting the placid idyll of the rhythms of her childhood, Fazel is taken with her family to a restaurant where they view a caged lioness:

Un giorno portarono come attrazione una gabbia con rinchiusa una splendida leonessa. Andammo tutti a salutarla, a tirarle gli avanzi di carne. Era triste vederla passeggiare nervosamente in quella gabbia. Su e giu, senza stancarsi. Batteva la coda e ruggiva.

(One day, they brought in, as an attraction, a cage enclosing a splendid lioness. We all went to greet her, tossing her leftover meat. It was sad to see her pacing nervously in that cage. Back and forth, tirelessly. Switching her tail and roaring.)[33]

The image is one of beauty and power and an unassuageable yearning for freedom. The lioness paces, suffering its imprisonment, grieving. Even the children, representative of Somalia's future liberated citizens, sympathize with the lioness's need to be released from her cage; Fazel invokes no fear in the reader that the lioness would rampage if set free. Throughout her autobiography, Fazel refuses to posit that Somalia's civil wars are inevitable results of the postindependence scramble to inherit colonialist (and anti traditional) boundaries of rule. She infers that Somalia's destruction is the result of greedy and shortsighted vainglory, of the kind one might attribute to the men who plotted against Ra. The rage in preindependence Somalia is, however, always latent.

The contemporary image Fazel constructs of Somalia is no longer Sekhmet in lioness aspect. The pacing sphinx has become a thin, desiccated Hathor, her breasts shriveled and incapable of giving nourishment to the offspring she, nevertheless, tries to suckle. Conflating apparently incongruous images, Fazel calls this skeletal mother of a dying child "Mother Teresa," exchanging Sekhmet's presumed sexual wantonness for a celibate's presumed virginity. Jungian Begg links black virginity with Sekhmet by recalling St. Mary the Egyptian's "long life of penance in the desert and, at death, a lion dug her grave,"[34] to say nothing of Mary the mother of Jesus, hiding in the desert from her son's enemies. The starving virgin who must yet nurture is Mary, succoring her child under the drought-stricken sycamore of Hathor:

La "mia" Madre Teresa ha la pelle nera ed il viso scavato dalla fame, ma non ha perso i lineamenti regali e fieri del suo popolo. I suoi occhi sono grandi, neri e portano dentro gli orrori dell'olocausto. Al suo seno, un tempo rigoglioso e sensuale, ora c'e attaccata la bocca grande di un bambino con la testa enorme e il ventre gonfio. Da quel seno non esce una goccia di latte.

("My" Mother Teresa has black skin and a face carved by hunger, but still retaining the regal, proud features of her people. Her big, black eyes reflect the horrors of the holocaust. At her breast, once so robust and sensual, sucks the large mouth of a child with an enormous head and a swollen stomach. Not even a drop of milk comes from that breast.)[35]

In Fazel's imagery, the once Hathorian, now starving virgin mother and kwashiorkor (severe malnutrition)-afflicted child are surrounded by parched land being watered with the blood of warring factions of men. Clearly, these ravages are not the doings of Sekhmet; there is no overly zealous justice afoot. Nor is this blood being poured out as a libation to a goddess.[36]

Fazel concludes this cameo with the thought that love is what is needed to nourish the land which should sustain these people, such as the love of the mother for the child. The implication is that this virgin mother icon's love is insufficient to heal the breach between the men who are, conversely, apparently not her children.[37] Has this mythatype given birth only to the political pawns, the victims of others' civil strife? Or must one suspect disavowal, maternal disownment, due to the betrayal of the mother goddess's ideals? For Xuela's and Neumann's dark mother mythatypes still claimed those of their children who killed each other as well as those who suffered unjustly.

It seems that both Kincaid's abundantly seductive and Fazel's desiccated Hathorian mythatypes ask nothing of their devotees except faith; in return, they give what magical or material comfort they can.

Such an act of faith and surrender in exchange for protection, empowerment, and beyond that, spiritual growth, drives the multivoiced narratives of Bambara's *The Salt Eaters*, to conclusion when the main character, Velma, experiences a power-filled conversion and transformation. Bambara's message is a paraphrasing of Fazel's: that to succeed without consuming the women who lead, serve, and support the revolution, the revolution itself must be spiritual as well as political and idealistic. Revolutionary women must open themselves to mythatypical paths; Velma must accept her gift of ancient power, find the space in her soul and psyche where *"the sky is lit by tomorrow's memory lamp."*[38] Until then, she is consuming herself in disillusioned and self-destructive depression, the equivalent of Nyasha's alternately furious or catatonic, self-cannibalizing anorexia.

Outside the site of Velma's transformation, her unfaithful, rationalizing husband falls face down like a worshipper at a shrine in the cleansing rain ("slate rained clean, a blessing"),[39] reaching toward the door beyond which Velma is rising, rejuvenated.

Min, Sophie, and Old Wife's shepherding of Velma toward rebirth recalls Mama Day's patient (and usually unrecognized) efforts on behalf of her granddaughter Coco in Gloria Naylor's *Mama Day*. But in both of these novels, the mythatype is incarnated in contemporary women who harness power—even lightning—through their own spirits and hands.

In the study of nurturing and destroying mythatypes, it is important to note that Diaspora and Continental African women's literatures depict few mothers who become spiritually empowered; Velma is an exception rather than a rule. Much more common is the anticolonialist depiction of a disempowering social order that makes an African-descent woman's effort to support her children a burden that will destroy her and/or them unless she abandons them first.

Gruelingly methodical portrayals of this process, the unrelenting destruction of mothers and children in colonized societies, are depicted in Buchi Emecheta's *The Joys of Motherhood* and Anne Petry's *The Street*. Nnu Ego and Lutie Johnson make every morally correct decision that they can, based on their values, work ethics, and upbringing. But the no-win binds that surround them become tighter and tighter clamps, reducing their goals to the single animalistic one of survival. Oddly enough, while Lutie Johnson's options are deteriorating, due to her victimization by the men who want her body and the social systems that do not find her and her son worthy of protection and support, Lutie's mousy neighbor, Min, is drawing on the widespread African cosmic symbol of the cross[40] to terrorize the tormentor that she and Lutie share in common. Min is empowered to walk out on her abuser and autonomously seek a new life; Lutie, who embraces the American work and profit ethics, is driven to desperation, murder, and fugitive flight.

Nnu Ego's life recounts no missed magical opportunities, only the eroding of her society's values so that she struggles to survive despite a growing conviction of disorientation and irreparable displacement. Igbo Nnu Ego and African American Lutie's stories illustrate Steady's "humanistic" feminist perspective that "racism remains the most stubborn and persistent form of oppression."

Nnu Ego's story seems to have been written in answer to the question Flora Nwapa posits as she closes her novel about a fellow Igbo woman, *Efuru*: why did her community of African women worship a childless goddess? The answer precedes the question: the childless goddess Uhamiri, dwelling at the bottom of her lake, gives beauty, wealth, and respectability. Emecheta's *Joys of Motherhood* paints a graphic picture showing that the colonized African world, shaped by European values, will privilege women possessed of those gifts valued by their colonizers. Others will have difficulty surviving.

In reading Pan-African women's works that outline the social decline mothers experience, one is well advised to keep in mind Steady's dictum that "the concern should focus more on the effect of neocolonial-

ism and the economic, political, and cultural domination of African societies." Steady explains economic and socio/familial deterioration in
colonized societies:

In the absence of a conducive economic infrastructure female self-reliance has
had negative effects. This is particularly true of situations where the larger so-
cioeconomic structure creates chronic unemployment among black males. . . .
Self-reliance has produced a hardship effect on women who have had to take on
additional burdens in meeting subsistence needs under conditions of extreme
poverty, and have had to assume the sole responsibility for their children. These
developments reflect consequences of economic changes which continue to mar-
ginalize the poor, especially blacks, erode family ties and render the black family
a cheap source of labor. . . . Female self-reliance becomes synonymous with male
peripherality.
    Some of these processes date back to slavery.[41]

These readings mitigate Velma's recovery in light of the fact that,
though she is emotionally abandoned, her husband is neither unem-
ployed nor absent. She struggles with the psycho/emotional burdens
left in the wake of the faltering civil rights revolution; the severity of
Velma's suffering does not lessen the fact that, compared to many Pan-
African literary mothers, the material security that leaves Velma enough
emotional space to become overwhelmed by relatively abstract ruptures
of her ideals (including her husband's interrupted sexual affair with another woman in the civil rights struggle) is, in itself, a rare and lovely
luxury.
    Ba's *Une si longue lettre* (*So Long a Letter*) well illustrates this point.
Abandoned emotionally and financially so that her husband can marry
the "other woman" (a bid for respectability that in no way makes the
Muslim heroine's pain less acute than the becoming-traditionalist
Velma's), Ramatoulaye and her children struggle to live with some dignity until his death. During her forty days of widowed seclusion,
Ramatoulaye examines her life in letters to her best friend. As the period
of seclusion ends, Ramatoulaye's letters show that her burgeoning commitment to independently formulated ideals will become the best assurance of her children's—and her continent's—healing. For example, she
writes

Avez-vous faconne le visage de l'Afrique Nouvelle? Reve assimilationniste du
colonisateur . . . Privilege de notre generation, charniere entre deux periodes
historiques, l'une de domination, l'autre d'independance.
    (Have you shaped the face of the New Africa? Assimilationist, colonizer's
dream . . . It is the privilege of our generation to be the turning point between
two historical periods, the one of domination, and the other of independence.)[42]

Ramatoulaye proceeds to refuse all offers of marriage (even that of her childhood sweetheart on the grounds that it might make his wife suffer just as Ramatoulaye has suffered) to give her oldest daughter legal authority to get back property unfairly given to the second wife, and even to protect and support another daughter who has taken a lover and is now pregnant.

Ramatoulaye is "shap[ing] the face of the New Africa" with every carefully weighed decision she must make. Ramatoulaye explains to her daughters that "Chaque femme fait de sa vie ce qu'elle souhaite." ("Each woman makes of her life what she wishes.")[43] This is a woman committed to human dignity, illustrating Steady's premises that "becoming westernized is not a necessary precondition for emancipation," and that "the centrality of children tend[s] to reduce emotional dependency of women on men."[44]

As if reflecting on Fazel's Mother Teresa image, Ramatoulaye writes,

Je pense a l'identite des hommes. . . . Pourquoi s'entretuent-ils dans des batailles ignobles pour des causes futiles en regard des massacres de vies humaines? . . . Et pourtant, l'homme se prend pour une creature superieure. A quoi lui sert son intelligence?

(I think about the similarity of men. . . . Why do they kill each other in ignoble battles for futile causes, considering the mass destruction of human lives? . . . And man takes himself to be a superior creature. Of what use to him is his intelligence?)[45]

This observation precedes Ramatoulaye's own most trying battle: deciding what to do when she discovers that one of her unwed college daughters is pregnant. In working out her decision, she speaks for Fazel's enigmatic starving mother, offering an empty breast in the desert:

On est mere pour comprendre l'inexplicable. . . . On est mere pour affronter le deluge. Face a la honte de mon enfant, a son repentir sincere, face a son mal, a son angoisse, devrais-je menacer?

Je pris dans mes bras ma fille. Je la serrais douloureusement dans mes bras, avec une force decuplee, faite de revolte paienne et de tendresse primitive.

(A mother understands the inexplicable. . . . A mother confronts the flood. Faced with my child's shame, her sincere repentance, faced with her pain, her anguish, should I have threatened?

I took my daughter in my arms. I squeezed her painfully in my arms, with tenfold strength born of pagan revolt and primitive tenderness.)[46]

Ramatoulaye's reverie answers the question of why Fazel's uncaged lioness has become the desiccated nurturer. Where is Sekhmet's rage?

The devourer mythatype nurtures those who turn to her, claim her, have faith in her and rely on her. Maybe she will come to forgive and nurture the others, those who spill precious human blood in antitheist intrigue, once they turn to her and seek to be forgiven.

NOTES

1. David Leeming and Jake Page, *Goddess: Myths and Legends of the Female Divine* (New York & Oxford: Oxford University Press, 1994), p. 46.

2. Ibid., p. 38.

3. Erich Neumann, *The Great Mother: An Analysis of the Archetype*, Ralph Manheim, Translator, (Princeton: Princeton University Press, 1963), p. 149.

4. Leeming and Page, pp. 51-53.

5. Ibid., p. 97-98.

6. Ibid., p. 43-44.

7. Ibid., p. 44-45.

8. Ean Begg, *The Cult of the Black Virgin* (London: Penguin Group, 1996), pp. 41 and 47.

9. Jamaica Kincaid, *The Autobiography of My Mother* (New York: Plume, 1997), p. 18.

10. Begg, p. 46.

11. Kincaid, pp. 37-38.

12. Ibid., p. 36.

13. Begg, p. 47.

14. Sheila Walker, personal communication on October 18, 1997.

15. Ibid., December 21, 1997.

16. Maude Southwell Wahlman, *Signs and Symbols: African Images in African-American Quilts* (New York: Penguin Group, 1993) p. 121.

17. Ibid., p. 78.

18. Barbara G. Walker, *The Woman's Dictionary of Symbols and Sacred Objects* (New York: Castle Books, 1988), p. 263.

19. *Awo* Fa'lokun Fatunmbi, *Yemoja/Olokun: Ifa and the Spirit of the Ocean* (Plainview, New York: Original Publications, 1993), pp. 3 and 14-15.

20. Robert Farris Thompson, *Flash of the Spirit: African and Afro-American Art and Philosophy* (New York: Vintage Books, 1984), p. 74.

21. Judith Hoch-Smith, "Radical Yoruba Female Sexuality" in Judith Hoch-Smith and Anita Spring, Editors, *Women in Ritual and Symbolic Roles* (New York: Plenum Press, 1978).

22. Kincaid, p. 19.

23. Wahlman, p. 78.

24. Thompson, p. 227.

25. P. Amaury Talbot, "Through the Land of Witchcraft: Part I," *Wide World Magazine*, (1913), pp. 428-437. Talbot writes of witnessing a man pulled overboard into a river by a crocodile and left to his fate by his companions, who agreed that the man's wife must have invoked Nimm to redress some wrong he had done her.

26. Sumerian goddess of death and the underworld, extensively interpreted

in Jungian analytical terms in Sylvia Brenton Perera, *Descent to the Goddess: A Way of Initiation for Women* (Toronto: Inner City Books, 1981).

27. Kincaid, p. 43.

28. Ibid., p. 83.

29. Ibid., pp. 96-97.

30. "Mother of the Waters," in Diane Wolkstein, Editor and Translator, *The Magic Orange Tree and Other Haitian Folktales* (New York: Schocken Books, 1980); Robert D. San Souci, *Sukey and the Mermaid* (New York: Four Winds Press, 1992); "The Apothecary and the Mermaid," in John Bennett, *The Doctor to the Dead: Grotesque Legends and Folk Tales of Old Charleston* (Columbia: University of South Carolina, 1995).

31. Simone Schwarz-Bart, *Pluie et vent sur Telumee Miracle* (Saint Amand, France: Editions du Seuil, 1980), p. 149.

32. Ibid., p. 223.

33. Shirin Ramzanali Fazel, *Lontano da Mogadiscio* (Rome: DATANEWS Editrice, 1994), p. 17 (my translation).

34. Begg, p. 47.

35. Fazel, p. 56 (my translation).

36. Perera explains "this archetype of exchanging energy through sacrifice" thus: "Nothing changes or grows without the food of some other sacrifice. This is the basis of women's experience of childbearing and of all blood mysteries that create and maintain life," p. 54.

37. Begg expounds that "one of the reasons given for the blackness of our virgins is that Mary, too, was very sunburnt. The most important function of the Black Virgin is her power to stay the destructive hand of God, tempering justice with mercy," pp. 47-48.

38. Toni Cade Bambara, *The Salt Eaters* (New York: Vintage Contemporaries, 1992), p. 293.

39. Ibid.

40. See Thompson, *Flash of the Spirit*, on *yowa* and *Zarabanda* cruciforms as complex multicultural fusions of Kongo, Yoruba, Dahomean, Roman Catholic, and other religious signs, pp. 109-113, and Wahlman, *Signs and Symbols*: "They (cruciforms) could have once been adopted because of a resemblance to the Yoruba belief in sacred crossroads, or the Kongo symbol for the four points of the sun," p. 91. They might even be used to represent "'danger, evil, and bad feelings,'" which would explain the superintendent's mounting paranoia Petry's *The Street*.

41. Filomina Chioma Steady, Editor, *The Black Woman Cross-Culturally* (Cambridge, MA: Schenkman Publishing, 1981), pp. 17 and 27-28.

42. Mariama Ba, *Une si longue lettre* (Dakar: Les Nouvelles Editions Africaines, 1987) pp. 39-40. (All translations of this work provided in this essay are my own.)

43. Ibid., p. 128.

44. Steady, pp. 26, 33.

45. Ba, p. 116.

46. Ibid., pp. 120-121.

4

Child Sacrifice and Salvation

Sometimes in African Holocaust women's literature, the sacrificial loss of children marks the beginning of a mother's or community's salvation. The mother rarely performs this sacrificial loss as a conscious and intentional ritual. Usually, it seems only circumstantial: circumstances drive a mother to such acts that her child is lost to her or dies violently; then the mother's or community's self-defined goals are met.

Deliberate ritual acts of child sacrifice are usually performed by the child's family or greater community, beyond the mother. This is the central plot of Head's "Looking for a Rain God." In this short story, South African writer Head describes a prolonged season of drought and the desperation of a family whose male members are eventually executed for the "ritual murder" of the family's little girls. The mothers have agreed to the ritual, which was suggested by an older male who remembers the precolonialist ways. The family's hope is to reach and appease a deity who will send rain.

The act is useless; no rain falls, and the women are left without the help and support of the men or the assumed pleasure of the little girls' presence.

However, one has to assume that "help and support" and "pleasure" ever made up a part of this family's life. Throughout the story, brittle desperation characterizes the feel of the drought, the slow suffering, and the building family tensions, reflected in the little girls' harsh play with their dolls. "Looking for a Rain God" continues and develops the atmosphere of bleak futility under colonial rule that distinguishes much of Head's work. What is inexorable throughout this story is that death of a meaningless, lingering, nontransformative kind will descend upon the

Mokgobja family and their community no matter what they do. The ugly irony is that futile death overtakes them, finally, as punishment for having acted in the hope of salvation.

The deaths of the little girls are revealed to be the simple acts of butchery that the colonialist government has pronounced them to be; yet it is bitterly pathetic to realize that the government that avenges the girls' ritual deaths had no intention of intervening to prevent their slow starvation. The girls who were so brutally misused by their disillusioned family are, in death, used by the government as a tool for further persecution of the African population. The executions of "the old man and Ramadi," who tried to take their family's survival into their own hands, signals the end of the last shreds of faith in the old ways while underlining the hopelessness felt under the regime of the colonizers: "The subtle story of strain and starvation and breakdown was inadmissable evidence at court." For, witnessing the executions, the Mokgobja family's community acknowledges—silently, through the narrator—that any of the rest of them might have also made such a sacrifice to relieve their own slow suffering:

All the people who lived off crops knew in their hearts that only a hair's breadth had saved them from sharing a fate similar to that of the Mokgobja family. They could have killed something to make the rain fall.[1]

These last sentences leave the reader with the shadowy realization that the government's execution of the Mokgobja men has been as useless an act of ritual murder as the men's killing of the little girls. Perera explains the uncertain dynamics of sacrifice:

We are forced to offer what we hold dear, what we have paid much to gain. And we cannot even know that the loss will be compensated in the ways we desire. The sacrifice may change the balance of energy somewhere in the overall psychic system where we did not even want a change.[2]

The Mokgobja sacrifice leads their community to an unwanted clarity of perception. What has been at stake in the traditionalist versus pro-colonialist struggle is a bid for highest authority, not a bid to be seen as beneficent ruler.

For just as the rain god may receive the sacrifice and yet withhold the rain ("Throughout that terrible summer the story of the children hung like a dark cloud of sorrow over the village"), so the government has witnessed the desperation of the people and yet refused to relieve it with any act other than that of a reciprocal pair of deaths ("and the sorrow was not assuaged when the old man and Ramadi were sentenced to

death for ritual murder"). The story closes with the implicit understanding that the colonized community must consent to labor under the
weight of hopelessness, no matter the ultimate authority to which it
makes its needs known.

The protagonist of another of Head's short stories, "Witchcraft," also
addresses the dilemma of lonely affliction suffered by the villager.
Mma-Mabele suffers a wasting illness: "The pain took precedence over
everything else she experienced. . . . Soon her whole village ward noticed
the struggle she was waging with death."[3] After struggling to afford the
means of pro-colonialist methods of healing, which all fail her, Mma-
Mabele is suddenly seen about the village again in robust, defiant health.
When asked if "a special Tswana doctor" has healed her "like the rich
people," Mma-Mabele rails, "'There is no one to help the people, not
even God! I could not sit down because I am too poor and there is no
one else to feed my children.'" The ironic implication here is that death,
debility, and even despair are luxuries that the colonized poor cannot
afford. But beyond, or perhaps preceding, this statement about the
worthlessness of changing government regimes to the masses is the
spiritual uselessness of their changing religious figureheads. When
Mma-Mabele earlier relates in terror to her doctor, "'This thing [afflicting
demon] which I see now laughs when I pray to the Lord,'" he explains
this unheard-of phenomenon as a result of Botswana's self-rule: "'We
can never tell what will happen these days, now that we have independence.'" At the end, Mma-Mabele has accepted her loss of faith in all the
propagandized protection of the colonialist regime, including the Christian religion's protection against indigenous malevolent spirits. What is
unique is her refusal to then return to a traditional Tswana way of faith
and healing. She will not make the mistake of the Mokgobja family; the
laughing demon episode has destroyed her faith in either system of re-
ligion-reflective-of-government. She has taken "independence" at its
word, and after lying "in her hut like one stunned and dead for many
days," she has apparently abandoned belief in any helpful agency outside herself.

The odd twist in this cosmic picture is the acceptance of afflictive
spiritual forces while denying the existence of beneficent ones. This
same graphic image of a woman's being forced to find in herself the perspectives and personal strength to resist and survive psychospiritual
persecution is amplified in Head's autobiographical, multilayered exploration of existence, *A Question of Power*.

The comparative images of spiritual cosmic evil fought with personal psychospiritual perspective and resolution are somewhat reversed
in devorah major's *An Open Weave*. The narrative voice of Hurston's

Their Eyes Were Watching God has warned that "real gods require blood." This thirst for the bloody bodies of sacrificial children, in particular, threads the scattered poignant tales of *An Open Weave*'s mothers and off-spring. In this tapestry about search and learning to have faith, the sacrificial loss of a mother's child—even when it is unintentional and lamented—always results in the personal salvation of the mother.

The first in the series of sacrificial deaths is that of Ezekiel, the lost resident male of the triplicity of psychic women whose home is the spiritual center of the novel's developments. Ezekiel's beating death, a relatively common racist mob activity until the last two American generations, secures for the three women who depend on him the house they have rented, in chronic danger of eviction: "You told him [the sheriff] he might quit living if he wanted to, but he sure wasn't going to quit you and yours out of your home."[4] Ezekiel won the deed to the house in a gambling bet with the owner; the beating death was meant to hush up the transfer of title.

The former owner and his accomplices come to evict Ezekiel's blind, second-sighted mother, Ernestine, the weaver and healer; his epileptic, visionary foster sister and former lover, Iree; and her telepathic little daughter, Imani. Another character has named these three survivors the Stairstep Ladies. They reflect the recurrent Pan-African women's literary mythatype of a triplicity of women representing divergent yet complimentary aspects of the goddesshead:

The triplicity of the Goddess is very important. This is not merely a multiplying by three, but rather a threefold manifestation; the Goddess reveals herself on three levels, in the three realms of the world and of humankind.[5]

Superficially, the women who will inherit the home for which Ezekiel died seem to be a rather straightforward representation of the goddesshead aspects of Virgin/Mother/Crone. This is perhaps the easiest representation with which people can identify as this triplicity corresponds to the three phases of a woman's life."[6] But as the story develops, the three women reveal characteristics more in keeping with an ancient Arabian triplicity that was first demonized by, and then absorbed into, Islam and its rituals. Daughter Imani is a loyal fighter and resembles Al-Uzza, "the mighty" warrior. Iree resembles Al-Lat, the "Goddess," who was "the Mother facet connected with the Earth and its fruits" and apparently even the history which the soil and sea contain and remember. For Iree demonstrates this gift of knowing the earth's and waters' needs and experiences. Menat, the Crone, who "ruled fate and death," is symbolized by Ernestine's weaving and the knowledge of the end of things that she gains at her shuttle.[7] Dealing, as they always seem to do, with knowing the hidden, bringing life to the dying, and foreseeing the impenetrable, Imani, Iree, and Ernie also begin to resemble "the Graeae—those female figures whose names are Fear, Dread, and Terror, and who live at the borders of night and death."[8] For Imani knows—and sometimes gets slapped for voicing—people's lonely secrets. Iree walks into the ocean on vacation and experiences the Middle Passage: "their fingers passing through my chest and coming out bloody. . . . They called me by my name and asked me to point them east."[9] The reader learns that Ernestine, whose nickname is "spider lady," routinely decides when to heal or save a life and when to let that person struggle with healing herself.

Ezekiel's ghost appears and shows where he hid the deed as he crawled home to die. The ghost leads Iree to the old oak tree that stands near and for their home. His skull pours blood upon the ground, as if feeding the worth of his life into, and thereby consecrating, the land he means to dedicate to his bereft family: "Blood started flowing all over again. . . . he was fading. Even his voice started sounding more like the wind and less like him."[10] Ezekiel's heroism in life and death assures his gifted, afflicted extended family of residence in the eerie psychic center of their community, the hill above town with its tree.

Iree, the epileptic visionary, suffers a terrible seizure in which she realizes that the site of their home wants a blood sacrifice, apparently in addition to Ezekiel's beating death:

She said real quiet, 'Nuthin's ever died here on this hill. Nothing with blood that is. . . . How come nothing but plants and insects have ever died here? . . . That's what keeps things going, the dying and the rotting and the soil that's made from the dead meeting with earth. . . . Do you think it wants me?'[11]

Iree is afraid that the land wants a living blood sacrifice, one that will touch and be swallowed into the earth while still alive. Perhaps this is the reason Ezekiel's blood is not enough, though it wins the three visionary women permanent residence on the site of the forthcoming live sacrifice.

Iree's feel for what the hill wants reads like Jungian analyst Neumann's description of the earth as womb and grave:

The hungry earth . . . which devours its own children and fattens on their corpses . . . the vulture and the coffin, the flesh-eating sarcophagus voraciously licking up the blood seed of men and beasts and, once fecundated and sated, casting it out again in new birth, hurling it to death, and over and over again to death.[12]

However, the cycle for the hill has been incomplete, and the land has evidently suffered because of this odd cyclic lack, becoming "too grey and dry."[13] While Ezekiel's blood will allow the women to stay there, the hill is giving them a permanent home in exchange for the fact that they will draw to it its first living sacrifice. So profoundly empathic is Iree in her sudden understanding of what the hill wants that she almost becomes this first consumed victim:

"I thought that if Iree could have been sucked into that hillside she would have been. For a minute, I thought I saw a cloud of dust just raising around her."[14]

Iree is rescued from assuming the place of the living sacrifice by another devoted male family member; this rescue is blessed by a cool(ing) breeze as the hill returns Iree to her family and awaits the upcoming sacrifice that will present the novel's climax. The living sacrifice that the land and tree await will come through Iree's daughter's best friend, Amanda, who is herself an intended sacrifice who was allowed to live.

To gain the freedom and autonomy she has always wanted, Amanda's mother, Lorraine, has tried to burn down the house she inherited from her own mother, with her daughter, Amanda, in it. Lorraine's alcoholic, married Euro-American lover, Ray, who has always denied that Amanda is his daughter, appears just in time to rescue Amanda from the basement, her crematorial crypt. This rescue is presaged by his once having saved Amanda from Lorraine's attempt to burn her hand on the stove to teach the girl not to touch what is hot.

After Ray rescues and, thereby, publicly acknowledges his daughter for the first time, Lorraine informs him that now the child is his:

"She's yours now," he heard Lorraine whisper. . . . "She came because you wanted her, not me. I kept her till you were ready. Now I'm done."[15]

Lorraine boards a bus to find a new town and begin a new life. What has been transformative for Lorraine is the sacrifice of her security, represented by her house, and the predictability of her relationship with her lover, which ends with the fire:

Lorraine always seemed to live her life in response to others, being moved and moving wherever she was pushed. . . . There was something about Lorraine that was too calm and ominous to let him stay long in her carefully laid-out home. He felt that she might gather the free will she never seemed to use and quietly cut his throat one night, acting on the bitterness of a life spent always being pushed by others.[16]

With astonishing consistency, this book portrays men fleeing in fear from the women with whom they have babies. Imani's biological father fears and flees Iree; Ray is justifiably afraid of Lorraine and her cruel passivity; and Amanda's boyfriend wishes to be supportive but seems none too sure about Amanda. This constantly implied threatening aspect of the fertile womb echoes and magnifies the hill's resemblance to "toothed vagina" symbols, described thus by Neumann: "the destructive and deathly womb, appears most frequently in the archetypal form of a mouth bristling with teeth . . . in an African statuette, where the tooth-studded womb is replaced by a gnashing mask."[17]

"Toothed vagina" is a demonized renaming of the cowrie shell, a Yemoja/sea goddess symbol. (Nnu Ego, "sacks of cowrie shells," critiques the colonialist disempowerment of Emecheta's heroine in *Joys of Motherhood*, reflecting in a mortal woman's life the erosion of spiritual values and social structures suffered by her colonized society.)

When Lorraine sacrifices the security of an emotional passivity that allows others to use and choose for her, she gains both the uncertainty and the freedom of starting a new life with nothing. Amanda's life was not a necessary part of Lorraine's sacrifice, and technically, Amanda could not be sacrificed by Lorraine because Lorraine did not value or want her. The book begins with two problems: that since Ezekiel's disappearance, Ernestine has never closed a weaving but left them all open, "a breath and a sleeping between the patterns,"[18] and the disclosure to Imani of her abused and neglected friend Amanda's pregnancy. The book closes with the joined images of Imani's woven baby blanket, Ernestine's first unfinished weaving, being tied shut with a twig by Iree, making a triangular[19] bundle of Amanda's miscarriage which was discharged beneath the family's oak. Iree buries the bundle under the tree, "a fragile gift."[20] The tree evidently accepts it as such; for immediately thereafter, Zelma and Al agree to take the abused, abandoned Amanda home with them and raise "'one last daughter.'"[21] The wrenching sacrifice of the baby straight into the soil, an act that almost cost Amanda her young, unhappy life, has evidently been received by the land and tree as a gift. For in exchange, Amanda receives the parents she always wished she had. The concluding implication is that the sacrifice that began with Ezekiel has been completed in the loss of Amanda's pregnancy a day and a night after Imani's birthday; that the hill, the tree, and the family caught together in Ernestine's "webs" have come through a pain like birth that has brought them together in stability; and that they will never lose each other. major's interwoven tale of fiery, cooling, and sacrificial powers concludes with the realization that this family can neither hold on to time nor release its members. [22]

Elaborate as is the gift of the miscarried fetus to the hungry hill, blood sacrifice in *An Open Weave* seems to be attended by fewer obvious signs of ritual than in other works. For example, the burning death of a daughter of the ancestress-becoming-deity in *Pluie et vent sur Telumee Miracle* is followed by isolation and renaming, so that when the bereft mother emerges as the Nameless Queen, her identity with ancient African goddesses who represent the wisdom gained through suffering seems clear. The scapegoat-beloved sacrifice of the youngest child in *Beloved* is attended with the mother/child reunion sharing of milk and saliva (motherhood/nourishment and the blessing of a sealed pledge), the sacrificed daughter's blood drunk by the surviving daughter along with her mother's milk, and sexual intercourse over the sacrificed child's gravestone, which emphasizes the regenerative end of death (in rebirth). In contrast with these more obvious sacrificial dramas and the fact that the novels develop around their beneficial results, the ending of *An Open Weave* with the act of sacrifice may feel nebulous and unresolved. More than the beneficial returns to the mother and the community following an act of child sacrifice, *An Open Weave* emphasizes instead the importance of the wisdom gained through suffering. At one point, Iree observes that growth is like the spiraling-out layers of an onion; her perception captures the expanding concentric circles of an onion but misses the fact that they ring each other like layers of a tree. The expanding circles she refers to are not connected, nor do they reach for levels beyond themselves.

But Iree's point may be that each step in growth is a leap to a new sphere that encompasses all that one previously knew and yet is a realm beyond, a revolution away. Jungian psychoanalyst Marie-Louise von Franz thus explains and describes spiral growth:

[Restoring] a previously existing order . . . giving expression and form to something that does not yet exist, something new and unique. . . . In the new order the older pattern returns on a higher level. The process is that of the ascending spiral, which grows upward while simultaneously returning again and again to the same point.[23]

Begg describes European returning interest to Black Virgin cults in similar spiraling terms: "She [the Black Virgin] is the spirit of evolutionary consciousness that lies hidden in matter. But evolution rejects the closed circle for the open spiral."[24] Iree conflates these two images in her onion analogy, implying closure together with expansion, an apt description of the spiraling-out healing effect the trilogy of women on the hill have on those who trust them. In this way, the female triplicity is a closed unit—a circle—that always radiates its influence outward to an open sphere—its community, past, present, and future—thus creating an ever expanding, spiral-like circle of reciprocity.   But the spiral-as-expanding-circles analogy works also as a description of each woman's spiritual reality. Holloway explains that

The persistent paradox in black women's literature is not simply that historic events often exist in the same space as the events of the present. In addition to literary synchronicity, a figurative sharing of metaphysical space between historically recoverable events and events metaphorically retrieved through the instantiation of memory and myth occurs.[25]

For example, when Imani is introduced to the ocean and Iree undergoes her Middle Passage experience, Imani is described as "being her mermaid self." This is an excellent example of the literary trait of recursion as it distinguishes African American and Continental women's writing:

No other women in the world have experienced a similarly shared and sundered historical connection like that between women of West Africa and women of the diaspora.[26]

Holloway posits these points of literary intersection as "bio-geographical and cultur[al]." In keeping with Holloway's analysis of recurrent "echoes of the original culture persist[ing]," the following readings trace ancestral memory as shared between the child, her mother, and the earth that cups the sea around them. Fatunmbi recounts praisesongs to the primeval Yoruba goddess Yemoja, addressing her as "Goddess of the Sea," "Queen of the Sea," and "Spirit of the Ocean."[27] Yemoja is often conceived of, and represented as, a mermaid. Describing an aspect of Imani as a "mermaid self" ascribes to the child the ancient, life-giving, wise attributes of the goddess. Another Yoruba goddess described sometimes as a mermaid is Oshun of the river. Oshun "creates beauty" and "teaches the mystery of the erotic."[28] Ascribing Oshun's attributes to a virgin child portends fulfillment in potential, the end in the beginning. Ascribing the nubile Oshun and the mother of all, Yemoja, to the playing child, Imani, acknowledges the child's imbibing the spirits of the deities worshipped by her ancestresses into the essence of her being; the term acknowledges Imani as a circular community of relationship, incarnate. Iree, in contact with people, plants, and animals through the messages of the earth, likewise embodies a community of earth goddesses whose attributes she exemplifies and in relation to whom she serves as a mortal devotee. Ernestine, healing and threading lives through time, is enclosed in a community with goddesses of fate. Each woman is at the center of a circle of healing that radiates outward to reflect her growth and her broader spiritual and material communities.

In this light, Iree's onion clarifies the concentric circles spiraling into growth that describe both the individual's experiences and the novel's representation of multiple levels of community interacting to heal. Begg contends that "against the frenzied fashion for denying, defeating, and transcending nature, the Black Virgin stands for the healing power of nature." Von Franz acknowledges this principle by pointing out one of the titles of Mary as "Queen of Nature," who reunited body and soul in her corporeal ascent to heaven.[29]   *An Open Weave* expands the mythatypical symbolisms of better-known Pan-African women's works, treating child sacrifice to include nature's devouring aspect as another beneficent female principle that embraces community and demands a reciprocal share of responsibility and benefit in reflective/reflexive growth. That is, the spiral/concentric circle aspect of growth in the story allows each character to participate in a story of the community in which the individual is not central, and concurrently in a story at whose center is the individual.

The hill has its own story whose "thousands of years" of hunger will be satiated with an act of the willful donation of a blooded life, casting back a reflection of destined nurturance on the parched years:

The distinction between the concept of aspect and the notion of time (especially a Western notion of time past, present, or future) expands the reflective/reflexive potential within the literary event. A consideration of aspect prompts a consciousness of being and existence more complex than a simple identification of the relationship between the moment of event and the nature of the character involved.[30]

Though literary analyst Holloway is using the above explanation to describe what happens in a text characterized by recursion as it relates to repetition, here the paragraph helps explain how the destitute hill fits into major's pattern of sympathetic heroines inscribed in concentric circles of need-filled experience. The hill is the sustaining base of a community of women who each reflect aspects of the whole community and are simultaneously seeking to perfect and more fully experience as a whole. The hill is also a feminine character whose timelessness and long-standing need are reflected in the women it sustains. At the same time, the hill experiences a need of acknowledgement that must be tended to by the women it houses and protects. The hill is in reciprocal relation with its inhabitants and visitors and refuses those sacrifices that are not destined to fulfill its need (those of Iree and Amanda). In this, the hill divests the most mystifying feminine destructive power of its terrifying aspect and invests it with wholeness by returning it to cooperative identification with its beneficent aspect. Theologian Long summarizes that,

Both East and West turned away from nature and the material, took little interest in observation and measurement of natural laws and seasons, and turned to personal salvation and eventually a hatred of the material world of everyday life, of "the body", and eventually of women.[31]

In contrast, by developing the benign aspect of the hill's demand for a living sacrifice in return for shelter and goal fulfillment, *An Open Weave* exhorts a conscious and deliberate turning again of communities to (specifically dark or earth-colored) women, the women who live in mutuality with the hill, with protective concern for their needs and reverence for their insights, as an act of communal healing that develops the concluding premise of *The Salt Eaters*.

The concentric-circle patterns of growth and meaning in *An Open Weave* also reflect the meaning of child sacrifice itself back onto the individual within the community. To participate in the death of one's child as an act of giving to appease or supplicate to a powerful goddess entity is also to participate in the excising of one's own childish self so that positive growth may take place. When Amanda miscarries her pregnancy into the soil beneath Imani's oak tree, she simultaneously loses the fear of becoming a mother in the image of her own mother, and does what her mother did not do for her: grieve at the loss of the child. In that grief, Amanda establishes herself as having grown past the emotionless acceptance of her mother's abandonment, which was at once a defensive posture and a bonded mimicking of the parent she regretted losing. When she grieves the loss of her frightening pregnancy and threatens to die with it, she must be coached by Iree, her temporarily borrowed foster mother, to let go of the inchoate child and see herself as separate from her. She is encouraged to disown whatever she is discharging as having never been hers, but always destined for the hill and the soil.

As she lets go, loses the fetus, and lives, Amanda also releases the sense of herself and her experiences as isolated from the world around her. She lets go of the internalized solitude for which her mother abandoned her. She breaks identity with her mother and with the fate she suffered as her mother's rejected child. She intuits that she, Amanda, may belong to a greater universe than that framed for her by her mother, just as her own fetus belonged to a greater existence than the one to be had by remaining in Amanda's body. The fetus belonged to the hill, a spiritual reality heretofore unforeseen by Amanda; perhaps Amanda also belonged to a spiritual reality she had never before perceived because it had not been defined in the terms of her mother's rejection. By releasing the fetus to the hill, Amanda releases herself from being narrowly defined as only Lorraine's daughter.

Ernestine also has experienced a spiritual redefinition and material benefit from the death of her offspring, though it was certainly not, in Ernestine's case, an act of voluntary sacrifice: Ezekiel's death. Ernestine is unaware that she has benefited from Ezekiel's death, and this sacrifice remains throughout the novel knowledge which she rejects. Ernestine's weaving becomes "open" simultaneously with her son's murder, "a cloth of too many woven strands. A cloth with too many memories."[32] The openness of Ernestine's weaving leaves a space in which to remember and incorporate Ezekiel, part of the family whom "none of them ever let go of all the way."[33] Though Ernestine might not have wished his sacrifice, Ezekiel's ghost seems cheerful enough and determined to stick to the worth of having exchanged his life for his mother's and family's security. His ghost banters with Iree and helps her fight off the sheriff and his men, while guiding her and little Imani to the deed that will protect their right to stay on their hard-won property.

An Open Weave is a multilayered tale whose message is the reverencing of women as the healing panacea of choice for Pan-African women's communities; this moral is foreshadowed in Grace Ogot's "The Rain Came." In this short story, an East African community besieged by drought is guided to sacrifice the chief's daughter to the spirit of the dried lake in exchange for rain. Oganda, the chief's daughter, walks bravely toward her death, but just before she can consecrate herself to the waters and the spirit that dwells there, the man she had once hoped to marry pursues and stops her. Hand in hand, they flee their homeland, their ancestors, and the "monster" of the lake, trying to reach the border of the "sacred land" before sunset—the scheduled time of Oganda's sacrifice—is done:

There was a bright lightning. They looked up, frightened. Above them black furious clouds started to gather. They began to run. Then the thunder roared, and the rain came down in torrents.[34]

The juxtaposition of the gift of rain with the missed sacrifice of the young woman leaves a potential interpretive space to read the end of the drought as the lake spirit's blessing on their love. While this tale can certainly be read as a condemnation of traditional beliefs, it can also be read as validation of the young woman's community-centered intention to sacrifice herself as being pleasing enough to the spirit. Just as Iree and Amanda are not allowed to confuse themselves with the gift of life that the hill craves, so the dream that willed Oganda to journey from her village to the sacred lake may also be reread, or read more closely. For the dream stated that Oganda must "offer herself as a sacrifice to the lake monster. And on that day, the rain will come down in torrents,"[35] while everyone else stayed home. Clearly, the villagers' assumption was that Oganda was not only to offer herself but be accepted into the lake. However, close reading of the prophecy privileges Oganda's intention, not the outcome. It is equivocal that the deity who sent the dream, or the lake monster (often a powerful but benign goddess, such as Uhamiri in Nwapa's *Efuru*), actually intended for Oganda not only to offer herself but also to die. The story's narrative voice leaves room for the reader's hopeful interpretation that perhaps the spirit of the lake took pity on Oganda's grieving mother; or maybe it merely desired to grant Oganda's secret wish, putting her in a position where she might receive her childhood sweetheart as a husband and as the spirit's gift. In either case, the spirit's merciful gift of rain upon the fleeing couple, their village, and all surrounding neighborhoods underlines the importance of the story's African-descent women's happiness in bringing about the well-being of their communities.

NOTES

1. Bessie Head, "Looking for a Rain God" in Bessie Head, *The Collector of Treasures and Other Botswana Village Tales* (Oxford: Heinemann, 1992), p. 60.

2. Sylvia Brenton Perera, *Descent to the Goddess: A Way of Initiation for Women* (Toronto: Inner City Books, 1981), p. 55.

3. Head, p. 55.

4. devorah major, *An Open Weave* (New York: Berkley Books, 1997), p. 95.

5. Adam McLean, *The Triple Goddess: An Exploration of the Archetypal Feminine* (Grand Rapids: Phanes Press, 1989), p. 14.

6. Ibid., p. 15.

7. Ibid., p. 80.

8. Erich Neumann, *The Great Mother: An Analysis of the Archetype,* Ralph Manheim, Translator, (Princeton: Princeton University Press, 1963), pp. 168-169.

9. major, p. 48.

10. Ibid., pp. 100-101.

11. Ibid., p. 209.

12. Neumann, pp. 149-150.

13. major, p. 5.

14. Ibid., p. 212.

15. Ibid., p. 88.

16. Ibid., p. 84.

17. Neumann, p. 168.

18. major, p. 30.

19. Maude Southwell Wahlman, *Signs and Symbols: African Images in African-American Quilts* (New York: Penguin Group, 1993) explains that "triangles in

a quilt signified prayer messages or a prayer badge, a way of offering a prayer, or asking for protection," p 110. Barbara G. Walker, *The Woman's Dictionary of Symbols and Sacred Objects* (Edison, NJ: Castle Books, 1988), p. 40, suggests that "the triangle became a common symbol for 'woman' largely because it was originally a symbol for 'Goddess' and many of the objects associated with her," identifying the triangle particularly with the mother and crone aspects of a European female trinity. The triangle, like the female trinity, oak tree, table, and *vagina dentata* suggestion of the hungry hill, seems to be another of the cross-cultural symbolic fusions of *An Open Weave*, available to multilayered interpretations of meaning that converge in an image of traditionally female power as a source of societal healing, similar to that in Toni Cade Bambara's *The Salt Eaters* (New York: Vintage Contemporaries, 1992).

20. major, p. 241.

21. Ibid., p. 242.

22. Ibid., p. 243.

23. Marie-Louise von Franz, "The Process of Individuation," in Carl G. Jung and Marie-Louise von Franz, Editors, *Man and His Symbols* (New York: Doubleday and Company, Inc., 1971), p. 225.

24. Ean Begg, *The Cult of the Black Virgin* (London: Penguin Books, 1996), p. 131.

25. Karla Holloway, *Moorings and Metaphors: Figures of Culture and Gender in Black Women's Literature* (New Brunswick: Rutgers University Press, 1992), p. 72.

26. Ibid., p. 167.

27. Awo Fa'lokun Fatunmbi, *Yemoja/Olokun: Ifa and the Spirit of the Ocean* (Plainview: Original Publications, 1993), pp. 21 and 24-25.

28. Awo Fa'lokun Fatunmbi, *Oshun: Ifa and the Spirit of the River* (Plainview: Original Publications, 1993), p. 15.

29. Begg, p. 131 and von Franz, p. 226.

30. Holloway, p. 74.

31. Asphodel P. Long, *In a Chariot Drawn by Lions: The Search for the Female in Deity* (Freedom, CA: The Crossing Press, 1993), p. 153.

32. major, p. 30.

33. Ibid., p. 243.

34. Grace Ogot, "The Rain Came," in Margaret Busby, Editor, *Daughters of Africa: An International Anthology of Words and Writings by Women of African Descent: From the Ancient Egyptian to the Present* (New York: Ballantine Books, 1992), p. 371.

35. Ibid., p. 366.

5

Rape
and Rage

Diaspora and Continental African women's literatures deal extensively with the personal and cosmic rage generated by sexual violations of women and girls, including seduction, marital cruelty, infidelity, and rape. In societies where the negative stereotyping and demonization of women of African descent serve multiple agendas by upholding imbalanced power hierarchies, antivictimization literature is a counteractive force that deserves greater attention and whose detraction should be more closely queried.

Working against the inherited force of racist assumptions, Christian explains that

Black women writers . . . highlight the art of daily living and give back to the community a mirror of itself; and in that mirror, they can correct the stereotypes about black life that seem to proliferate so irresponsibly in our society.[1]

Cannon further develops this argument by pointing out that "the majority of Black women who engage in literary compositions hold themselves accountable to the collective values that underlie Black history and culture," creating a literary space that authenticates "how they affirm their humanity by inverting assumptions, and how they balance the continual struggle and interplay of paradoxes."[2]

One story of inverted assumptions and the interplay of paradoxes is Diallo's *Le fort maudit (The Cursed Fort)*. Critic Susan Stringer has pointed out that Diallo's work does not express hostility toward colonization. The implication is, clearly, that Diallo's work lacks a literal reaction against European colonization in Africa. This is arguably so, not only for

Diallo, but in the writings of many other Continental African women who feel Islamic strictures more immediately than they do Europe's imposed cultural imperialism, which sometimes seems in these women's writings to offer a comparative taste of freedom.

While Diallo's *Le fort maudit* is certainly vulnerable to criticism as a procolonialist account of African interethnic warfare before the European invasion, it also drives a wedge into the racist stereotyping of enslaved women of African descent as willing and voluptuous sexual-discharge receptacles. By defamiliarizing the enslavement discourse, taking race out of the equation by proposing an historically accurate setting of African nation against African nation, Diallo's story allows a re-examination of the racially biased assumptions about African docility, bestiality, and stupidity that have held sway when European colonization becomes a dialogic factor. Benin literary critic D'Almeida explains the subtle revolt in Senegalese Diallo's writing:

She acknowledges the importance of Islam and embraces it; however, she does so as would an "iconoclast," a Muslim defined by Mbye Cham as one who professes belief in Islam but criticizes its interpretation and practice. She remains closely attached to the "traditional" world of her origin, even as she suggests how that world is unfair or inadequate.[3]

D'Almeida's analysis highlights antipatriarchal resistance in Diallo's autobiography, *A Dakar Childhood*, even as Diallo celebrates elements of her Muslim tradition. Diallo's narrative voice "is one that praises tradition while denouncing and opposing certain negative elements of that same tradition." In *Le fort maudit*, Diallo creates a Muslim heroine who eschews what Diallo describes in her autobiography as qualities expected of well-brought-up African Muslim girls: "'the virtues of humility, silent endurance and self-effacing patterns of behaviour.'"[4]

To vindicate her enslaved nation, the captured princess Thiane subjugates the above traits to the service of a level of goal orientation and heroism traditionally reserved for boys: "'to go out there and triumph and survive.'"[5] Thiane becomes a loyal supporter (traditional Muslim female) to her own incentive (traditional Muslim male) to formulate and execute a plan for revenge and overthrow of the tyrant's invading forces that will tactically employ her sexuality—and her enemies' expectations about her sexual self—as weapons in her own arsenal. That is, Thiane will subjugate her feminine characteristics to the service of her will to wreak vengeance on her people's enemies, acting at once as female pawn and (traditionally patriarchal) strategist.

Had her father lived to execute this plan and used Thiane as bait, the reader would have been obligated to protest. Since it is instead Thiane who plans and executes the overthrow alone, the reader is forced to ponder the implications of her usurping the role of strategist while calculating the usage and successful deployment of her own female sexuality.

Diallo has isolated the situation of enslavement and successfully reversed the yoke of negative assumptions about the enslaved African female, attributing to her protagonist the ability to calculate her enemies' expectations of her limitations while steeling herself to act independently of her own traditionally instilled values. That is, Thiane will surrender herself to rape in order to avail herself of a unique opportunity to murder the enemy prince's chief commander of armed forces.

This strategy is similar to Brent's calculations in *Incidents in the Life of a Slave Girl*. Brent foresees that if she agrees to what would be statutory rape by modern legal standards (she was only fifteen), at the hands of a wealthy and politically influential Euro-American man, circumstances would most likely develop that could be maneuvered toward arranging her and her (unborn) children's freedom from another Euro-American, who was fast arranging a situation of coercive rape. Brent is at pains to explain to her readers the importance of freedom of choice in the sharing of one's sexual self; what may be impossible to explain to anyone who has not experienced it is the negligibility of concern for one's supposed honor when one is in a situation in which degradation is assumed by others to be one's normal state. That is, perhaps the never-enslaved reader would assume that it was more honorable for Brent to await forced rape at the hands of her owner than to submit willingly to another after extracting from him all necessary self-protective verbal agreements. Perhaps a reader may also reasonably assume that it is more honorable for Thiane to witness the rape and murder of mother, family, and nation, and then to kill herself out of despair rather than knowingly place herself in a position of rape in order to catch her opponent in his most vulnerable (orgasmic) state. The comparative acceptability of arguable alternatives is less the issue here than is Diallo's and Brent's converging portrayals of enslaved African women whose strategic use of their sexual vulnerability enables them to outmaneuver and defeat their enslavers. These heroines concurrently challenge, if not defeat, those pervasive, procolonialist negative stereotypes that portray African women in captivity as lasciviously enslaved to their own sexual appetites and incapable of complex rational thought. In *Reconstructing Womanhood: The Emergence of the Afro-American Woman Novelist*, Carby describes these stereotypical sexual metaphors as extending from the passionate and apparently quite willing whore to the cringing, helpless victim, the range of which both Brent and Thiane's stories assiduously deny.

After murdering the general and the prince he served, sacrificing the virginity she had hoped to share with her fiance to her fiance's murderer and her mother's rapist and murderer, Thiane seeks peace in an anti-Islamic act of suicide. Following the death of the prince:

Thiane etait au sommet de l'extase. Elle eprouva une sensation de bien-etre, une paix immense comme si son corps, son couer, son etre tout entier etaient a jamais debarrasses du poids de toutes les souffrances de son existence. Elle s'enfuit dans le crepuscule et vint s-asseoir pres de ses soeurs sous le baobab. La . . . elle s'enfonca le rabou dans le couer.

(Thiane was ecstatic. She felt such well-being, such tremendous peace as if her body, heart, and entire self were freed as never before from the weight of all she had suffered during her lifetime. She fled toward the dawn and went to sit with her sisters beneath the baobab. There . . . she stabbed the [poisoned] twig into her heart.)[6]

Diallo completes this rewriting of historical perspective by including heroic praisesongs for the girl who plotted to sacrifice her virginity, commit murders, and send herself to the spiritual world to be with her murdered loved ones after defeating an enemy her father's army could not resist. Thiane's story can certainly be interpreted as supportive of procolonialist arguments that intertribal conflicts necessitated and continue to excuse European invasion and imperialist theft of natural and human resources from the African continent. However, the reader gains appreciable insights into the female character of resistance by appreciating Diallo's stringent querying of racist and misogynistic stereotypes about enslaved African women.

It is necessary to note, however, that a procolonialist reading of *Le fort maudit* would be supported by comparison with other of Diallo's works, such as *Awa, la petite marchande*. In this young adult novel, a Senegalese girl suffering from class discrimination goes to France and suffers from racial bias. But her European education and appearance win her respect and envy when she returns to her former community back on the Continent. The message of *Awa* seems to be that Africans can experience and benefit from the same kind of class jumping that Europeans did and do (invading the Americas, Africa, and Australia) by accepting the grudging opportunities offered in Europe. If a reader is opposed to class bias, *Awa*'s message is potentially quite positive. Just so, *Le fort maudit* can quite appropriately be read as a mythatypical epic that queries paternalistic and racist stereotypes about who possesses and what constitutes courage, ingenuity, and the potential for an unflinching commitment to a difficult purpose, attributes long denied women of African descent in the literatures of European-descent writers and multicultural men. *Le fort maudit's* mythatypical perspective is supported by decolonialist histories such David Sweetman's *Women Leaders in African History* and Giddings's *When and Where I Enter: The Impact of Black Women on Race and Sex in America.*

An even more aggressively womanist rewriting of European invasion of Africa is Emecheta's historical fiction, *The Rape of Shavi*. In this novel, Emecheta posits the crash landing of a bunch of disenchanted Europeans in an isolated African community. The Europeans are made welcome according to the community's traditional customs and housed and tended to by the community's own royal women. Procolonialistically misreading the host community's every action and intention, the invading group leaves havoc in its wake, including the rape of the community's virgin princess, Shavi, the community's namesake, before it finally returns to England to recount its adventures.

Shavi's fiance and prince has stowed away with the Europeans. The prince returns to his home carrying the infection of European weaponry to marry a bride now infected with syphilis. Shavi's women have captured and secretly killed her rapist, but the reader watches in helpless horror as Emecheta makes it clear that the women have no means of understanding or curing Shavi of Europe's trademark disease. The novel closes as syphilis races to the crown prince's brain, spurring him on to greater acts of atrocity with his European tools of genocide, inspiring him to the conscienceless bastardization of his African powers of kingship. He is fast depleting his people's sacred and natural resources for more European means of mass destruction. Rebellion and chaos are spreading in the wake of Europe's destabilizing intrusion into a delicately balanced African society, imitating in *The Rape of Shavi's* fictional microcosm the Continental African history whose immediacy and racist media treatment often make it difficult to objectively understand.

Shavi's women consult and cite tradition and women's wisdom in their decision to cage the rapist so that he may die of thirst and sunstroke in the desert; their futile but intelligent retribution calls to mind the doomed efforts of Nyale. Judith Gleason describes Nyale as

Goddess of fire-and-wind in the upper Niger, Malinke culture area. A rebellious feminine principle, Nyale was demoted by the powers of reason and balance to the status of "little old woman with white hair."[7]

Nyale is a weakened but, oddly, still witchlike perception of womanly sedition. Shavi's women invoke feminine efficiency and unclouded judgment as the authority that empowers them to take the punishment of the rapist into their own very capable hands, thereby reuniting "reason and balance" with the "rebellious feminine principle."

The plight of Shavi recalls Lorde's depiction of the demonized warrior goddess, Seboulisa, and Lorde's assertion in a poem that "the snake" (wisdom and regeneration) remains "aware" though "sleeping" under the narrator's "blood,"[8] which apparently unites menstrual flow with rain and rebellion, as in Jamaica Kincaid's post-abortion scene following the protagonist's statutory rape in *The Autobiography of My Mother*.

Perhaps the fictional work which most irrevocably calls up a black female deity to avenge rape, and ties this figure in as the patroness of anticolonialist revolutionaries, is written by a Bengali.

Before they were invaded by brown-skinned Aryans, the black-skinned inhabitants of the Indus Valley worshipped a goddess named for her blackness, "Kali." It is in Kali that the Eurocentrically negative definition of blackness comes full circle to indicate the ultimate victory of the vanquished: "Kali reigns supreme as the goddess of fatality who determines the destiny of things."[9] Kali, "the great protectress," survived the Aryan invasion, became integrated into the conquerors' religion, retained dominion of the city named for her—Kalighata, anglicized into "Calcutta"—as well as her hold on the cosmic consciousness of both India's colonized blacks and their brown-skinned Aryan colonizers. There is a depiction of Kali that shows her beheaded, standing on two copulating bodies, which Adam McLean explains represent "the divine principle as the male and female forces in nature and the human realm," while the goddess's two female servants and her own severed head drink the three founts of blood that spurt from the goddess's neck. This is the depiction of Chinnamasta, a self-surrender to which Kali inspires the reflective soul for, McLean advises, "this horrific and terrible Triple Goddess figure, in fact, contains a profound wisdom of the inner functioning of our psyches."[10] Edward C. Whitmont explains that, psychoanalytically,

Offering oneself for beheading implies a renunciation, temporarily at least, of "head control," of the objectifying sense of order and collective rule upon which the ego has relied. One faces into the dark maw of one's own nature, into one's needs and hurts, one's affects and instincts, including the two demonic aspects of "devouring passion and bestial stupor," in their tempting as well as destructive forms.[11]

Chinnamasta represents the balance of opposing drives in the lower soul, "the dark, inert, feminine" and "the radiant, expansive, masculine," resulting in a balanced "upper-head consciousness."[12] This balancing of female and male aspects of the individual, and from this, the individual with the world around her or him, is mirrored in *Ifa* (traditional Yoruba religious) teachings, as explained by Fatunmbi.

In *Ifa* myth, expansion and light are frequently identified with Male Spirits called *"Orisha'ko"*. Contraction and darkness are frequently identified with Female Spirits called *"Orisha'bo"*. Neither manifestation of *ase* is considered superior to the other and both are viewed as essential elements in the overall balance of Nature.[13]

Psychoanalyst Charles Muses analyzes the peculiarly imbalanced excesses of materialism and abstract reasoning that

[Lead to] patterns of paranoid power-seeking that, by and large, tend to seize control of world society in the dark ages of the latter twentieth century . . . [promoting] the shabby and shoddy creed of hopelessness. . . . That there is (1) no scheme of things other than the molecular one in which we live on earth, and (2) no higher than human intelligence and ability, and hence (3) that individualized personality and living form cease with the physical dissolution of the molecular body . . . made the basis of our educational system, leading at once to both a jungle-law society and, in other aspects, to an essentially hopeless and comfortless collectivism which ultimately reduces all individual suffering and learning to meaninglessness.[14]

The world in the wake of European imperialist expansion suffers from the divorcing of mind and soul, desire and reason. It is the goal in a worldwide modern society that embraces expansionist theories to feed these drives inordinately. But not to unite or balance them, tempering the urges of one against the limiting influence of the other. This leads to a world crippled by the demands of mind and body running separately amok behind the devouring implements of the industrial revolution. Kali is sometimes depicted dancing on the bleeding body of her "sometime husband, the Great God [Siva] himself. In this depiction, Siva is often in a state of sexual arousal."[15] Benjamin Walker explains this symbolism thus: "There is a tantric saying, 'Shiva (Male Principle) without Shakti (Female Principle) is a corpse.'"[16] Steady explains modern imbalance in terms of a nature/culture perceptual divergence, leading to the same ruinous world crises:

Another point of departure from Western interpretations involves the viewpoint that nature is necessarily inferior to culture and consequently, in keeping with views of female inferiority, correlates female with nature and male with culture. When one thinks of how, in the name of culture, technology will very nearly destroy all that is natural and good on the planet earth and replace it with nuclear technology and pollution, one wonders why there has been such overvaluation of so-called progress. . . . Our energies might be better spent if we focus on the more critical fact, namely, that the earth's resources (nature), on which technology (culture) depends, are finite.[17]

Kali is the "dynamism of the cosmos."   If a colonized and polluted world will survive, this "avenging side; the terror side" of "an all-pervading female potency that suffuses the universe like a vast web in which the manifest world is enmeshed"[18] must be incorporated some-how, represented in the wake of colonialism's worldwide grasp. Kali gives the world its "shape and reality but also a fierce vital energy," and if the world collectively wishes to exist and learn to confront its ills, its Kali aspect must necessarily be reckoned with, as there is no existence possible without it.

Similarly, through the consuming, transformative power of Kali's appearance in black women's literature, it is to be hoped that the world's history will cease to be hearsay, the egomaniacal cant of displaced plun-derers, and become instead an echo of "the creative and destructive breathing of the universe"[19] in which all peoples and all things have their point of balance. David Leeming and Jake Page liken Kali to the Yoruba "instrument of death," the goddess Oya, who is also "one of the guardi-ans of issues related to the fair treatment of women."[20] Indeed Kali, her baby throat slit, as was Beloved's, shares with Oya, "mother of children and mother of corpses," the additional designation of "bringer of jus-tice."[21] In fact, just as Kali dances for female power in the balance of the universe, so do Oya and all the Yoruba riverain goddesses, "famed for their 'witchcraft,'"[22] protect traditional societies from sex and class re-pression and its excessively imbalanced distributions of power. Ideally, in these colonialist times, these goddesses have extended their "radical female power" to aid in the struggle against economic imperialism. In *The Sword and the Flute*, David Kinsley describes how Kali's energy "pitilessly grinds down" differences. Perera explains that Kali "is the destructive-transformative side of the cosmic will."[23] Alice Walker's genitally mutilated African protagonist, Evelyn-Tashi, invokes Kali when she wishes to have enough arms to hurl stones and fend off her husband's interracial lovechild:

A large jagged stone, grey as grief, struck him just above the teeth. I began to throw the stones as if, like Kali, I had a dozen arms, or as if my arms were a mul-tiple catapult or windmill.[24]

The "destructive-transformative" aspect of this "great protectress" is consummately depicted in Devi's short story, "Draupadi," translated and criticized by Spivak in *In Other Worlds: Essays in Cultural Politics*. "Draupadi" is about the efforts of the black-skinned Bengali migrant workers to rebel against their brown-skinned Aryan landlords, the privileged descendants of India's Hindu Aryan colonizing invaders. The story's use in this Pan-African collection reflects my agreement with, and desire to illustrate, Kathleen Cleaver's categories of "colonized" and "colonizers" as necessary terminologies in a worldwide dialogue that opposes economic imperialism and continuing erosion of human rights in a technological age. Also, the following analysis demonstrates the efficacy of freeing the interpretation of the subaltern's literature from the analytical devices of the colonizer's methodology through the overlay of culturally relevant mythical precedents.

The title character in "Draupadi" is named for a Hindu heroine who could not be raped. This story's "tribal" protagonist, not a Hindu, has been given the name as an act of benevolence, translator Spivak explains, on the part of the landowner's wife for whom the protagonist has worked. Spivak suggests that "Dopdi," which the title character is called in her mind and by her corevolutionaries, is a tribal mispronunciation of the Sanskrit "Draupadi." Perhaps "Dopdi" is even the original tribal name that was eventually bastardized into the Sanskrit "Draupadi."[25] In any event, the "tribal" title character initially defends her claim to inviolability by putting out the eyes of the Aryan landowner, as he is terrorized and killed by the revolutionaries, because he used to look at her with lust.[26] But "Dopdi," the black Bengali tribal, is not "Draupadi," the privileged descendant of upper-caste Aryan Hindus. When Dopdi is ambushed and captured for the murder of the lustful landowner, she is stripped—although Draupadi of the legend could not be stripped—tied spread-eagled in a tent, and raped countless times under the "vomited" light of the moon.

This brutalization, obviously, is intended to humiliate and terrorize the widowed Dopdi. But in the morning, Dopdi, the spelling of whose name has now metamorphosed to "Draupadi," refuses to wash or dress, just as during the rapes she refused herself the consolation of more than the first involuntarily shed tear.

Draupadi will not present humiliation or fear to her captors. Instead, she shreds her garment with her teeth, an act legend says that Kali performed as well to strangle the enemy demons who only multiplied when she stabbed them. An astonished messenger carries to the commander news of Draupadi's Kali-like action before she goes, in all the horror of her violation, to face this man who engineered her capture and prescribed the method of her torture.

The rapes were meant to put Draupadi, the tribal, in her place, to remind her of her station and her vulnerability in the hands and judgment of the procolonialist law. Instead, the rapes have thrown the protagonist back into a power base lost in time and history to her tribe's persecutors. Haglike, her breasts "two wounds" (like the worm-eaten left breast of Seboulisa), blood matted and running from her pubic area,

Draupadi spits "gore" from her bloodied mouth upon the commander and challenges him to see how she has been "made," which is his own term for her rape. She has been "made" into an image remarkably like that of Kali: the blackness, the nakedness, the bloodshot ("red") eyes and tangled hair, and the blood-dripping mouths are shared in common between Dopdi the rapeable and Kali the dispenser of harsh justice, particularly to those who harm women and children.[27]

Draupadi laughs in the commander's face and says in a "terrifying" voice that

"You can strip me, but how can you clothe me again? Are you a man? . . . There is not a man here that I should be ashamed. I will not let you put my cloth on me. What more can you do? Come on, *counter* me."[28]

The story closes upon the commander's unexplained fear of his prisoner.

Devi's and Spivak's insistent use of the word "made" for Dopdi's ravaged transformation suggests an unwitting agency on the part of her captors by means of the multiple rapes they perpetrated upon her. Draupadi's black, bleeding, mangled body opposes that of the inviolable Hindu Draupadi in every aspect, even in Dopdi's refusal to let herself be dressed again in the cloth that the god Krishna made miraculously unwindable on the praying Draupadi of Hindu legend.

Dopdi, unlike her foreign and privileged namesake, has not only been stripped but physically violated. But unlike Draupadi, the conqueror's symbol of purity, Dopdi, the tribal, emerges from this ordeal spiritually empowered by her captors' acts of debasement. She was not "unmade" by this ordeal, as was intended, but truly "made." The only question is, "made" into what? This is what the commander asks as he is struck by her transformation: "'What is this?'"[29]

Dopdi's flaunting of her ravaged self signals her rejection of the values of the conquering Hindu culture whose tactical war agent she now confronts. She has been made, but made into something besides the aspiring admirer of an unreachable culture and status that the "benevolent" bestowal of her foreign name implied. She has become something outside that theological and philosophical system. By emphasizing to his prisoner that she is not her namesake, Draupadi, the eternally clothed and eternally chaste, the commander has only emphasized to himself that she is protected, not by a male god who wants his women devotees to be passive suppliants, but by an older, angrier deity who historically inspires her devotees to kill men and offer her their blood.

Kali seized the latecoming European conception of terror through such devotees as the Thugs, highwaymen who practiced a strangling ritual in honor of one of Kali's aspects, Bhavani, and worshipped her sacred pickaxe.[30] Thugs were usually not Hindus, as Dopdi, the "tribal," is not a Hindu, but the goddess and the ritual murderers embraced each other, anyway, just as Dopdi and Kali have done.

It would be infinitely interesting to know how Devi, the writer, might have interpreted the "made" Dopdi. However, Devi's possible interpretation of "Draupadi," the story, is not included with Spivak's own argument against Devi's interpretation of another of her short stories, "Breast-Giver."

In fact, the whole of Spivak's and fellow postcolonialist theorist David Hardiman's arguments over the right to interpret, excluding and overriding Devi's own offer of interpretive theory,[31] makes for a troubling reenactment of what Henderson, in "Re-Membering the Body as Historical Text," has called the white male who writes and the white female who reads upon the body of the black female.

Spivak argues against Devi's reading of the "Breast-Giver" story, of the subaltern (unempowered woman) as a metaphor for her nation.[32] For Spivak's postcolonialist theoretical approach to Subaltern Studies, this refusal of Devi's reading may be understandable. In this separation of the author's intended collapse of history and literature into metaphor, what is left unanswered by the translator's rejection of the author's analysis is how Spivak's rejection reflects upon what Morrison summarizes in "Rootedness: The Ancestor as Foundation" as the individual life that is also representative. Clearly, Devi reads in her own writing a solitary life that reflects a community's experience as well as its prognosis: cancerous death. In this light, Spivak's dismissive discourse, which advises Devi out of the historico/literary dialectic about her own work, might be answered by Holloway's point that

The perceptual "outsidedness" of these authors (a factor of both gender and culture) propels a revision in the critical discourse about their literature. In such a discursive space, "shift" becomes a necessary mediation between the reader and the text and encourages a dialogue among critical postures within the interpretive community. Shift positions the alternative interpretations represented by the assertions of gender and culture within the textures of this literature. The critical result is a theoretical acknowledgment of the multiplied text. . . . Whose point of view is privileged?[33]

In reading this "multiplied text," perhaps an alternative analytical phraseology to the subaltern-as-nation metaphor might still permit the overlay of the individual, the community, and in reflective/reflexive interaction with and transformation through individual and community, their culturally-relevant mythatypes. In other words, is Dopdi's emergence into Draupadi's "made" black body an "activation in the face of stasis, a restoration of fluidity, translucence, and movement to the traditions of memory?"[34] Specifically as they apply to black women, these words demarcate a theoretical boundary separating the empowerment of decolonialist theory from the silencing presumption of postcolonialism.

In Bengal, where "the worship of Kali remains widely prevalent" and is closely associated with that of the warrior goddess Durga, the colonizing forces that sought to suppress Dopdi seem to have "made" her into a reflection of divine retribution. "Kali is what we call history," Leeming and Page summarize, "the Mother of eternal Time," and if her manifestation through the raped black body of a migrant farmwoman signals their being championed by her bloody rage, it might also herald the advent of the time when "she gathers them as seeds to begin anew the everlasting creation."[35]

This note of bloody, lament-filled promise is echoed in Cliff's exceptionally ambitious decolonialist work, *Free Enterprise*. Cliff shares Emecheta's use of syphilis and rape to distinguish Europe's impact on the foreign cultures it claims to civilize—"'We had been syphilized, my friends, cured of our savage state,'"[36]—adding to this metaphor the use of leprosy to represent anticolonialist rebellion. These symbolic tools spread with poetic irony a storytelling net that catches and drags the putrefactive face of European colonialism's story into coherent and appalling relief, shattering stereotypes in the light of their own reflections: "They were no more gods than we were, but seemed unsure of that. They helped themselves to the world as though they had created it."[37]

The story is about the women behind and beyond John Brown's precocious plunge into rebellion; among them are Mary Ellen Pleasant, entrepreneur, and Annie, a once privileged Jamaican of mixed race. As in "Draupadi," *Free Enterprise* ties rape to startlingly successful reversals in the revolution against racist colonialist domination. But in the anguish of Cliff's gathering tale, one may miss the transition point of Annie's capture, imprisonment, and repeated rapes as the Civil War breaks out and—dispassionately, without commitment to her ideals—ends the chattel slavery against which Annie fought and for whose preservation she has been captured and tortured.

One may read past this turning point, assuming, as does the character of Annie, that her contribution to the cause has come to nothing. However, the interpretive use of available mythatypes would argue otherwise. For it is Annie's menstrual blood that gives away her identity in the prison camp. She is pitied by the escaped enslaved men who are brought, "for the daily entertainment," to rape her. Though West African Oya is represented by volcanic eruption,[38] Cliff assures the reader that it is Pele, the Polynesian volcano goddess, who is called to the reader's mind by Annie's show of menstrual flow: "When Pele stomps her feet in anger at human insults, the earth shakes and lava flows from her volcano vulva."[39]   Pele's blood has revolutionary consequences: "Pele makes her will known on earth, and when it is gainsaid . . . she will explode in rage."[40] Perhaps Annie's blood shares the revolutionary traits of Pele's. For when she is released from prison, heartsick and trauma-tized, she wanders the scorched and defeated former slave states until she finds a leper colony in which to seclude herself, contemplating the world in which she has been an unknowing force.

In sharp contrast to Annie's emergence from captivity and rape is Frances E. W. Harper's Iola Leroy. Sold and, apparently, sexually as-saulted, as must be assumed from the protagonist's statement that "I was abused, but the men who trampled on me were the degraded ones,"[41] Iola is freed and emerges as the opposite of the similarly riches-to-rape traumatized Annie. Iola becomes the incarnation of all that Annie's es-caped Nanny was named to be: industry. Iola will uplift herself and her lately identified people (she used to see herself as European American) by advocating and exemplifying the moral worth of wage-paid labor. Annie, instead, hopes that her own nurse, fitted with a bit until she grinned against her will like Sethe's mother (in *Beloved*), has escaped to blend and become one with the legendary Nanny of the revolutionary maroons, much as Sethe's wetnurse, Nanny, and Janie's grandmother, Nanny (in *Their Eyes Were Watching God*), speak for escape and the seiz-ing of dignity. Kenneth Bilby and Steady explain that

An important personage named Nanny really existed. . . . It is believed that her ethnic background was Akan and that she was born in Africa. There are refer-ences to her in the contemporary British literature as a powerful obeah-woman, or sorceress...Whether or not she ever actually joined in combat is uncertain, but there is no doubt that she wielded great authority, military and otherwise, as a result of her ritual status.[42]

Cliff summarizes and poetically paraphrases this biography of an ancestress becoming a deity as she describes Annie's devoted admiration of Nanny and her own progressive conflation with a companion revolu-tionary mythatype, Annie Christmas.

Commemorating this legendary, revolutionary Nanny, and her fighters, with the glass bottle tree is the mythatypical symbol of Annie's gradual spiritual reorientation and healing:

Today the function of similar expressions presiding over Kongo graves is the blocking of the disappearance of the talents of the important dead. Lifting up their plates or bottles on trees or saplings also means "not the end," "death will not end our fight," the renaissance of the talents of the dead that have been stopped, by gleaming glass and elevation, from absorption in the void.[43]

Annie is building herself a spiritual community of fellow revolutionaries, maroons, runaways, and lepers, all social outcasts who take no joy in the politicized, spiritually noncommittal defeat of the chattel slavery phase of colonialism.

This becomes clear as Annie relives the anticolonialist revolution with her friends in the leper colony, linking hope, mother, spirituality, and nanny with the fight for freedom:

"The most important tributary of the Hope River was the Mammee, the Akan word for mother. Names are extremely important. . . . The source of the healing stream and the Mammee was in the Blue Mountains, near the site of Nanny Town. . . . The source is to be found in the cascade of water which washes the mountain, near where a flock of white birds, the souls of Nanny and her soldiers, gathers each evening at dusk."[44]

In the Diaspora, the color blue represents Yemoja/Yemaya.[45] This symbol, along with Annie's many references to water and healing, leads one to suspect that, in her solitude with spirit bottle tree and lepers where the Mississippi River meets the ocean, Annie is being healed by the mother spirit whose power "is to transform traumatic experience by providing a soothing and comforting sense of the transcendent."[46]

Free Enterprise abounds with mythatypical symbols, including the Kongo Cosmogram and the saddened snake god, Damballah, or could it be the orphaned rainbow serpent, Bunzi? The story presents an image of a snake trampled underfoot by suffragette little girls playing at politics and power with issues that are life and death to the enslaved and their descendants. The many symbols' interactive interpretations add layers of multiplied meaning to the text and enrich Cliff's already vivid presentation of the transcendence of time and the reality of spiritual communities in the wars for liberation waged in the material world.

NOTES

1. Barbara Christian, *Black Women Novelists: The Development of a Tradition, 1892-1976* (Westport, CT: Greenwood Press, 1980), p. 144.

2. Katie G. Cannon, *Black Womanist Ethics* (Atlanta: Scholars Press, American Academy of Religion, 1988), p. 77.

3. Irene Assiba D'Almeida, *Francophone African Women Writers: Destroying the Emptiness of Silence* (Gainesville: University Press of Florida, 1994), p. 37.

4. Ibid., p. 43.

5. Ibid., p. 42.

6. Nafissatou Niang Diallo, *Le fort maudit* (Paris: Hatier, 1980), p. 125 (my translation).

7. Judith Gleason, *Oya: In Praise of an African Goddess* (New York: Harper-Collins, 1992), p. 306.

8. Audre Lorde, "Dahomey" in Audre Lorde, *The Black Unicorn: Poems by Audre Lorde* (New York: W.W. Norton and Company, Inc., 1978), pp. 10-11.

9. Benjamin Walker, "Kali," in Richard Cavendish, Editor, *Man, Myth and Magic: An Illustrated Encyclopedia of the Supernatural* (New York: Marshall Cavendish Corporation, 1970) p. 1556. These volumes are all the literature that I was allowed to inherit from the extensive library of an aunt who supported my abstract intellectual interests with uncompromised encouragement and undiluted theoretical challenges. Her independent research was my inspiration. This chapter is written in memory of Ruth Johnson Thornton, who earned unrecognized degrees in Comparative Religion and Philosophy.

10. Adam McLean, *The Triple Goddess: An Exploration of the Archetypal Feminine* (Grand Rapids: Phanes Press, 1989), pp. 98-100.

11. Edward C. Whitmont, *Return of the Goddess* (New York: Crossroad, 1990), pp. 175-176.

12. McLean, pp. 100-101.

13. *Awo* Fa'lokun Fatunmbi, *Yemoja/Olokun: Ifa and the Spirit of the Ocean* (Plainview, NY: Original Publications, 1993), p. 12.

14. Charles Muses, "The Ageless Way of Goddess: Divine Pregnancy and Higher Birth in Ancient Egypt and China," in Joseph Campbell and Charles Muses, Editors, *In All Her Names: Explorations of the Feminine in Divinity* (New York: HarperCollins, 1991), p. 132.

15. David Leeming and Jake Page, *Goddess: Myths and Legends of the Female Divine* (New York & Oxford: Oxford University Press, 1994), p. 24.

16. Walker, "Tantrism," in Cavendish, Editor, p. 2778.

17. Filomina Chioma Steady, "The Black Woman Cross-Culturally: An Overview" in Filomina Chioma Steady, Editor, *The Black Woman Cross-Culturally* (Cambridge, MA: Schenkman Publishing Company, Inc., 1981), p. 31.

18. Walker, "Kali," pp. 1554, 1556.

19. Leeming and Page, p. 24.

20. *Awo* Fa'lokun Fatunmbi, *Oya: Ifa and the Spirit of the Wind* (New York: Original Publications, 1993), p. 10.

21. Leeming and Page, pp. 24-25.

22. Robert Farris Thompson, *Flash of the Spirit: African and Afro-American Art and Philosophy* (New York: Vintage Books, 1984), p. 74.

23. Sylvia Brenton Perera, *Descent to the Goddess: A Way of Initiation for Women* (Toronto: Inner City Books, 1981), p. 24.

24. Alice Walker, *Possessing the Secret of Joy* (New York: Pocket Books/Washington Square Press, 1993), p. 145.

25. Gayatri Chakravorty Spivak, "Entering the Third World," in Spivak, *In Other Worlds: Essays in Cultural Politics* (New York: Methuen, Inc., 1987), p. 183.

26. Ibid., p. 193.

27. The compared descriptions of Kali and the "made" Dopdi are from

Benjamin Walker, "Kali," p. 1556, and Spivak, p. 196.

28. Spivak, p. 196.

29. Ibid.

30. Benjamin Walker, "Thugs," in Cavendish, Editor, pp. 2835-2836.

31. Spivak, p. 268.

32. Ibid., p. 244.

33. Karla Holloway, *Moorings and Metaphors: Figures of Culture and Gender in Black Women's Literature* (New Brunswick: Rutgers University Press, 1992), p. 64.

34. Ibid., p. 68.

35. Leeming and Page, p. 24.

36. Michele Cliff, *Free Enterprise* (New York: Dutton, 1993), p. 49.

37. Cliff, p. 47.

38. *Awo* Fa'lokun Fatunmbi, *Oya: Ifa and the Spirit of the Wind* (New York: Original Publications, 1993), p. 16.

39. Leeming and Page, pp. 25-26.

40. Ibid., p. 26.

41. Frances E. W. Harper, *Iola Leroy*, in William L. Andrews, Editor, *The African-American Novel in the Age of Reaction: Three Classics* (New York: Mentor, 1992), p. 88.

42. Kenneth Bilby and Filomina Chioma Steady, "Black Women and Survival: A Maroon Case," in Filomina Chioma Steady, Editor, *The Black Woman Cross-Culturally*, pp. 459-460.

43. Thompson, pp. 144-145.

44. Cliff, p. 53.

45. Fatunmbi, *Yemoja/Olokun: Ifa and the Spirit of the Ocean*, p. 16.

46. Ibid., p. 11.

6

Air and Fire, Bringing Rain

In *Oya: In Praise of an African Goddess,* Gleason shares with the reader the difficulties she faces in discussing an African goddess in an academic text. Yet the goddess whose attributes Gleason is attempting to encapsulate in written words has the capacity to facilitate her own intercultural transcription. Gleason describes the goddess Oya as a bridge between cultural expectations and gender prerogatives. Gleason explains that Oya's qualities preempt social roles ascribed to men among the Yoruba, traditionally Oya's principal worshippers. As well, attempting to express the qualities and nature of the goddess in an academic frame necessitates a mythatypical focus expressed in a traditionally procolonialist mode:

Oya is the goddess of edges, of the dynamic interplay between surfaces, of transformation between one state of being and another. . . . What is especially interesting about Oya in Yoruba cultural context is her refusal to stay out of the enclaves of ideology and social control long, long ago preempted by men.

To speak of Oya between the covers of a book and with an audacity befitting her own, it has been necessary to attempt to combine two ways of thinking: African and European. . . . The following presentation of Oya's various meteorological and hydrologic theophanies aims to reverse this depersonalizing trend. One hopes, by responding imaginatively to Oya's power, one may coax her natural turbulence to enter the text as directly as possible![1]

Two novels dramatically depict the course of "coaxing" Oya's "natural turbulence to enter the text" through both the authors' and their fictional heroines' spiritual apprenticeships with the goddess. These chronicles of the growth of self-actualization and the struggle to reconcile satisfying one's deepest drives with one's socially imposed limitations are Hurston's *Their Eyes Were Watching God* and Warner-Vieyra's *Juletane*. In these works, the reader witnesses the sudden, erratic, and pain-filled infusions of "vital woman-power" in both the language and imagery of the authors as the tales gather momentum, sweeping their heroines into an unconscious affinity with "the generative power of the feminine, promising loyalty in return for continued homage."[2]

Apprenticeship to Oya promises that writers and protagonists will escape the sad fate of a similarly endowed—but trapped and restrained—goddess, Nyale. Oya is feminine evolution beyond Nyale, appropriating traditionally masculine qualities to the service of her own tumultuous, imbalancing aims. "Fire and wind, burning wind, are considered feminine elements in that part of Africa evoked by the poetry of Senghor," Gleason explains, translating a West African equation of femininity with air and fire as she prepares the reader for her comparison of Oya to Nyale. Gleason next relates Nyale's tale of humiliation:

Suddenly god thought. And that "suddenly" . . . became known as Nyale.
   Pure impulse.
   . . . Nyale dispersed creation's word throughout space. Touching all four directions into existence, she traveled as a whirlwind. Alone, born of herself by her own impetuosity, Nyale carried on this self-appointed task. So air, striking against air, ignites fire, further accelerating air's displacement.[3]

But creation was a spoken act, and "as one speaks, from the mouth issues a mist." The spirit of water "was concealed within the vibration of that creative word Nyale was spreading through space." Nyale felt "the drag of this moisture" and "sped up . . . effectively evaporating all the moisture enveloping the word. The moisture shriveled into a scum."

That scum solidified itself, acquired bulk, and became the second and final obstacle to her power. . . . With the creator's help, Water and Earth conspired to banish Fire-Wind from the ostensible scheme of things.

Nyale was subdued and imprisoned in the water and earth that her own creative ecstasy had brought into being. Gleason ends this tale ambivalently, conceding first that "enveloped in water, [Nyale's] fiery soul keeps within bounds, recovers direction and meaning in what otherwise would remain mere impetus." Gleason reasons approvingly that "the appeal is to reason," a necessary faculty "to build up in someone overwhelmed by primal terrors and vortical depression," which are the effects of the air-fire goddess's ardor running rampant through human lives. But immediately after giving rationalized consent to Nyale's containment, Gleason disrupts her own tone of quiescence. She recounts asking about Nyale in a village in Mali and being introduced to "the little old woman with white hair," a woman in the image of the captured creative spirit:

The ribald, cynical townspeople literally shoved her into my presence, as if to say, "Write *this* in your notebook." Sparse white hair clung like the scum of myth to her aged scalp. Her eyes swept distractedly through the crowd. But when they turned toward the visitors, there was sorrow and humiliation in their look. "I used to live in the water," the crazed woman apologized through an interpreter, "but now I live on land, most of the time." It was a terrible occasion.[4]

Perhaps Gleason is espousing a limited rational containment such as the context into which she herself is attempting to coax Oya, between the covers of an analytical text. Undefeated thief of lightning and fire, re-vivifier of the male god Shango, her second husband, Oya resists containment.

Oya's name means "she tore," and this translation allows Gleason to further implicate Oya in relation to Harrakoi Dikko (Mother of the Waters) and her river's own creation myth. A princess was instructed to shred a black cloth to protect her father's kingdom from invasion. When she did, the cloth's two pieces fell to the ground and formed the two major tributaries of the Niger that surround and isolate the island where recognition of Oya began. Princesses used to be sacrificed to this river, as "half gods are worshipped in wine and flowers," but "real gods require blood."[5] The more uncommon, precious, and even revered the life of the blood-shedder, evidently, the better received by the deity.[6]

This concept of fatal self-sacrifice, represented by bloodletting, surfaces in the evidence of suffering and vulnerability experienced by the writers and readers who empathize with Oya's agency in a protagonist's life. It is well expressed in Gleason's description of her own struggle with the goddess's impact on her concepts and language. Listing Oya's praises, including "purifying wind . . . sky-sent power . . . whose uplifting strengthens me," Gleason concludes that, under the goddess's influence, her own discourse must "move jaggedly" between science, myth, and lived experience, always with the intense desire to convey and persuade.[7]

This description of "wounds that heal us, sanctifying madnesses" that writers feel under the influence of "numinous archetypal forces"[8] recalls an incident Christian relates in *Black Feminist Criticism*. Christian attended a conference of African American critics and writers, during which Alice Walker attempted to convince listeners that in Hurston's *Their Eyes Were Watching God*, Tea Cake died as a punishment for his abuse of Janie. Christian notes Walker's distress and urgency; perhaps these contributed to the other critics' resistance to Walker's point of view. The following analysis of Janie's coming under the protective influence of Oya is intended to elaborate upon Walker's extraordinarily unique insight that "Hurston's book, though seemingly apolitical, is, in fact, one of the most radical novels (without being a tract) we have."[9] Cannon agrees with this assessment but focuses it upon the heroine: "In sum, in *Their Eyes Were Watching God*, Hurston developed a new character type, who embodies in creative ways radical aspects of the Black community."[10]

Walker writes empathically for women of African descent who strive to free their creative selves from the mire in which Nyale is punished and contained. In the essay "In Search of Our Mothers' Gardens," Walker describes "these crazy, loony, pitiful women" who "were our mothers and grandmothers," mirror images of the village idiot woman on behalf of whom Gleason felt such pained empathy in Mali. Gleason and the French countess who told her Nyale's story had felt together the horribly chthonic pull of Nyale's fate:

We had hit the bottom and stayed there wordlessly, stayed with it—that streak of uncontrolled energy, that primary illusion of omnipotence by which impulsive women have been just as suddenly mortified as we were then.[11]

Walker, forcefully self-expressive after her postabortion attempts at suicide, looks into that threatening scum and describes "our mothers and grandmothers['s]" efforts to liberate their own creative force:

They forced their minds to desert their bodies and their striving spirits sought to rise, like frail whirlwinds from the hard red clay. And when those frail whirlwinds fell, in scattered particles, upon the ground, no one mourned. Instead, men lit candles to celebrate the emptiness that remained, as people do who enter a beautiful but vacant space to resurrect a God.[12]

Their Eyes Were Watching God and *Juletane* are two works that celebrate "radical Yoruba female sexuality," in which riverain goddesses' power of witchcraft, such as Oya's, is "supreme in the arts of mystic retribution."[13] Gleason states that "all female Orisha are not only rivers but witches."[14] Oya's radical witchcraft, rather than succumbing to the androgynous dousing of water, subsumes water into its own explosive expression of determined will in her appropriation of lightning, hurricane, and tornado. Oya's descendants are not left subdued in the earth and falling rain. *Their Eyes Were Watching God* and *Juletane* depict how, on behalf of even her unwitting followers, "Oya's protective gesture . . . tears social reality to shreds," for "it is the goddess herself who will magically meet the threatening situation for us." When Oya comes forth on behalf of her women, "the war no longer exists. Whatever drama there was takes place on another level."[15]

Due to her commitment to the flow between heroine, community, and ancestors, Hurston has left a meticulously crafted chronicle of the blossoming powers and learned self-acceptance of an unwitting witch in *Their Eyes Were Watching God*. Morrison writes that

Studies in American Africanism, in my view, should be investigations of the ways in which a nonwhite, Africanist presence and personae have been constructed—invented—in the United States, and of the literary uses this fabricated presence has served.[16]

The writings of Zora Neale Hurston, when they fictionalize this "presence and personae," serve as excellent analytical vehicles for the study of Pan-African women's mythatypes because she wrote with such blunt and naked subject empathy. Hurston embraces her ethnic inheritance with unapologetic acceptance. She celebrates it, isolates, insulates, and magnifies it:

[*Of Mules and Men*] was my first indication of the quality I feel is most characteristic of Zora's work: racial health; a sense of black people as complete, complex, *undiminished* human beings, a sense that is missing in so much black writing and literature. (In my opinion, only Du Bois showed an equally consistent delight in the beauty and spirit of black people.)[17]

June Jordan points out this celebratory quality in *Their Eyes Were Watching God* as, "Blacklife freed from the constraints of oppression."[18] While Hurston cherished the distinguishing qualities of the African presence in America, her convictions about African American communities' survival needs were strong. According to Walker:

[Hurston's work,] far from being done carelessly, is done (especially in *Their Eyes Were Watching God*) almost too perfectly. . . . It seems to me that black writing has suffered because even black critics have assumed that a book that deals with the relationships between members of a black family—or between a man and woman—is less important than one that has white people as primary antagonists.[19]

Cannon expands this evaluation by explaining that generally,

Black women writers find value consciousness in their home communities which serve as the orthodox framework for their circular literary structure. As insiders they venture into all strata of Black life. Black women writers transform the passions and sympathies, the desires and hurts, the joys and defeats, the praises and pressures, the richness and diversity of real-lived communities into the stuff for art through the medium of literature.[20]

Christian points out that, specifically in *Their Eyes Were Watching God*, Janie "gives the meaning of her story back to the community."[21] Christian uses this text as an example of the reciprocity she perceives between African American women writers and their communities. Joy James explains the concept of community to women of African descent who are living thinkers:

Community extends through time and space to include the ancestors, those now physically present, and future children. . . . You determine not whether or not you belong but the nature of the relationship and the meaning of belonging.[22]

Holloway explains the dynamic of reciprocal representation between the woman writing in, to, and through a community in a material world, observing and absorbing the reflection the writer sees in the spiritual, which concurrently beholds, shapes, and defines the writer:

Recursive structures accomplish a blend between figurative processes that are reflective (mirror-like) and symbolic processes whose depth and resonance make them reflexive. The combined symbolic-figurative process results in texts that are at once emblematic of the culture they describe as well as interpretive of this culture. Literature that strikes this reflective/reflexive posture is characteristically polyphonic.[23]

Cannon explains that Hurston's emphasis on "life within the community, not the conflict of outside forces" may have been the cause of her works' denigration by African American male critics and writers:

The protagonist in the Black man's literary tradition moves quite differently. Christian contends that Black men are less circular in movement. The movement for the Black male writer is outward and downward. The prominent Black male writers develop story lines that move horizontally within the community with the major development occurring once the characters have moved away from their natal roots.[24]

In contrast, the reflexive circularity of women's writings in relation to their communities develops heroines who are "ordinary women who embrace the great wealth of knowledge amassed by the Black female community over the years," placing these women in the position of acting as their communities' "cultural custodians."[25] More far-reaching in scope than even this reciprocal relationship between a heroine and her community is a larger concept whose circularity expands to include the community's ancestresses and goddesses in the reflective/reflexive pool. Both Hurston's vulnerable storytelling candor and her loving community scrutiny reflect her being "incapable of being embarrassed by anything black people did." These vitalizing qualities make *Their Eyes Were Watching God* a particularly clear mirror of dynamics beyond that furthest border where the goddess enters into interaction and, suddenly, "concept verges upon transformative action."[26]

In *Their Eyes Were Watching God*, Janie's grandmother is called Nanny. Her name signifies that Nanny is a caretaker of others. Her own desires are unacknowledged and unfulfilled. Juxtaposed with Janie's crucial coming-of-age scene, Nanny appears as an angry, dying tree, the spiritual mother at the transformative crossroads. However, this spiritual mother, full of "ancient, useless power," is demanding that Janie sell herself as a desirable object of marriage in exchange for safety from rape and shame. This is the best that the formerly enslaved Nanny can envision for a woman of African descent, "the mule of the world." Nanny's own experience as a sexually used slave, and her daughter Leafy's rape by a freeman schoolteacher and subsequent traumatized acting-out in prostitution, have desensitized Nanny. She is scornful of Janie's notion that love is a valid consideration for a young and beautiful woman of African descent. Nanny simply wants Janie to be financially secure and placed out of the way of easy rape or sexual misusage.

Analysts have suggested that the browbeating of Janie into marrying Logan Killicks reflects an early abandoned marriage in Hurston's own life. Kafka persuasively argues that Nanny's position on marriage is "influenced by [Booker T.] Washington's stress on economic success and by traditional African concepts of marriage (which are economic and political, not romantic)." Conversely, Kafka states that "Janie's concept of marriage, however, is European American."[27]

While the assessment of Booker T. Washington's influence on Nanny's values is highly perceptive and convincing, I would like to qualify the dismissal of love as a European American marital criterion. Simply among the works previously cited in this work, Nwapa's *Efuru* and Ogot's "The Rain Came," well-raised young women in traditional African societies allow personal attraction to outweigh all other considerations in their choice of husbands. Diallo's *Le fort maudit*, Ba's *Une si longue lettre*, and Fazel's *Lontano da Mogadiscio* all describe at length and with conviction the importance of love in African women's acceptance or refusal of, and happiness in, marriage in traditional Muslim African societies. Clearly, it is men who choose and women who accept or refuse. But even beyond the works cited here, the theme of love's importance in marriage in historical and contemporary African societies crops up with tenderness and pathos in African fiction (written by both women and men) so regularly that it might be safest to steer away from an absolute qualification. Perhaps it is most fair to say that economic, social, and political considerations are crucial—if not deciding—factors in African marriages, just as they are in European American and African American ones. In pressuring Janie to marry Logan Killicks, Nanny is probably being pragmatically cross-cultural. (Let it not be overlooked that it will never be Nanny who has to "turn over in de bed and stir up de air whilst he is in dere.") Be all this as it may, the coerced self-selling into marriage is intended, as far as Nanny is concerned, to end in Janie's realization of safety and contentment.

Instead, a down-in-the-mouth Janie confronts her grandmother with her bitter distaste for her husband, instead of the hoped-for gratitude and pride. The newlywed Janie pronounces, "Some folks never was meant to be loved and he's one of 'em." If pride of property and married status will never make this marriage into a voluntary compromise, then Janie's trade of self for safety clearly harks back to Nanny's own experience of sexual helplessness in chattel slavery. This was not what Nanny had intended. Helplessly seeing the enormity of her error, Nanny "entered this infinity of conscious pain again" and died within one month.

Janie's calculated trade of youthful beauty for limited protection is marked in terms of a rite of passage from girlhood innocence: "Janie's first dream was dead. So she became a woman."[28] This need for a dreamy teen girl to deny her own desire to love and instead plot to share herself strategically so as to gain an approximation of security reflects Brent's dilemma in *Incidents in the Life of a Slave Girl*. Set four generations earlier than Janie's story, Brent must send away the freeman who wishes to marry her and give herself, apparently at age fifteen, to a local politician. In nearly the same words as those Hurston gives Janie, Brent marks this surrendering of the desire to love her future sexual partner, possibly even in marriage, with the observation, "The dream of my girlhood was over."[29]

Brent's hope is that her influential lover will keep his promise to buy and free any children they may have, thereby helping her achieve her goal of escaping her sexually aggressive owner. Commanded by her owner to confess whether or not she loves his rival, Brent says she is thankful she does not despise him.[30] It is well worth noting that Brent never panders to the Victorian mores of her readers by suggesting that her heart eventually followed where her body had been given, and she learned to love the father of her two children, thus elevating their union to an approximation of idealized marriage. Avoiding rape by settling for lack of love unites both these young teens, Janie and Brent, through time and forms a community theme. Their quests center on the pursuit of personal and legal freedom, but their rites of passage into womanhood are marked by surrendering—irrevocably for Brent—the dream of one day sharing themselves in a bond of mutual love.

Janie's intense desires and resentments have invoked Oya:

The unique function of *Oya* within the realm of *Orisha Awo* (Mysteries of Nature) is to provide those changing conditions that force consciousness to grow, expand and transcend its limitations.[31]

Oya's presence in Janie's text begins with the teen's first encounter with sexual wonder and her resistance to her grandmother's admonitions: "The Wind as Spiritual Principle brings the unexpected, the chaotic, the transformative and the overwhelming."[32] Oya's involvement continues to pique Janie, escalating her very healthy sense of discontent with what her society conspires to mete out to her.

It is Oya who empowers Janie's words to usher in Nanny and Joe Starks's deaths, at once ridding Janie of obstacles to her pursuit of love and providing living sacrifices to the goddess:

Oya is a verb form conveying her passage as an event with apparently disastrous consequences. *O-ya* means "she tore" in Yoruba. And what happened? A big tree was uprooted, literally and figuratively: the head of the household, the one in whose shade we felt secure, suddenly perished. She tore, and a river overflowed its banks. Whole cloth was ripped into shreds. Barriers were broken down. Tumultuous feeling abruptly destroyed one's peace of mind.[33]

Adeleke Adeeko notes, "Whenever this woman [Janie] speaks, someone dies."[34] The "someone" is the person who has attacked Janie's freedom by curtailing it. Though personal freedom is Janie's goal, it is only a means to the end of finally experiencing mutual sexual love. Tea Cake seems to be the cathartic gift through which will come self-actualization, which Janie is being offered in exchange for her receptivity to the agency of the goddess who frees Janie from poverty, tyranny, and even the anger of her two communities—the African American township and the migrant farmworkers on the muck—following the deaths of both Starks and Woods. Tea Cake's proper name, Vergible Woods, is an even stronger signifier than his nickname, as to the sexual sharing that he is meant to offer Janie. For if one pear tree in bloom promises Janie an orgasm, then Vergible Woods as "Tea Cake" ("'So you sweet as all dat?' . . . 'You better try me and see,'"[35]) offers her a *veritable forest* of such delights.

Just as Janie inherits the assets that she helped Jody amass, so she seems to have inherited the "ancient power" that "no longer mattered"[36] in Nanny. This power is far from useless or dormant in Janie. It surrounds her and works through her, often against her will and without her knowledge (see involuntary witchcraft comments in chapter three).

Oya is "one of the guardians of issues related to the fair treatment of women."[37] Oya made a gift of Tea Cake to Janie, not the other way around. By the time they have been married two years, Tea Cake has stolen and gone gambling with the money Janie brought with her, abandoned her in an unfamiliar city, tussled in the cane field with a young girl, and beaten Janie to demonstrate his phallicity to a rival on the muck. Janie makes generous excuses for Tea Cake's every act of thoughtlessness and downright cruelty:

The tornado—generative power of the feminine, promising loyalty in return for continued homage, will bracket its destructive potential and move in. Even the best-intentioned men are likely to sometimes forget that continuous need for homage, lack of which is apt to send Oya off into a tailspin.[38]

That tailspin reminds all that it is Oya's mission to "give human consciousness a sense of mortality and humility."[39]

Tea Cake's beating of Janie begins a whirlwind of events that will test to the limit Janie's ability to make sense out of, and peace with, her life. Oya, "strong wind who knocks down trees everywhere in the wilds,"[40] first sends a violent storm that drives the couple and their friends in terror from their shacks:

Sometime that night the winds came back. . . . Through the screaming wind they heard things crashing and things hurtling and dashing with unbelievable velocity. . . . [The wind] woke up [the lake] and the lake got madder and madder.[41]

As the terrified couple lie shivering between rushing streams of water and debris, Janie spies a piece of roofing "hung against a tree," as if it were an offering. "The very thing," she thinks to herself. Janie would like to get it, to shelter "poor Tea Cake." The rapid events that lead the couple to their tragedy are replete with goddess signs:

She crept up on hands and knees to the piece of roofing and caught hold of it by either side. Immediately the wind lifted both of them and she saw herself sailing off to the fill to the right, out and out over the lashing water.[42]

There is a cow swimming "in an oblique line" toward the fill. Janie's screams awaken Tea Cake, and he shouts to her how to swim to the cow and grab its tail to stay afloat. Something is wrong. There is a vicious dog atop the cow:

The dog stood up and growled like a lion, stiff-standing hackles, stiff muscles, teeth uncovered as he lashed up his fury for the charge. Tea Cake split the water like an otter, opening his knife as he dived. The dog raced down the back-bone of the cow to the attack and Janie screamed and slipped far back on the tail of the cow, just out of reach of the dog's angry jaws. He wanted to plunge in after her but dreaded the water, somehow. Tea Cake rose out of the water at the cow's rump and seized the dog by the neck. . . . They fought and somehow he managed to bite Tea Cake high up on his cheek-bone once. Then Tea Cake finished him and sent him to the bottom to stay there. . . .
    "Po' me, he'd a tore me tuh pieces, if it wuzn't fuh you, honey."
    "You don't have tuh say, if it wuzn't fuh me, baby, cause Ah'm *heah*, and then Ah want yuh tuh know it's uh man heah."[43]

Here it is important to remember that princesses used to be sacrificed annually to Oya's river (a tributary of the Niger). After patriarchal religions spread in the region, the river's spirit became masculinized. But significantly, the sacrificial object remained female: an annual heifer. However, while it is true that "One does not throw a female animal to a male divinity,"[44] Oya will accept certain male animal sacrifices, preferably ram.[45]

With the above facts in mind, reading the signs of the events after Oya's stormy arrival explains why Walker was justified in her analysis that Tea Cake died for beating Janie. Oya's wind has driven the couple from home and carried the tantalizing offer of shelter to Janie, teasing her eternal desire to "mama" Tea Cake. The couple has sought brief asylum between two instant moving bodies of water, recalling the two instant black rivers that resulted when the king's daughter tore the black cloth to surround and protect Oya's island. The gift of yet another way to show tenderness to Tea Cake is hung seductively on a tree, symbol of a woman's spiritual transformation. The combination of wind, storm, tree, and proffered shelter indicates that the goddess Oya is making an aggressive interruption in the couple's lives so that Janie can be coaxed to a level of spiritual transformation that she might not have willingly approached while being so content with the goddess's gift of a *veritable forest* of love. The reader is assured that spiritual transformation is at stake because of the references to trees throughout the storm scene. While Tea Cake sleeps, Janie is virtually alone in interaction with the goddess who has adopted her.

No sooner does Janie seize the lure hung on the tree than she is carried off with it to the flash flood rushing water, enacting the ancient fate of the sacrificial princess, what Perera calls the scapegoat-beloved.   To reinforce the meaning of Janie's screaming plunge into the water and subsequent sparing of life, a sacrificial cow, the princess's replacement, appears in time to effect a rescue. The Oya system of elements that threatened Janie is now offering to save her, doubling the message of *goddess* sacrifice by sparing Janie's life through the agency of the most customary gift of a cow.

The cow and the safety that it offers are the goddess's gifts. So was Tea Cake. The threat of the dog atop the cow illustrates to the reader (and probably should but does not to Janie) what Janie's position in life with the goddess's other gift, Tea Cake, has become. His marital infractions have incrementally increased in severity until, by the time the storm arrives, Janie is clearly in danger due to her lack of influence over Tea Cake's assaultive behavior. The dog, too, is visibly rabid, threatening Janie only because it must take out its madness on some living thing. This is exactly the same realization that Janie will have about Tea Cake in the last stages of his own delirium.

It is crucial to decide whether or not Tea Cake had other rescue options besides attacking an obviously abnormal dog. The dog was afraid of the water; the narrative voice points this out through the observations of Janie, hanging onto the cow's tail. It is worthwhile to consider if Tea Cake might possibly have saved Janie by helping her swim to the fill, since the dog was not willing to pursue into the water. If, in fact, the situation the narrator describes does leave reasonable room to assume that rescuing Janie might have worked as well as grabbing the dog, a relevant question is why Tea Cake chose this more indirect, risky mode of assistance. Based on Tea Cake's own comments after the dog's death, when he restated his manhood as he did after beating Janie, it seems reasonable to conclude that attacking the dog was an act of phallocentric preference, asserting Tea Cake's territoriality just as he did in beating Janie. At this point, it is important to note that the dog is also acting out, to an exaggerated degree, a normal claiming of territory. This unreasoning territoriality acted out by the rabid dog mirrors the senseless brutality of Tea Cake toward Janie, beating her despite the fact that he himself acknowledges she has done not a thing that he can fault. Obviously, this would explain the violence in Tea Cake, not excuse it: "'Ah didn't whup Janie cause *she* done nothin'. Ah beat her tuh show dem Turners who is boss.'"[46] Kafka notes that "Tea Cake undergoes transformation into a mad dog and ends up being shot down like one."[47] This observation is astute but misses the fact that Tea Cake's mad dog transformation begins before he is bitten. Before the rabies infection, Tea

Cake witnesses for himself Janie's candid declarations of loyalty; yet he sullies his relationship by assaulting her. The point of these observations is that had Tea Cake not acted out again with the dog the same exaggerated territoriality that led him to beat Janie, it seems unlikely that the infectious bite could have taken place. Tea Cake's own proclivity toward violent and unreasonable claiming of Janie's person as territory to be contested establishes that, given the presence of the mirroring mad dog, Tea Cake will take steps that ensure he will become infected. The healthy female cow, a prescribed and acceptable sacrifice, is spared and tows Janie to land, while the rabid male animal sinks to the bottom of the storm goddess's sudden pool of swirling water, signaling a similar death for its mirror, Tea Cake.

After the dog bite, Tea Cake's suspicions have increased in their angry intensity but maintained an equivalent degree of unreasonableness. However, at least it can be surmised that Tea Cake's suspicions are now founded on at least some degree of observation: Janie is not by his side when he wakes; he hears that Miz Turner's brother is back; therefore Janie must have sneaked off to see Miz Turner's brother. Tea Cake is moved by the same jealousy and suspicion that afflicted his wife before his bite, but now he acts more swiftly and irrevocably in his madness. There is no longer any lag time, a gap for healing and reconciliation of some kind.

The storm and its flash flood sacrificial drama have set events in motion that will *force* Janie to act out a self-defense toward which she was not otherwise inclined. (Tea Cake reports that when he beat her, Janie would not so much as call out in anger or for help; she would only cry.[48])

When Janie describes in court the shoot-out in which she killed Tea Cake, she explains it not as self-defense, which seems most reasonable, but in terms of liberating Tea Cake's personality:

Tea Cake couldn't come back to himself until he had got rid of that mad dog that was in him and he couldn't get rid of the dog and live. He had to die to get rid of the dog. But she hadn't wanted to kill him.[49]

Freed of the madness, Tea Cake goes home with Janie to the large house where they first made love. Having experienced love, Janie can now pull "in her horizon" and call "in her soul to come and see" the "life in its meshes."[50] It is Oya who assures that "the soul, too, changing its colors, slips away, to return."[51] Oya has carried Tea Cake's purified soul back to Janie.

In *Juletane,* Guadeloupean Warner-Vieyra also chronicles the intervention of Oya in a marriage unalterably turned toward unfairness and the evident reuniting of the couple in the spiritual world on more equal terms.[52] *Juletane* is the story of a Diaspora woman who has nowhere left to turn. Orphaned in the Caribbean and raised in France, the death of Juletane's guardian pushes her into a love affair with a Senegalese student. They marry, and she returns with him to West Africa. En route, she discovers that she is his second wife. She feels this polygynous situation is repugnant. After a miscarriage and successive mental breakdowns, the reader is introduced to a severely-disturbed Juletane who lives in a bedroom that is suffocatingly small and pours her heart into her private journal. Warner-Vieyra presents Juletane's journal through a woman called Helene, the unhappy social worker who offered too little help, too late, to the disoriented Juletane. Helene examines her own life and choices as she is swept up in the record of Juletane's self-empowerment, whose climax is the murder of the first wife's children and the disfigurement of the husband's third wife.

While acknowledging that for Jacobs's Brent, her "socially unacceptable, and morally reprehensible" actions are justified by the attainment of her goal of "freedom,"[53] Francoise Lionnet imposes patriarchal measures of failure upon her reading of *Juletane*. Lionnet's statement of a positive analytical goal is quickly undermined in her analysis of *Juletane* by her abandonment of the African-descent woman's right to "personal agency," in deference to Paul de Man's view that journal writing is self-decapitation. Lionnet begins to lose the thread of African womanly empowerment as she introduces de Man's reading of self-frustration in the writing of one's own story: "'Autobiography veils a defacement of the mind of which it is itself the cause.'"[54]

This is a paradoxical conclusion to a series of arguments that began with the defamiliarization of social values implied in Jacobs's *Incidents in the Life of a Slave Girl* and prepared the reader for a close reading of *Juletane* with the apprehension of "alternative models and strategies proposed by heretofore 'muted' groups."[55]

As if aware of "alternative models" latent in the layering and tripling of *Juletane*, Lionnet acknowledges the work's "principle of doubling," the triplicity of the three cowives, and the heroine's return to Africa to reclaim identity as "a black woman."[56] But these raised signifiers fall mute upon the introduction of de Man's critical perspectives, which treat neither the doubling and tripling of women nor the reclaiming of African identity. The following analysis reorients Lionnet's criticism toward the cultural reinscription that she proposed and did not fulfill.

Juletane finds herself in an untenable position when she learns that her new bridegroom, Mamadou, has every intention of continuing to pursue the African tradition of polygyny, no matter the sufferings imposed upon Juletane.[57] Mamadou eventually adds a third wife and thus completes the patterning of his household on that of the Yoruba god of thunder, Shango, Oya's second husband. Shango also had three wives.

The triple goddess is a widespread preancient mythatype.[58] Sometimes the triple goddess serves as a dualistic figure: two members of the triune (three-in-one) deity represent apparent polar opposites, such as sexual promiscuity and vengeful death, or virginity and motherhood, while the third figure stands between them and mediates their interactions with each other and with their human suppliants.

The Juletane, Awa, and Ndeye triplicity of wives may be taken to symbolically represent the roles and influences of Shango's three wives, Oya, Oba, and Osun, at work in the Mamadou household. The triune goddesses' influence may have been drawn in by any of three ways. First, the mythatypical influence may have been introduced once the triune marital arrangement had been made; that is, it began once the flirtatious Ndeye, reflecting Osun's influence, had joined the word-exercising Juletane, influenced and eventually championed by Oya, and the child-bearing first wife, Awa, reflecting Oba. Or maybe the hint to the reader of Awa's resorting to a shaman to rid herself of Juletane as a competitor for bearing Mamadou's first son may have been a quiet sign of Oya's introduction into the marital situation. Mamadou's niece hints to Juletane by that Awa might have acted to insure her role as sole mother by having a shaman sterilize the pregnant Juletane so that Mamadou would bring Awa back from the countryside to live with them. This makes the offer of Awa's first son to the grief-stricken Juletane take on the aspect of guilty propitiation. Oya "makes an unbreakable treaty with anyone wanting a child,"[59] and it has been generally recognized in Mamadou's family that the birth of a son would save Awa's supreme position. What might have been Awa's "unbreakable treaty"? Kindness to the childless Juletane, who could never again rival her for power? In this case, the sacrifice of the children would represent payment of a broken bargain between Awa and the goddess Oya. The goddess's entry into the workings of the household seems most fully announced by the incidents surrounding the deaths of Awa's three children.

Or finally, Juletane's writing, her endless wielding of one of Oya's mediums, the avenging word, might have been a tireless, unconscious invocation of the goddess to intervene in Juletane's unjustifiable persecution.

Juletane's alienation from West African culture renders her incapable of reading the possibilities still open to her for pursuing her own avenues of power. Of course, even if she could read them, it is necessary to acknowledge that Juletane might not find the pursuit of West African motherless women's power options personally satisfying as did Nwapa's Efuru. Still, Niara Sudarkasa's article, "The 'Status of Women' in Indigenous African Societies,"[60] raises questions about the somewhat determinist presentation of Juletane's emotional and mental decline. Juletane's estrangement not only from West African but also from Caribbean cultures might make her incapable of consciously perceiving and satisfactorily carrying out her self-assertive options. However, her recall of her Caribbean childhood would be enough to point out to Juletane the relative vulnerability of her rootless state. Nancie Solien Gonzalez emphasizes the importance of consanguinity and, conversely, the lack of surviving or intervening blood relations as a trait shared between West African and Afro-Caribbean communities.[61] (It may well be that the social importance of having consanguine relations to protect one from domestic and personal injustice is manifest in most Pan-African communities.) Juletane would therefore be doubly aware of her disadvantages without a compensating grasp of her enabling options. Incapable of defining and defending her rights in a polygynous marriage, Juletane is confronted with a self-denying identity bind: if she will not accept polygyny as her husband and the other two wives present it to her, Juletane is not truly "black." Though she rails poignantly against this whitewashing of the depths of her inheritance, writing feverishly in her journal that "mes peres avaient durement paye mon droit a etre noire" ("my forefathers have paid bitterly for my right to be black"),[62] her household's denial continues to affect her. As her efforts at self-fulfillment in an environment she does not understand continue to meet with failure and dismissal, Juletane isolates herself more entirely in the world of her journal writing, where she creates undiluted self-affirmation:

Je n'avais jamais imagine que coucher ma peine sur une feuille blanche pouvait m'aider a l'analyser, la dominer, et enfin, peut-etre, la supporter ou definitivement la refuser.

(I would never have imagined that setting down my pain on a white sheet would help me analyze it, dominate it, and finally, perhaps, learn to bear it or reject it, once and for all.)[63]

Oya is goddess of the justifying word: "Particularly associated with female strength, it is she who stands behind any individual's ability to use the spoken word as a weapon."[64] Limiting Oya's influence to the spoken word may be a gesture toward the European appropriation of the history of writing while attributing orality to Africa, an historically unsound theoretical bias. The goddess's traditionally defined verbal power is extended in this essay to the written word. Therefore, the years of Juletane's self-explanatory, self-exploratory, self-justifying journal writing would serve as apprenticeship to the goddess of words and justice, Oya: "Where there is violence, there is Oya."[65]

Once the triplicity of wives is in place, Mamadou and Ndeye are guilty of overt emotional and, in Ndeye's case, physical assault on Juletane's precarious well-being. Even the mild and motherly Awa begins to participate in the put-downs of childless Juletane, signifying with her eyes that Juletane's uselessness is analogous to that of the infertile mango tree outside her window:

Awa m'a dit que ce devait etre un manguier sterile—son regard me disait <<comme toi>>. . . . Mamadou n'avait pas eu la main heureuse, dans les deux cas.

(Awa told me that the mango tree must be sterile. Her look said, "Like you." . . . Mamadou was unlucky, in both choices.)[66]

Awa may have served a mediating purpose between the mourning hag Juletane and the wanton Ndeye until she destroyed the remnants of her own neutrality by agreeing with Ndeye's assault on Juletane's deculturating, pacifying European music. Could the foreign Beethoven have acted as an estranging element that kept Oya from fully manifesting herself through Juletane? Ndeye's aggressive flaunting of her beauty and subsequent influence over Mamadou may have made Juletane finally open herself up to Oya's devastating capacity to level all competitors. Ndeye breaks the record album that is Juletane's last tie with her deculturating influence, France, and soundly strikes Juletane's face. (Recall that nights of partying with Bahaman musicians preceded Oya's manifestation in Janie's life in *Their Eyes Were Watching God*.) At last, Juletane admits to herself that she is cornered and ready to fight back, for her precarious balance of almost all-rightness is permanently threatened. Juletane decides in the darkness of her closet-sized room that she must act, not only to curb Ndeye/Osun's ascendant influence, but to destroy the household that has become a shrine to Mamadou's phallic status.

Oya enters and immediately destroys the symbols of Mamadou's phallic power, beginning the process of destruction that will finally leave Juletane as his last surviving wife, in monogamous marriage with Mamadou.

"Patroness of childbirth, and the instrument of death . . . mother of children and mother of corpses,"[67] Oya's signs of harsh justice accumulate as the story reaches its climax. Juletane loved two of Awa's children: the firstborn girl, already five when Juletane met her, and the boy presented to her at his naming party as Awa's peace offering. If it was Juletane's hand that moved to initiate their deaths, guided by the goddess who steps in to battle for her devotees, then it seems reasonable to

see their deaths as a great sacrifice. Most invocation rituals that attempt
to draw down the influence of goddesses and gods who deal in life and
death involve blood sacrifices. The more precious the victim, the more
potent the power invoked on the sacrificer's behalf. If Juletane's writing
has drawn Oya into the household, then the sacrifice of the children immediately upon the goddess's entrance serves double duty as both an
invoking ritual and an initial act of vengeance. If Awa's position was
supposed to be one of peaceful neutrality, then it can be concluded that
Awa has broken her treaty and drawn down vengeance on her own head
via the loss of the goddess's gift of her children. Immediately after the
death of the children, Juletane's memory of having perpetrated the act is
erased. As "patron of justice and memory," Oya's eradication of Juletane's memory would be a merciful concession to the woman's inability
to accept the goddess's scale of action.

Next, Oya's penchant for balancing things in the manifestation of
justice literally places Awa in the well in which Awa's position as first
wife had figuratively placed Juletane. Awa flings herself into a well to
drown just as Juletane feels she has finally crawled out of the well that
was her psychoemotional place of imprisonment: "J'ai enfin trouve sous
la glaise des parois la faille qui m'a permis de sortir du puits." ("I finally
found the fault in the wall that would allow me to climb up out of the
well.")[68]

In her new state of internalized liberty, Juletane describes herself in
terms akin to Oya's image as madwoman-turned-wisewoman: "Me rev-
eiller dans un autre monde ou les fous ne sont pas fous, mais des sages
aux regards de justice." ("To waken in another world where the mad are
not mad, but wise, when it comes to justice.")[69] If Oya's actions as manifest through Juletane seem monstrous, it is Juletane who offers the reader
the alternative view of seeing justice in Mamadou's mutation of Juletane's character returning, like Frankenstein's monster, to visit its mon-
strosity upon its creator: "Celui qui fabrique un monstre de douleur ne
doit pas s'etonner d'etre un jour detruit par lui." ("He who creates a suffering monster shouldn't be surprised, one day, when it destroys him.")[70]

As if aware of the preancient animist forces contending for dominant
manifestation in his home, Mamadou next turns to fundamentalist Islam.
Juletane, or Oya influencing Juletane, quietly scoffs at this patriarchal
stratagem.

But Ndeye finds her powerful position in the household radically
threatened. Her childlessness was inconsequential as long as Awa's
children lived as testimonies to Mamadou's phallic potency. With the
death of the children, Ndeye's beauty becomes as superfluous as her ac-
cumulation of golden bangles in a home badly in need of repair. Ndeye

is worried about the overthrow of her dominion but mistakes the direction from which this overthrow is coming. For it is not Mamadou, but Juletane under Oya's influence, who wreaks a vengeance upon Ndeye as terrible as that wrought upon Awa and Mamadou.

Juletane contemplates a quick and relatively clean dispatching of Ndeye with a knife while Mamadou is out of the house. The knife is not one of Oya's symbols of power, but fire is; and a death that leaves Ndeye's beauty intact is apparently not to the goddess's taste. Oya is, after all, part of a religious system for which death is merely a transition to another state of continued existence. Some traditional African religious belief systems hold that a body disfigured in death will mark the soul that inhabited it, should it return in rebirth. Oya's capital punishments, as meted out to Awa, Ndeye, and Mamadou, will render them all disgraced before their own influential deities.

Oya will not allow Juletane to bungle her vengeance by dispatching Ndeye to a state of eternal wanton beauty. Oya overcomes Juletane with the heat and smoke of her element, fire, as if the goddess would manifest herself and take matters into her own hands. When Juletane recovers from her fainting hallucination of knifing Ndeye, she is unaccountably moved to heat oil to the boiling point. She uses this scalding oil on Ndeye's face, torturing and permanently disfiguring the powerful representative of Osun the beautiful.

If Juletane was formerly seen as the figuratively monstrous and crippled wife, it is now Ndeye's turn to be seen literally in those terms. Again, Juletane has switched places with a wife whose ascendancy she could not formerly challenge. Oya again strips Juletane of her ability to remember and, hence, confess her crime until she is safely sheltered in an insane asylum. Juletane's catatonic state renders Mamadou, who has been effectively castrated by his "Europeanized" wife, incapable of carrying out any vengeance upon her. Juletane lives in sheltered comfort, revelling in those episodes of her revenge that she may guiltlessly enjoy and continuing to benefit from Oya's expunging of those incidents whose memory would destroy her exultation with horror or regret.

Juletane's only regret is that Mamadou dies before he learns that it was she, Juletane, who acted as the arbiter of her own revenge. Oya also swiftly corrects this regret. (This goddess does like to be appreciated by her beneficiaries.) Rather than leaving Juletane to languish dissatisfied and ultimately defeated in a material world whose spiritual workings she cannot perceive, Oya, "mother of corpses . . . she carries the dead on her back, the dead returning,"[71] immediately carries Juletane to the spiritual world where the lasting effects of her vengeance will be evident to her.

Mamadou, who misrepresented himself in order to marry Juletane and bring her to West Africa, is disgraced before both his male deities, Shango, whom Oya loved so much she resurrected him, and Allah, who extols truth and fairness toward wives.[72]

Finally, Helene benefits from her study of Oya's workings through Juletane. As if made cognizant of the manifestations of the spiritual through the physical world, Helene decides to marry her young and adoring lover. The history of goddesses choosing to marry devoted and self-effacing young consorts is legion: "Her consort . . . slain for the sake of renewal . . . the phallic power of aggression and assertion devoted to the feminine, to life universal."[73] Such patterned marriages with a son-like male have sometimes provided an effective option for avoiding the bitter contests of power that Oya has just manifested through the life and death of Juletane. But if not, Oya can handle the developments, as has been seen in her intervention between Tea Cake and Janie.

Oya will always keep her devotees from succumbing to the pull of the storm and the drag of the heavy world, striving through pain toward a horizon where they see their dearest wishes coming true.

NOTES

1. Judith Gleason, *Oya: In Praise of an African Goddess* (New York: Harper-Collins, 1992), pp. 2 and 18.

2. Ibid., pp. 45-46.

3. Ibid., pp. 24-25.

4. Ibid., pp. 25-26 and 45.

5. Zora Neale Hurston, *Their Eyes Were Watching God* (New York: Harper & Row, 1990), p. 139.

6. This creation myth is recounted in analytical detail in "Oya's River," Gleason, pp. 47-58.

7. Ibid., pp. 9-10 and 19.

8. Ibid., p. 14.

9. Alice Walker, "From an Interview" in Alice Walker, *In Search of Our Mothers' Gardens: Womanist Prose* (New York: Harcourt Brace & Company, 1983), p. 260.

10. Katie G. Cannon, *Black Womanist Ethics* (Atlanta: Scholars Press, American Academy of Religion, 1988), p. 132.

11. Gleason, p. 26.

12. Walker, p. 232.

13. (Judith Hoch-Smith quoted and explained in) Robert Farris Thompson, *Flash of the Spirit: African and Afro-American Art and Philosophy* (New York: Vintage Books, 1984), p. 74.

14. Gleason, p. 70.

15. Ibid., p. 50.

16. Toni Morrison, *Playing in the Dark: Whiteness and the Literary Imagination*

(Cambridge: Harvard University Press, 1992), p. 90.

17. Walker, p. 85.

18. June Jordan, "On Richard Wright and Zora Neale Hurston: Notes Toward a Balancing of Love and Hatred," *Black World*, vol. 23 (April, 1976).

19. Walker, p. 261.

20. Cannon, p. 88.

21. Barbara Christian, *Black Women Novelists: The Development of a Tradition, 1892-1976*, (Westport, CT: Greenwood Press, 1980), p. 241.

22. Joy James, "African Philosophy, Theory, and 'Living Thinkers'," in Joy James and Ruth Farmer, Editors, *Spirit, Space & Survival: African American Women in (White) Academe* (New York: Routledge, 1993), p. 32.

23. Karla Holloway, *Moorings and Metaphors: Figures of Culture and Gender in Black Women's Literature* (New Brunswick: Rutgers University Press, 1992), p. 55.

24. Cannon, pp. 87-88.

25. Ibid., p. 89.

26. Walker, p. 260, and Gleason, p. 65.

27. Phillipa Kafka, *The Great White Way: African American Women Writers and American Success Mythologies* (New York: Garland Publishing, 1993), pp. 164 and 172.

28. Hurston, pp. 22-24.

29. Linda Brent, *Incidents in the Life of a Slave Girl* (New York: Harcourt Brace Jovanovich, 1973), p. 42.

30. Ibid., p. 60.

31. *Awo* Fa'lokun Fatunmbi, *Oya: Ifa and the Spirit of the Wind* (New York: Original Publications, 1993), p. 3.

32. Ibid., pp. 12.

33. Gleason, p. 5.

34. Adeleke Adeeko, Lecture notes, University of Colorado (Fall 1993).

35. Hurston, p. 93.

36. Ibid., p. 12.

37. Fatunmbi, p. 10.

38. Gleason, pp. 45-46.

39. Fatunmbi, p. 13.

40. Gleason, p. 7.

41. Hurston, pp. 150-151.

42. Ibid., p. 157.

43. Ibid., pp. 157 and 159.

44. Gleason, p. 57.

45. Fatunmbi, p. 19.

46. Hurston, p. 141.

47. Kafka, p. 163.

48. Hurston, p. 141.

49. Ibid., p. 178.

50. Ibid., p. 184.

51. Gleason, p. 51.

52. This analysis is abbreviated from Alexis Brooks De Vita, "Wresting Order from Chaos: Reading Mythological Influences in Myriam Warner-Vieyra's

Juletane," The Griot, 16.1 (Spring 1997). In that essay, I occluded Shango's identity by conflating him with Ogun in order to describe a male, resistant force opposed to Oya's, without (I hoped) risking blasphemous disrespect. In this revision, Juletane's husband Mamadou simply represents a patriarchal element. No misrepresentation of Shango's relationship with Oya, or among Oya, Osun, and Oba, is intended.

53.   Francoise Lionnet, "Geographies of Pain: Captive Bodies and Violent Acts in the Fictions of Myriam Warner-Vieyra, Gayl Jones, and Bessie Head," *Callalloo* 16.1 (1993), p. 132.

54.   Paul de Man quoted in Lionnet, p. 140.

55.   Lionnet, p. 136.

56.   Ibid., p. 139.

57.   Filomina Chioma Steady, "The Black Woman Cross-Culturally: An Overview," in Filomina Chioma Steady, Editor, *The Black Woman Cross-Culturally* (Cambridge: Schenkman Publishing Company, 1981) describes social and financial strengths for African women in polygynous marriages.

58.   Adam McLean, *The Triple Goddess: An Exploration of the Archetypal Feminine* (Grand Rapids: Phanes Press, 1989), pp. 7-17.

59.   David Leeming and Jake Page, *Goddess: Myths of the Female Divine* (New York & Oxford: Oxford University Press, 1994), p. 25.

60.   Niara Sudarkasa, "The 'Status of Women' in Indigenous African Societies," in Rosalyn Terborg-Penn, Sharon Harley, and Andrea Benton Rushing, Editors, *Women in Africa and the African Diaspora* (Washington, DC: Howard University Press, 1987), pp. 25-41.

61.   Nancie Solien Gonzalez, "Household and Family in the Caribbean: Some Definitions and Concepts," in Steady, pp. 421-429.

62.   Myriam Warner-Vieyra, *Juletane* (Paris: Presence Africaine, 1982), pp. 79- 80. (All translations of this work in this essay are my own.)

63.   Ibid., p. 60.

64.   Leeming and Page, p. 25.

65.   Ibid.

66.   Warner-Vieyra, p. 134.

67.   Leeming and Page, p. 25.

68.   Warner-Vieyra, p. 135.

69.   Ibid., p. 141.

70.   Ibid., pp. 134-135.

71.   Leeming and Page, p. 25.

72.   Marnia Lazreg, "Between God and Man" in Lazreg, *The Eloquence of Silence: Algerian Women in Question* (New York: Routledge, 1994), pp. 209-222.

73.   Edward C. Whitmont, *Return of the Goddess* (New York: Crossroad Publishing Company, 1990), p. 33.

7

Cruelty, Castration, and Claiming

In *Exorcising Blackness*, Harris states that African American women rarely describe in their literature the historical lynch/castrations of men of African descent in European American society. She quotes Richard Maxwell Brown's description of the lynch/castration hysterical phenomenon:

They came regularly to be subjected to fiendish tortures that had seldom been inflicted on the white victims of lynch law. They lynching of Southern Negroes came to be accompanied routinely by the emasculation of males and the burning of both sexes.[1]

Exceptions to this literary silence among women are oddly obfuscated. When ritual racist lynch/burnings and castrations are depicted in African American women's literatures, they are oblique, seen through a distorted lens that mitigates the visceral impact of the assault by emphasizing its social ramifications following a comparatively brief description of the physical suffering of the victims. For example, in her magazine novel *Winona*, Pauline Hopkins has the castration of an imprisoned African who was probably escaping enslavement, briefly witnessed by an imprisoned man of European descent:

One day he was aroused to greater indignation than usual by hearing heart-rending cries come from the lower room. Hurrying to the stove-hole he gazed one moment and then fell fainting with terror and nausea upon the floor. He had seen a Negro undergoing the shameful outrage, so denounced in the Scriptures, and which must not be described in the interests of decency and humanity. . . . Unhappily we tell no tale of fiction.[2]

The reader is spared proximity to the brutalization of "the Negro" by witnessing his assault through the buffer of the European American man's suffering on his behalf. Oddly, the most tense anticipation of the reader's possibly being forced to witness a lynch/castration in this story comes as a proslavery mob descends upon, and prepares to burn alive, this same European American man.

Though castration as a facet of capital lynching increased in frequency and severity after the Civil War, Bebe Moore Campbell's *Your Blues Ain't Like Mine* opens with the shooting execution of a young African American from Chicago who is visiting Mississippi and is not, during the lynch ritual, emasculated:

Armstrong heard the click of the trigger, and he took a deep breath. He felt his bowels ripping through him, then a soft, warm mushiness in his pants. He heard an explosion; fire seared the inside of his chest. His head slammed into the dirt. . . . As he heard the retreating footsteps in the air around him, he thought: *My daddy could whip all of you.*[3]

Though the complex human relationships in *Your Blues Ain't Like Mine* are described in convincing and realistic detail, the central event, Armstrong's murder, is stripped not only of castration but of the beatings and tortures historically known to have accompanied racist lynchings throughout post-Civil War America.

Yet it would be inaccurate to state that Pan-African women are not describing castrations. In fact, their literature describes castrations in excruciating detail. However, most of these literary castrations are enacted by women who are claiming or controlling men to whom they have committed themselves, either psychoemotionally or through marriage.

The most blatant depiction of castration as claiming is described by Jones in *Eva's Man*. This book is about confusion: protection of innocence is confused with permission for the innocent to self-endanger, as when Mama entrusts the housebound teenage Eva to her philandering and violent cousin, Alfonso; trust is taken as an opportunity to abuse, as when Tyrone takes Mama's cooking bouts in the kitchen as opportunities to sexually entrap her daughter, Eva. Even who abuses and who protects remains entangled and confused throughout the novel; besides the above examples, Mr. Logan, who sexually abused Miss Billie as a child, becomes the protective witchlike owl who interrupts Tyrone's aggressive assault of the adolescent Eva. The confusion reaches its climax in the work's title, as Eva claims Davis Carter, another woman's husband, as "her" man by taking his life and the physical symbol and tool of his manhood from him, demonstrating the "queen bee" quality of women's love that she has feared since childhood. Eva's lifelong study of the people around her teaches her that women, victimized, unwillingly carry the power to destroy the men they love, as is plaintively explained in the suicidal plight of the original queen bee: "When they found the queen bee, it went all around the neighborhood. The cops didn't know why she did it, but the people in the neighborhood did."[4]

What everyone in the neighborhood understands is that the queen bee must destroy the man who loves her, for this is her nature, and she cannot help this inevitable result of the power of her contact with men. Mama and Cora Monday have foreseen the queen bee's suicide as inevitable should she become afflicted with love and concern for one of the ninety-nine out of a hundred men who must be destroyed by close association with her. It is not the helplessly destructive nature of the queen bee that the gossiping neighbors question, but only what caused her to be so "marked."

In fact, the series of violently subdued women in *Eva's Man* demonstrates that it is erroneous to assume that the queen bee was especially "marked." The repetitive tales of male violence and women's tenderness with their own kind builds the tenuous theory that the only safe outlets for women's sexual power are venting it with men whom they do not love or with other women. Mama vents her sexual power in her lengthy affair with Tyrone, then sustains beating and rape by her husband as punishment. This triangle explains the odd trilogy of Jean's loyalty to the cruel Alfonso, who regularly beats his wife in front of hotels, hivelike structures, until he is stopped by his brother, Otis. Alfonso chronically subdues the queen bee aspect of Jean, and the only restraining power to which he responds is male, Otis, acting protectively on Alfonso's behalf to prevent his arrest, not to save his victim's life.

In the final analysis, *Eva's Man* is about the destructive, meaning deadly, nature of women's love for men, symbolized by the lubricating phallic sausage cooked with labial-flowering cabbage and covered with anal mustard, which Eva eats as she draws Davis Carter to her at the story's opening and when she celebrates her claiming of him in murder and castration. Women's life-giving fertility, bastardized into sexuality, is also under examination, as Davis Carter and Eva discuss the eggshells sucked empty and filled with oysters at Easter, the time of male resurrection, to which Davis Carter alludes bitterly as he waits for Eva's menstrual flow to cease so that their sexual intercourse may begin:

"I thought you'd be through," he said, changing the subject, sitting close beside me on the bed, till I could feel his thigh, firm and muscular through his pants.

"Three days I said."

"Christ could rise in three days," he said, touching his crotch.

"Then let him. I'll be grateful."[5]

Male sexuality revelling in female suppression is the ongoing theme of this book; the innocent Eva must discover why a woman or girl must be subdued and forced, or coerced and abandoned, in order to be enjoyed:

"I'ma put my thing in you like Mama's men put it in her."
I didn't try to run. I just stayed with him. . . . Then he kept looking from my eyes to his thing. And then all of a sudden he pushed me away from him, and turned and zipped his pants back up, and went upstairs. I didn't know what he'd seen in my eyes, because I didn't know what was there.[6]

At the novel's climax, Davis Carter has entrapped Eva in his hotel room strictly for the enjoyment of sexual activity. He tells her that if he lets her out, he believes that she will return to streetwalking, either becoming sexually promiscuous or a prostitute. Wanting to prove her loyalty to Davis Carter, Eva becomes afraid to leave and lose their relationship. Her entrapment in the dingy hotel room causes her emotional and physical constraint to the point of suffering: "I punched my belly, swollen with too much eating in, and being constipated. I'd get nervous with him there, and nothing would come out."[7] Eva's entrapment in the hotel and physical self-constraint in order to keep Davis Carter is symbolized by her painfully distended stomach, Oya's purifying winds trapped inside: "He belched, said excuse me. . . . I held my own belch in, till it made me feel sick. All that gas inside."[8] Eva incubating in the hive of Davis Carter's dark room, becoming a woman in love, is desperately in need of "exactly what Oya, properly reverenced, does: clears the air. . . . Storms clear the air and dispel pollution."[9] Eva's psychoemotional relief and release are signaled, at the moment of Davis Carter's poisoning death, with releases of this putrid gas: "I had my back to him and didn't watch. But he gripped my waist hard enough to break my ribs. 'Bitch.' I belched."[10]

Oddly enough, Eva's murder and claiming of Davis Carter come just as he has promised to give her a key to his unpaid hotel room so that she may come and go. Here, the novel's confusion of opposites surfaces again. For in making the hotel room Eva's home by offering her freedom of movement to and from it, Davis Carter confirms to her his opinion that she is a loose woman, available to other men. At the same time, he announces to her that he is, in fact, married and unable to pay for the room, and therefore, may be moving on without her. Eva's murder of, and sexual revelling on the corpse of, Davis Carter proclaim his belonging to her and the release of her furious tension:

I opened his trousers and played with his penis. My mouth, my teeth, my tongue went inside his trousers. I raised blood, slime from cabbage, blood sausage. Blood from an apple. I slid my hands around his back and dug my fingers up his ass, then I knelt down on the wooden floor, bruising my knees. I got back on the bed and squeezed his dick in my teeth. I bit down hard. My teeth in an apple. A swollen plum in my mouth . . .

I got the silk handkerchief he used to wipe me after we made love, and wrapped his penis in it. I laid it back inside his trousers, zipped him up. I kissed his cheeks, his lips, his neck. I got naked and sat on the bed again. I spread my legs across his thighs and put his hand on my crotch, stuffed his fingers up in me. I put my whole body over him. I farted.[11]

The sexual coming together in the hivelike hotel (many small, dark rooms) of Eva and Davis Carter ends in his genital blood and her claiming of him, conversely to its beginning in her genital blood and his claiming of her. Freed of her fear of losing or being undervalued by the man she saw as almost a husband, Eva is now free to celebrate their consummated commitment by taking the key he had promised and leaving the hotel to wander and feast on her favorite sexual foods. Exultant in her survival at her lover's expense, Eva thinks that with her hair unbound and wild she resembles, first, the Medusa and, next, a lion. She distorts the traditional idea of the North African Gorgon Medusa, who turned men's bodies to stone, claiming for herself the power to harden men's penises. Though it is male lions who have her wild mane, it is the female sphinxlike power to devour males and know the secret of life that Eva is claiming. She recalls Carter's watchful envy of her ability to devour: "You eat food like you're making love to it."[12]

Davis Carter's death by poisoned, sexually symbolic food finally allows both Eva and the reader to interpret the *vagina dentata* (toothed vagina) symbols of desirous female sexuality as ravenous, consuming, and castrating. These symbols have riddled Eva's story from childhood to imprisonment and are emphasized in the passing reference to the lioness/devourer Sekhmet image: "The queen bee. Men had to die for loving her. . . . He said he was dying to kiss me. . . . He said my kiss was full of teeth."[13] The power of women's unbridled sexuality affords them a strength that is superior to the abusively dominating power of men who beat and rape. The queen bee is only apparently a woman who has rejected the sexually subjugated role which is suffered by women whose love is constrained by abuse and who do not kill their men. Eva has discovered that in actuality, the queen bee who kills and the subjugated woman who is sacrificially consumed are precariously one and the same woman:

The queen bee, sitting on the toilet throne, wipes between her legs. Her nipples are full of blood.

"They told me her father abused her mother when she was pregnant, and she came out gumming her own umbilical cord—she couldn't gnaw because she didn't have no teeth—so she came out gumming."[14]

Couples and couplings encountered in the novel's course make it clear that men and women have no recourse to sexual sharing in which one partner will not be sacrificially consumed or destroyed by the other: "Otis said it was like they were working some kind of blues ritual. . . . A man sucking milk from her breasts. He is sucking blood."[15] Sexual relations between men and women, or between the socially powerful and the apparently disempowered, are enshrouded with someone's destruction fueling another's power: "'She won't bother you because she's afraid of you. '. . . Sour cabbage and spoiled sausage spread with turd mustard."[16]

But the queen bee has only seemed to cut the umbilical cord that ties her to her ancestresses and their sexual subjugation. The releasing of her destructive passion only returns her to entrapment. The novel closes by fusing Eva with the image of her grandmother buried in the sand of a dried riverbed, symbol of dessicated female power: "All female Orisha are not only rivers but witches."[17] Once swimming with fins, mermaidlike in the power-filled image of Yemoja and Mami Wata, the grandmother/ancestress, symbol of all sexually subjugated women to the imprisoned and disillusioned Eva, dies disempowered and trapped in the earth like Nyale, with a hole over her face to allow her to give sexual pleasure to the men who buried her, not to allow her to breathe. Eva, imprisoned, reviews the choices available to her as a sexually desiring woman: to be trapped and used, or to consume, destroy, and be imprisoned again:

He pushes my face into his lap. He combs my hair with his long fingers. I am afraid.
    We are in the river now. We are in the river now. The sand is on my tongue. Blood under my nails. I'm bleeding under my nails. We are in the river. Between my legs. They are busy with this woman.[18]

Another riverain goddess who takes a mermaid form is Oshun, who has "skill in the art of mixing deadly poisons" and owns "the inner court, where witch lays her eggs."[19] The power of the owl shapeshift of West African witches and priestesses of Nephthys, known as Lady of the Castle and Isis's "dark" (underworld) sister, has been appropriated by the sexually assaultive man who saves Eva the child from rape. The owl returns to its symbolizing of female empowerment as Eva explains to the dead Davis Carter, to whom she is telling her life's story, that she is considering sexual fulfillment with her cellmate:

An old owl sucks my blood. He gives me fruit in my palms. We enter the river again . . . together.

They are doing with this woman. See. They are doing with this woman. See what they are doing with this woman.

Last night she got in bed with me, Davis. I knocked her out, but I don't know how long I'm going to keep knocking her out.[20]

Eva's Man rejects the mutual dispensing of pain that will eventually allow reconciliation between Ursa and Mutt in Jones's *Corregidora*. In this work, the protagonist Ursa's great orality, her blues singing and her enactment of a near castration of the repentant Mutt, who has deprived her of the ability to bear children as witnesses to her ancestresses' enslavement, leads to tearful and pain-accepting reunion:

A moment of pleasure and excruciating pain at the same time, a moment of broken skin but not sexlessness, a moment just before sexlessness, a moment that stops before it breaks the skin: "I could kill you. . . ."

He came and I swallowed. He leaned back, pulling me up by the shoulders.

"I don't want a woman that hurt you," he said.

"Then you don't want me. . . . "

He shook me till I fell against him crying. "I don't want a kind of man that'll hurt me neither," I said.

He held me tight.[21]

However, in Jones's subsequent work, the odyssey of Eva's silent self-understanding begins as an answer to the late Davis Carter's questions about her life, made when he was still alive and trying to picture her as the non-demanding woman he took her to be, ends as Eva discovers the uncompromised pleasure of sexual sharing with another imprisoned and equally disempowered woman:

"Tell me when it feels sweet, Eva. Tell me when it feels sweet, honey."

I leaned back, squeezing her face between my legs, and told her, "Now."[22]

Contrary to the earlier *Corregidora*, in which Mutt's acceptance of Ursa's gesture toward an equalizing castration brings their turbulent reciprocal dispensing of pain to a standoff closure, *Eva's Man* posits swiftly and bluntly that ideal sexual sharing should lack contests of pain-giving domination and self-expressive destruction of the partner.

Head's Dikeledi in "The Collector of Treasures" shows a few strong points of both similarity and dissimilarity to Jones's Eva and Ursa. Unlike Eva and Ursa, Dikeledi's castration of her husband is not an act of claiming relational equality with him or even of claiming him as her own. Dikeledi's husband is morally monstrous:

It was as though he was hideous to himself and in an effort to flee his own inner emptiness, he spun away from himself in a dizzy kind of death dance of wild destruction and dissipation.[23]

For Dikeledi, castration of her husband is an act of personal responsibility for the tenuous dignity that she has established in her life since her husband's abandonment of her and their three children eight years earlier. She loves, works for, and is cared for by her neighbors. She sews, knits, and is "the woman whose thatch does not leak." When, in a fit of unwarranted sexual jealousy, Garesego announces his return to her, Dikeledi is horrified:

Her life had become holy to her during all those years she had struggled to maintain herself and the children. She had filled her life with treasures of kindness and love she had gathered from others and it was all this she wanted to protect from defilement by an evil man. . . . She turned her thoughts this way and that and could find no way out except to face him.[24]

Dikeledi does not bother to kill her husband before castrating him, as did Eva, who was still in love. The reader is left to wonder whether or not Dikeledi even knew that her act of castration would be fatal:

With the precision and skill of her hardworking hands, she grasped hold of his genitals and cut them off with one stroke. In doing so, she slit the main artery which ran on the inside of the groin. A massive spurt of blood arched its way across the bed. And Garesego bellowed. He bellowed his anguish. Then all was silent. She stood and watched his death anguish with an intense and brooding look, missing not one detail of it.[25]

The story has opened as Dikeledi, named for her mother's widowed tears, is imprisoned for the castrating murder of her husband. Unlike Jones's Eva, Dikeledi in prison does not find that she is an oddity to be questioned and studied; she finds that her four cellmates have all murdered their husbands, and that one, Kebonye, castrated hers with a razor. Kebonye's husband was an "education-officer" who abused his administrative position by seducing schoolgirls; Kebonye sees her execution of this man as a public service:

"The last time it happened the parents of the girl were very angry and came to report the matter to me. I told them: 'You leave it to me. I have seen enough.' And so I killed him."[26]

Besides, Kebonye's husband was cruel to her, an apparently common complaint, the narrative voice explains, among the women married to colonialism's broken and demoralized men.

'Our men do not think that we need tenderness and care. You know, my husband used to kick me between the legs when he wanted that. I once aborted with a child, due to this treatment.'[27]

Before the story circles back to explain Dikeledi's predicament, however, the narrative voice pauses at the close of Dikeledi's first imprisoned day to explain that Dikeledi has already found something to treasure while incarcerated:

She had always found gold amidst the ash, deep loves that joined her heart to the hearts of others. She smiled tenderly at Kebonye because she knew already she had found another such love. She was the collector of such treasures.[28]

In contrast with Eva, who found sexual sharing with her cellmate in prison but, as far as can be discerned, not love, Dikeledi has found love with her cellmate in prison but, as far as can be discerned, not sexual sharing. Dikeledi has made it clear to her neighbor, a woman who offers to share her husband, that she has never cared for sexual relations. Yet Dikeledi and this neighbor's husband are rumored to be lovers; it is jealousy about this man and this rumor, which Dikeledi's husband has himself spread, that brings the philandering Garesego home.

The narrative voice is at pains to make it clear that Dikeledi and the man with whom she has come to be as a second wife in all ways, except the sexual, actually care deeply about each other:

Two soft pools of cool liquid light were in his eyes and something infinitely sweet passed between them; it was too beautiful to be love.

'You are a good woman, Mma-Banabothe,' he said softly.

It was the truth and the gift was offered like a nugget of gold. Only men like Paul Thebolo could offer such gifts. She took it and stored another treasure in her heart.[29]

Ironically (and magically), the very issue that brings Dikeledi and her chaste admirer to her husband's attention is resolved by Garesego's murder and Dikeledi's imprisonment. After murdering Garesego, Dikeledi sends her son to fetch the police and have her arrested. As she waits, the story closes on her admirer's last words to her:

Out of the dark Paul Thebolo stepped towards the hut and entered it. He took in
every detail and then he turned and looked at Dikeledi with such a tortured expression that for a time words failed him. At last he said: 'You don't have to
worry about the children, Mma-Banabothe. I'll take them as my own and give
them all a secondary school education.'[30]

These closing lines explain Dikeledi's contentment as she learns that
her cellmates in prison will be made up of at least one good friend. Now
she and her children have everything: the "treasures" of affection and
dear memories which were threatened by Garesego's return, and even
the secondary education that Dikeledi unfortunately went to Garesego to
ask him to help her afford. The act of murderously castrating Garesego
has preserved and precipitously added to Dikeledi's store of treasures.

Guadeloupean Warner-Vieyra creates a protagonist whose dilemma
combines the conflicts faced by Jones's Eva and Head's Dikeledi and Kebonye. Warner-Vieyra's Sidonie, in the short story of that name, has left
Guadeloupe with her brother, who is pursuing his education and career
in Paris. She is soon paralyzed below the waist in a car accident. The
driver, a spoiled joy-rider named Barnard, marries Sidonie. Soon, their
happiness dissipates in bitter arguments over his repeated acts of infidelity. The story opens shortly before their worst crisis; Sidonie is about
to discover that her husband and his young cousin, who has come to
clean house for her and whom she has loved like a sister, are expecting a
baby. They are also expecting that Sidonie, paralyzed and incapable of
bearing children, should be happy to accept and raise the child.

Sidonie is outraged. She has lately taken up writing, sublimating her
own loneliness in a tale about another young woman's unrequited love.
She has been happily occupied with her writing; now she burns it. She
refuses food and water; when her husband plays music to lighten the
unexpectedly morose atmosphere that has descended upon their apartment, Sidonie breaks the music disc.

Throughout the story, Sidonie's plight is contrasted with that of her
brother's wife, who feared that she was too fat to be loved and married,
and who willingly tolerates her husband's infidelities, simply grateful
that he always returns home. Sidonie's plight is further contrasted with
the young cousin, Yolene's, rather mindless pursuit of sensual pleasure.
In close and intense comparative contact as Sidonie's crisis becomes
clearer and her desperation heightens, the reader becomes aware that
health, beauty, and sensuality are of relatively little use to any of these
women in terms of helping them shape their relationships with the men
in their lives. In fact, one might be led to conclude that attractiveness

might predispose men toward a dismissive attitude; Sidonie's brother married Nicaise because he could see that her poor self-image predisposed her to bear any negligence or infidelity at his hands without complaint.

Poverty and helplessness render both Yolene, the young cousin, and Sidonie vulnerable. Yolene has spent her life in want, and she does not wish to follow in her mother's birth-bedraggled footsteps. She links birth with supernatural female power and death; yet, despite her recall of a symbolically rich experience, she is as unable as everyone else in Sidonie's life to foresee what the news of this last infidelity is driving Sidonie to do:

Une nuit que son pere etait absent, elle dut aller querir la sage femme au bourg. Elle devait avoir six ou sept ans. Elle marchait pieds nus. A certains endroits, elle sentait la terre chaude sous ses pas; selon la legende, cela signifiait qu'un mort y etait enseveli. Cette nuit-la, elle eut l'impression que tout le chemin n'etait qu'un cimetiere. Elle redoutait qu'a tout moment, un spectre ne se dressat devant elle. En arrivant au bourg, un grand chien blanc lui barra la route. Elle cria. L'animal grogna et brusquement disparut, comme absorbe par le sol: c'etait sans doute la vieille madame. . . . On disait qu'elle se metamorphosait en bete, pour circuler la nuit. Elle avait connu a cet instant la plus grande peur de sa vie.

(One night when her father was not home, she had to go get the wisewoman from the village. She must have been six or seven. She walked barefoot. At certain places, she could feel that the earth was hot under her feet; according to the legend, that meant that a corpse was buried there. That night, she had the feeling that the whole road was nothing but a cemetery. She had no doubt that, at any moment, a ghost might appear in front of her. When she got to the village, a big white dog barred her way. She screamed. The animal growled and suddenly disappeared, as if it had been absorbed into the soil: it was, without doubt, the old lady. . . . It was said that she could become an animal and go around at night. That was the most frightening moment of her life.)[31]

Like the old and power-filled wisewoman, Sidonie appears all in white, going about the house in the dark of night to avenge the ultimate betrayals with which her longsuffering has been met. Blood, death, and devastation will cut a path through the lives of all the people who counseled her to accept Bernard's latest—and grossest—act of infidelity. Her newfound writing vocation abandoned, it should be—but is not—evident that, in their home, Sidonie has joined the circle of birth to death.

Sidonie asks her husband to attend her bath and help her dress for bed because she will have nothing more to do with "his concubine." Expecting that his docility in these little attentions will smooth the way to his wife's acceptance of his lover's child, Bernard acquiesces. He even refrains from arguing—at much length—about her insistence on playing opera music as he falls asleep.

As the night progresses, Sidonie behaves as if possessed by the "darker side" of the riverain goddess of love, Oshun, "using knives as she flies through the night."[32] Fasting, extraordinarily distressed, Sidonie manages to get into her wheelchair and select a knife from the kitchen. She returns and slides between the legs of her sleeping, unfaithful husband. Warner-Vieyra describes Bernard's and Sidonie's final confrontation:

Bernard fut reveille par une impression de lourdeur au bas-ventre qui s'imposa en brusque elancement. Il eut la sensation de manquer d'air, entendit d'abord le fou rire hysterique de Sidonie avant de decouvrir son visage luisant de sueur, deforme par un rictus dementiel. La douleur lui montait au coeur, un rideau noir tomba devant ses yeux. Il saisit Sidonie, eut conscience de la tenir a la gorge. Malgre lui, un hurlement de bete ecorchee vive jaillit du fond de ses entrailles, tandis qu'il serrait qu'il serrait de toutes ses forces.

(Bernard woke with an impression of heaviness in his abdomen that suddenly became piercing. He felt he couldn't breathe, and he first heard Sidonie's crazy, hysterical laughter before he discovered her face, shiny with sweat and deformed by a demented rictus. The pain climbed to his heart, and a black curtain fell before his eyes. He seized Sidonie; he was aware that he had her by the throat. Despite himself, a bellow as of an animal being skinned alive rose from the pit of his gut, while he strangled her with all his might.)[33]

Meanwhile, Sidonie's brother has been dreaming of her walking with him in a flower garden; she is weeping inconsolably. He awakens to the ringing of his telephone, convinced that the dream is an evil augury. He rushes to the apartment to find ambulances and police; Bernard is carried away, near death, and Sidonie has been killed.

The thoughts that close the sad account are the brother's. He remembers loving Sidonie and wishing to make her happy after their mother's death. He does not recall taking her educational sacrifices for granted; he loves her more than he loves the woman he married. He thinks sympathetically of Bernard, hoping that for his own sake, Bernard will die. Yet, even in his reverie, Sidonie's brother seems oblivious to the implications of his own memories. How can a woman who was her brother's "only good thing" (as Beloved was Sethe's "best thing" in *Beloved*) ever learn to settle for being as neglected, abandoned and humiliated as the brother's own wife? What good did once being treasured do Sidonie, except to build in her unfulfilled expectations of continuing to be treasured? (Bernard has repeatedly justified his treatment of Sidonie by comparing it to her brother's treatment of his wife.) The obvious question goes unanswered: what did the brother do to effect positive change in the deteriorating marriage, except counsel Sidonie to accept and adapt? Clearly, nothing.

As the brother goes out of the blood-washed apartment, he looks back, not to learn, but to seek comfort in memories of his love for his sister during earlier, happier times: "Dehors, la brume froide d'une nuit d'automne l'enveloppa de nostalgie." ("Outside, the cold mist of an autumn night enveloped him in nostalgia.")[34] This is a comfort that was unavailable to his sister, who was forced to live, and finally chose to share death, with her husband, as she was swept into the current of rapid and traumatic changes she found herself powerless to modify or control.

Sidonie's castration of her husband serves to render him as impotent as a man as he had rendered her helpless and incapable of childbearing, as a woman. Sidonie also ensures that should Bernard survive his wounds, his wanton career of seducing women is, nonetheless, over. Whatever he may live to enjoy sexually, in future, he will experience the extreme limitations that were suffered by his wife. Sidonie's castration of Bernard can be seen as an act of claiming her husband and concurrently claiming the power of moral agency; but beyond all this, Sidonie's act has served to reverse the fortunes of all who claimed to love her while subjecting her to emotional torture and psychological cruelty. Now it is Bernard, the spoiled and devil-may-care, who may live—or die—in shame, pain, and that peculiar loneliness that accompanies humiliation. Bernard's shocking mutilation at the hands of the woman who was devoted to him, like Garesego's, serves to remind that the goddess who incarnates "both fertility and love" also "represents the motivating factor for social justice."[35]

NOTES

1. Richard Maxwell Brown, "Legal and Behavioral Perspectives on American Vigilantism," *Perspectives in American History* 5 (1971), p. 105, quoted in Trudier Harris, *Exorcising Blackness: Historical and Literary Lynching and Burning Rituals* (Bloomington: Indiana University Press, 1984), p. 7.

2. Pauline Hopkins, *Winona*, in Pauline Hopkins, *The Magazine Novels of Pauline Hopkins* (New York and Oxford: Oxford University Press, 1988), p. 385.

3. Bebe Moore Campbell, *Your Blues Ain't Like Mine* (New York: Ballantine Books, 1993), p. 39.

4. Gayl Jones, *Eva's Man* (Boston: Beacon Press, 1987), p. 60.

5. Ibid., p. 61.

6. Ibid., p. 120.

7. Ibid., p. 122.

8. Ibid., p. 126.

9. Judith Gleason, *Oya: In Praise of an African Goddess* (San Francisco: HarperCollins, 1992), p. 46.

10. Jones, p. 127.

11. Ibid., pp. 128-129.

12. Ibid., p. 130.

13. Ibid., p. 131.

14. Ibid., p. 152.

15. Ibid.

16. Ibid., p. 153.

17. Gleason, p. 70.

18. Jones, p. 176.

19. *Awo* Fa'lokun Fatunmbi, *Oshun: Ifa and the Spirit of the River* (Plainview, NY: Original Publications, 1993), p. 14, and Robert Farris Thompson, *Flash of the Spirit: African and Afro-American Art and Philosophy* (New York: Vintage Books, 1984), p. 80.

20. Jones, p. 176.

21. Gayl Jones, *Corregidora* (Boston: Beacon Press, 1986), p. 185.

22. Jones, *Eva's Man*, p. 177.

23. Bessie Head, "The Collector of Treasures" in Head, *The Collector of Treasures and other Botswana Village Tales* (Oxford: Heinemann, 1992), p. 92.

24. Ibid., pp. 93 and 101.

25. Ibid., p. 103.

26. Ibid., p. 90.

27. Ibid., p. 89.

28. Ibid., p. 91.

29. Ibid., p. 98.

30. Ibid., p 103.

31. Myriam Warner-Vieyra, "Sidonie" in Myriam Warner-Vieyra, *Femmes echouees* (Paris & Dakar: Presence Africaine, 1988), pp. 138-139. (All translations of this text are my own.)

32. Thompson, p. 80.

33. Warner-Vieyra, p. 142.

34. Ibid., p. 146.

35. Fatunmbi, p. 7.

8

The River and the Wall

Pan-African women's literature often follows the psychological, social, and spiritual quests for personal fulfillment of motherless heroines. The motherless state of these women of African descent in societies at once racist and sexist clarifies for the reader the heroines' lack of protective guidance and role modeling. These heroines are socially abandoned and psychoemotionally assaulted by the rigorously competitive and relatively conscienceless societies into which they must fit if they would find belonging and personally meaningful goals both to nurture and structure their lives. Even highly commercial works often feature motherless heroines of African descent whose loss is central to the driving quest of the novel.

For example, in Margaret Cuthbert's *The Silent Cradle*, the heroine's adolescent witnessing of her mother's death in childbirth is not only the impetus for the girl's growing up to become an obstetric surgeon but drives her to become an idealistic and self-motivated protector of her charges, the laboring mothers and their helpless newborns. As well, the heroine's motherlessness supplies the reader's understanding of her often repeated sense of isolation in her highly competitive professional environment, her aloneness in the face of bias and dismissal, and her questlike forging ahead into relatively uncharted territory as she continues to assume authority that no one surrenders to her without a fight.

By comparison with motherless heroines, however, in a relatively rare gesture of blunt social commentary, Dangarembga does away with the tool of motherlessness to depict twin heroines who openly reject, if not their mothers, then the social positions and lifestyles that their mothers represent. In *Nervous Conditions*, the narrator, Tambu, and her cousin, Nyasha, attempt to shape satisfying destinies for themselves as their colonized homeland of Rhodesia shapes itself into the independent fragments of Zimbabwe.

For Tambu, the goal is easy to define though its achievement is grueling and seems, at times, as if it must be impossible for a girl whose parents, siblings, and most familiar social traditions are all opposed to her pursuits. Tambu wants to earn the highest educational degrees available to colonized Africans, even if this means farming her own maize to go to elementary school, then going away from her home to live with her paternal uncle and his family, and, eventually, boarding at a prestigious school for European-descent girls that assuages its racist collective administrative conscience by taking in a token number of African girls. Someday, the reader is led to understand, Tambu is perfectly willing to cross the ocean to England to continue pursuing ever higher educational degrees. She has spent her young life helping her mother farm, cook, clean, and tend the babies that are the lot in life of country women in colonized, traditional African societies. Tambu does not want this grim, hand-to-mouth, subsistence-farmer's-wife lifestyle for herself. Tambu's ideal lifestyle, for an African woman, is that of her paternal cousin Nyasha and Nyasha's mother, Maiguru.

It is a disconcerting surprise, two-thirds into the book, to discover that Nyasha's mother has already achieved all Tambu's educational goals, including that of an English master's degree. Maiguru's lot is an unenviable one, though Tambu is too driven by fear of the kind of helpless poverty in which her own mother lives and suffers to have any spare emotional space for contemplating the comparatively rarified suffering of privileged African women. However, the reader, who is probably as educated and possibly less socially constricted than Maiguru, is given ample opportunity to contemplate the entrapment of the educated and privileged African woman. Maiguru's teaching paycheck goes straight into her husband's account to be disbursed among his relations, to whom he is a conquering hero; she spends her holidays at his traditional homestead, cooking traditional meals, without the benefit of either refrigeration or electricity, for his dozens of visiting relatives; she takes the blame for his chastisement of their daughter and the unbridled freedom of their son whether or not she approves of her husband's childrearing decisions. As Head aptly explains in "The Collector of Treasures," the triple burdens of tradition, the gluttonous free-for-all that was colonization, and the chaotic power scrambles of independence combine to subjugate African women, some of whom are still shackled by traditional expectations poorly translated into rapidly changing societies: "To this day, women still suffered from all the calamities that befall an inferior form of life."[1] Maiguru, who Tambu explains should have everything a woman could want, has only the material advantage over her village sisters of knowing that she and her children will not be forced to starve. Dangarembga arranges to address this last point, the village woman's fear of her children's starvation, poignantly and ironically in the course of Nyasha and Tambu's pursuits of self-defined achievements.   For Maiguru's relatively privileged daughter Nyasha will prove to be dying of a psychospiritual starvation that will manifest itself physically.

To appreciate Dangarembga's denunciation of the social deadend faced by African women in colonized societies, it is necessary to review the life-sustaining goals that she presents as tempting and driving these societies' colonized members. Poor village boys may aspire either to successful subsistence farming or, more prestigiously, to education and its attendant careers, income, security, and status. The competitive, tradition-rejecting ambitions of the village boy who wishes to divorce himself from the poverty and helplessness of the colonized man is depicted by Tambu's brother, Nhamo, whose death opens the novel. Nhamo had stolen and treated his school friends to Tambu's crop of maize ("mealies"), with which she intended to continue providing herself with an elementary education. Tambu's narrative voice draws the reader into the story by explaining that she did not mourn her brother's passing because it signaled the advent of her own opportunity to become highly educated in his stead. Her father's older brother, who symbolizes the epitome of success for the colonized African male, descends upon Tambu's bereaved homestead to announce that it has fallen to Tambu to take her brother's place in his home and at the school where he is headmaster.

Tambu clearly steps into the limelight at this point, representing the pinnacle of the village girl's possible achievements. She is slated to become her parents' source of pride and financial well-being in their declining years. Tambu moves out of the brick and dung-and-wattle homestead on loan to her parents from her uncle, and into the large, carpeted, European-style home of that paternal uncle and his divided, suffering family.

Here the reader becomes acquainted with the opportunities and goals — or lack thereof — facing those colonized Africans who have achieved the prospects poor villagers so desperately pursue. Chido, Nyasha's brother, has been educated side by side with neighboring "white Rhodesians" whose father has assiduously secured him a place in their schools, as a token "good" African:

So determined was this good missionary that Chido should have the best in life that he personally drove my cousin to Salisbury. . . . Not surprisingly, since Whites were indulgent towards promising young black boys in those days, provided that the promise was a peaceful promise, a grateful promise to accept whatever was handed out to them and not to expect more, Chido was offered a place at the school and a scholarship to go with it. . . . "So Chido gets his scholarship and Mr. Baker feels better about sending his sons there in the first place!"[2]

Chido now spends his vacations and free time with this family and, at this rate, is expected to one day marry the daughter. His prospects are defined by the accomplishment possibilities open to the European colonizers; Chido's father's standing with their traditional, patriarchal family ensures him adequate status—should he ever concern himself with traditional matters—in his African society. Chido is free to pursue the status and role of the colonizer. Stepping into the shoes of, and eventually replacing, the European colonizer is the pinnacle of achievement to which the colonized African male may aspire.

As has been explained, Nyasha and her mother Maiguru represent the hollow and precarious heights of achievement available to colonized African women. Maiguru's education and career go unrecognized and unappreciated, except as a source of income for her husband's family. Maiguru is voiceless and overworked. She resents the burdens placed upon her by the traditional roles whose translation into contemporary colonized African society has crippled her with both cultures' responsibilities and expectations, but with neither societies' freeing options.

This lack of freedom of aspiration and behavior is represented in Nyasha. But Nyasha no more wishes to step into the dual-colonized drudgery and spirit-crippling remnants of tradition that characterize her mother's life than Tambu has wanted to inherit her mother's grubbing poverty. However, unlike Tambu, Nyasha has nowhere to go to escape; she has no optional goals. Like Chido, Nyasha has been raised relatively ignorant of traditional ways. Unlike Chido, Nyasha has not been given full permission to pursue a Europeanized lifestyle, education, and spouse to adopt the only lifestyle she fully understands. These children's stay in England, while their parents attained master's degrees, has equipped the boy to fully understand and acclimate himself to the world of the colonizing European. It has rendered the girl a stranger to her traditions and the strengths they may have offered to save her as she faces the crisis of her dearth of choices. If she cannot understand or tolerate the traditions that afflict and render her mother the voiceless property of her father, then what other options can Nyasha pursue?

The novel's climax and decline present Tambu moving on to the Catholic boarding school and the assurance of college, someday, in Europe; meanwhile, Nyasha consumes herself with self-imposed starvation and the obsessive study of world history as if, by understanding how her society came to be as it is, she might create or discover an avenue of survival in it for herself.

Nyasha's anorexia is a classic futile gesture at warding off impending womanhood. She refuses to inherit her mother's hollow status and unrecognized achievements, which are all appropriated by a demanding and spoiled husband; yet, Nyasha is aware of no other womanly roles to which African girls may aspire. Nyasha opts to endlessly deny and put off the inevitable discovery that her adult life will never reflect the values that her close association with the colonizer's culture has taught her to value. Colonizing society's abandonment of Nyasha is brought home to the reader by the closing information that a European doctor refuses to treat her in crisis, too thin and weak to walk but demonically destructive of her room, her books, and her precious pots of riverbed clay, because he believes that African girls are too psychoemotionally coarse to suffer from "nervous conditions." The doctor counsels that Nyasha's overbearing father take her home and be even more firm with her.

Though an African doctor is found who agrees to try to treat Nyasha, the book closes on her questionable chances of survival, as Tambu draws closer to the achievements whose inherited emptiness are destroying her cousin. Was there no solution to the meaningless intellectualized enslavement of the educated, professional African woman?

The optional solution to contemporary highly-educated servitude has been acted out for the reader by the women whom no one wishes to emulate, Tambu's impoverished, hardworking mother and her paganistically wanton sister, Lucia.

Having lost her son in her brother-in-law's home, been forced to participate in a Christian wedding nearly twenty years into her marriage, and now losing her daughter to a distant boarding school, Tambu's mother sinks into a catatonic decline after announcing that

'Truly that man is calling down a curse of bad luck on my head. You have survived the mission so now he must send you even further away. I've had enough, I tell you, I've had enough of that man dividing me from my children. Dividing me from my children and ruling my life. He says this and we jump. To wear a veil, at my age, to wear a veil! . . . If I were a witch I would enfeeble his mind, truly I would do it, and then we would see how his education and his money helped him.'

My mother declined so rapidly after that it was as though she was the one who had been cursed.[3]

The mother's youngest baby develops diarrhea, and both mother and child seem to be dying. Tambu's father wants to take his wife and child to "a medium," but Tambu intervenes, afraid that her mother will persuade the medium to, indeed, curse her uncle and prevent her attending the Sacred Heart boarding school. So instead, the father settles for calling in the mother's sexually free sister to see if she may not help matters. This sister's first act is to take the afflicted woman and child to the local river, idealized by Tambu in the opening pages of the novel as an edenic counterpoint to the village's growing capitalistic poverty:

First Lucia made my mother walk to Nyamarira, quite simply by strapping Dambudzo to her back, grasping my mother round the waist and walking her there. Then she made my mother wash herself and the baby. 'Sisi,' she threatened, wading calf-high through the water and depositing Dambudzo on a boulder, 'watch me. I am putting him on this rock and leaving him there, right in the middle, in the middle of the river. If he slips into the water because you do nothing to save him then you will truly go mad. Because this time you will be guilty.'

And so when other women came to wash or to draw water they saw my mother and Lucia and Dambudzo leisurely waiting for their clothes to dry, which is a normal sight at Nyamarira. In addition, they were all very pleased to see Lucia and so they were lively and gay when they came over to greet my mother. . . . It was all very good medicine.[4]

Oshun, though haling from West Africa instead of Southeast, is a "Goddess who freely gives medicine to cure mother and child;" Lucia, the loving and loyal, seems perpetually guided by the "Spirit of the River who Teaches the Mystery of the Erotic." In Tambu's descriptions, the river consistently functions as a source of contact with a tradition that is beautiful, timeless, and joyful, all gifts of Oshun, whose impulse it is "to maintain balance and harmony within the natural environment."[5]

The river Nyamarira remains throughout the story a focus of community well-being. As Tambu leaves her parents' home to pursue her dream of higher education at her uncle's mission school, she does not anticipate missing her family, including,

My anxious mother, [who] was no more than another piece of surplus scenery to be maintained, of course to be maintained, but all the same superfluous, an obstacle in the path of my departure.

But dramatically, she does anticipate missing this river:

Nyamarira which I loved to bathe in and watch cascade through the narrow outlet of the fall where we drew our water. Leaving this Nyamarira, my flowing, tumbling, musical playground, was difficult.[6]

When forced to visit her father's inherited homestead during vacations, increasingly troubled Nyasha develops a hobby that allows her, too, to return to the positive traditional feel of the river: she makes herself little clay pots with its soil. Interestingly, when she returns with her family to the mission school, Nyasha uses the handmade clay pots to hold the accoutrements of her Europeanized existence: her "buttons and jewellery and pens."[7] This is a staving-off gesture toward containing her colonized form in a traditional mold. However, it remains no more than a gesture, for as Nyasha poignantly laments to Tambu, she knows nothing of her traditional beliefs.

Possibly hoping to spare her daughter the burden of unevenly interpreted traditional African ways as applied to educated African women, Maiguru has kept her daughter alien to all things traditional, as far as she is able. This is made clear with Nyasha's first appearance in Tambu's story, when she and her brother accompany their parents to the homestead to be greeted by relatives upon their return from England. The family is dancing, and Nyasha, who has been painfully embarrassed about her English minidress and ignorance of greeting customs during dinner, is finally willing to join the family in this ancient form of celebration. But Maiguru will not let her. So Nyasha retreats further into her sense of being alien, of being "shocked" by her own inherited culture. Long specifically links the patriarchal prohibition of "frenzied dancing" in goddess worship with modern women's psychoemotional ailments:

The Goddess at the feast 'delights in drums' and is the 'frenzy-loving, joyful one.' I feel the importance of this very strongly as it has been denied us for so long. When it emerges it is so often distorted and turned against us or against others who do not deserve it and whom we do not wish to hurt. We have the capacity for orgy, for frenzy, for demonic release, and we can use this safely if we have space for it, and if it is sanctioned and in the service of our deepest feelings. How many women are locked up in psychiatric hospitals, or at home in the prison of valium and other anti-depressants, only because they have nowhere to work out their life-loving frenzy? In love there is space, but because of the age-old tyranny of patriarchy frenzy can so often only manifest itself in male violence.[8]

Sadly and prophetically, the next time the reader encounters Nyasha trying to enjoy the sensual freedom and association of the feminine, divine sensuality of dance is at the mission school. A dance is being held for the students. Chido dances all evening with the "white Rhodesian" daughter of the family that has adopted him and monopolizes his free time; Nyasha, similarly, has spent the evening dancing with one of the "white Rhodesian" brothers. As the group wanders home, Nyasha and this friend of Chido's are still practicing a dance step together. Understandably, Nyasha is reluctant to end the evening and return to the morbid study and diet regimens that make up her teen existence.

True to his description as a "good boy," Chido makes no effort to warn his friend that Nyasha will be in trouble if she continues to dance with him at the head of the driveway while their father waits. Instead, Chido and Tambu try to sneak into the house, leaving Nyasha blissfully dancing. When Nyasha's father discovers what she has been doing, he does indeed beat her. The beating intensifies as she tries to defend herself. The horrid scene ends with everyone's awareness that this family has lost something irretrievable.

Nyasha despises and pities her father, who restricts and condemns her, refusing to question the dangerous double standard his interpretation of tradition and colonialist religion has established in the disparities in personal liberty, future aspirations, and public behavior he allows his two children. To her downfall, Nyasha has embraced her father's interpretation of the colonizer's Christianity. Tambu explains that Nyasha "liked having causes and the Christian cause, which was conformist but could clandestinely be translated into a progressive ideology, was ideal for her."[9] Nyasha disputes this assumption:

When I confronted Nyasha with this evidence of the nature of progress, she became quite annoyed and delivered a lecture on the dangers of assuming that Christian ways were progressive ways. 'It's bad enough,' she said severely, 'when a country gets colonized, but when the people do as well! That's the end, really, that's the end.'[10]

However, the study of Christianity is available to idealistic Nyasha in her colonized country while the study of traditional religions, goddesses, and heroines is not. Nyasha's ambivalent but intense embracing of Christianity proves to be a double-edged sword, as it enforces in Nyasha's mind her father's interpretation of her rebelliousness as "evil."

For Nyasha, the "evil" of her rebelliousness is also her only salvation from buckling under the colonialist heel and conforming to the highly educated slavery that claims her mother's accomplishments and individuality. Rapidly reaching a crisis of psychoemotional rupture, Nyasha rants to Tambu, who has come visiting from Sacred Heart:

'They've deprived you of you, him of him, ourselves of each other. We're groveling. Lucia for a job, Jeremiah for money. Daddy grovels to them. We grovel to him.' She began to rock, her body quivering tensely. 'I won't grovel. Oh no, I won't. I'm not a good girl. I'm evil. I'm not a good girl.' I touched her to comfort her but that was the trigger. 'I won't grovel, I won't die,' she raged and crouched like a cat ready to spring.

Note the cat transformation, recalling Bast the black cat goddess healer or Pasht, Bast's avenging/destroying aspect, as Nyasha's critical breakdown strips her of her remaining shreds of Anglicized, restrained comportment. (See analysis of Sekhmet and the Black Virgin in chapter three.) Tambu goes on to describe Nyasha's furious rebellion and collapse:

She rampaged, shredding her history book between her teeth ('Their history. Fucking liars. Their bloody lies.'), breaking mirrors, her clay pots, anything she could lay her hands on and jabbing the fragments viciously into her flesh. . . . 'They've trapped us. They've trapped us. But I won't be trapped. I'm not a good girl. I won't be trapped.' Then as suddenly as it came, the rage passed. 'I don't hate you, Daddy,' she said softly. 'They want me to, but I won't. . . . Look what they've done to us,' she said softly. 'I'm not one of them, but I'm not one of you.'[11]

Nyasha rages, desperately in need of the riverain goddesses' cooling and soothing powers, destroying her tenuous links with the Oshun-like "Spirit of the River, Mother of the Mirror, Owner of the Dance, who Transforms" and "guides my Character."[12]

The power of Nyasha's global and personal outrage recalls the furious eye toward social justice and equality of the riverain goddesses, whose study is lost to Nyasha due to her parents' (probably well-intentioned) deculturation of both their children. Indeed, were Nyasha acquainted with riverain goddess/"witches," she would realize that she shares with them the patriarchal colonizer's appellation of "evil." She would also realize that they are her intellectual and spiritual mythatypes, her role models, and the course through which she might first steer a precarious path to self-salvation, if not immediately to the salvation of her nation and people. Priestesses of Oshun "have a key role in maintaining the communal standards of justice and equality."[13] Thompson explains that riverain goddesses' powers undermine "Western technocratic structures" in that

Imperially presiding in the palaces beneath the sands at the bottom of the river, the riverain goddesses are peculiarly close to Earth. In the positive breeze of their fans, the ripple of their water, there is coolness. In the darkness of their depths and in the flashing of their swords, there is witchcraft.[14]

Nyasha uncooled and about to rampage crouches like a cat, also recalling the link between riverain goddesses and West African leopard societies: "'*mermaids* showed us how to write *nsibidi*.'" *Nsibidi* is the

five-hundred-year-old African ideographic script whose signs defied the
European incursion and embodied "many powers, including the essence
of all that is valiant, just, and ordered."[15] It is fitting that Nyasha, overwhelmed and horrified, might blindly incarnate the power of these secret
societies for "Only a woman can call the leopard spirit back because, so it
is believed, the leopard society was first a women's society."[16] Clearly
and tragically, Nyasha was not an indoctrinated devotee of Oshun, Spirit
of the River, the mermaids Yemoja or Mami Wata, Nnimm the Terrible,
Ebongo, mother of the sounding leopard, or Sikan, the bride of God.[17]
But one is forced to marvel at how perfectly the study of these goddesses' traditional religions and tenets might have calmed, guided, and
transformed the self-consuming, raging Nyasha, who suffers from ter-
minal self-alienation. Only the clay of the little river Nyamarira which
grounds Tambu is ever shared between the girls; any empowering or
magical stories it sustains remain unmentioned in their (unwitting or
unwilling) pursuits of colonialist solutions to deculturation.

Another African-descent woman's work that develops the relationship between women and the secret leopard societies is Octavia Butler's
Wild Seed, in which the Igbo heroine is a shapeshifter whose most frequently resorted-to shape, in times when self-defense is paramount, is a
leopard. Oddly and significantly enough, in this work also, however, the
magically empowered heroine eventually speaks the mantra of Tambu's
radically disempowered mother: "When had it ever mattered what she
said to him? He did as he pleased." In fact, as if symbolizing the historic
overtaking of leopard societies by men, *Wild Seed's* heroine eventually
tells her nemesis (who is both enemy and lover) that it is he who is the
leopard while she and her people are his prey, though this statement is
clearly somewhat tongue-in-cheek as she and her people are, to some
extent, escaping this spirit man.[18]

Might her own people's rapidly vanishing pantheon of deities have
offered Nyasha a healing mythatype as well? Nyasha unhappily reaches
for her alien origins through Tambu, who is racing to escape those
poorly grasped origins so that she may fit more comfortably into the
world of her country's colonizers. Sadly, in *Nervous Conditions*, neither
of the young and vulnerable heroines is able to fully nurture or ade-
quately forewarn the other, nor assist each other's efforts at cross-
cultural bridging.

The problem of splitting the whole heroine into the personae of two
protagonists is a frequent one in Pan-African women's literatures; however, this pairing is often difficult to recognize because the themes split
between the two girls or women often reflect differing issues across cultures and generations. Still, it is relatively safe to summarize that the

pairs most often seem to reflect the issues predominantly facing their generation of colonialist resisters. That is, roughly, that older pairs of heroines seem to be grappling with the stereotypes of the mammy and the whore, which capitalist colonizers of European descent foisted upon women of African descent for obvious reasons of economic gain and hierarchical privilege. Younger pairs of women are often faced with the dichotomy of developing spiritual versus material skills for coping in a colonized but hypocritically democratic world community and economy.

Diaspora and Continental women's literature that presents older pairs of women dealing with the racist images thrust upon them of mammy and whore, are reflecting these women's internal responses to the external expectations of societies at once racist and sexist. An example of this kind of dilemma is in Toni Morrison's *Sula*, which has been analyzed by Mary Helen Washington as a work in which Sula and Nel represent opposing halves of one fully integrated and maturely developed female personality. Further, Sula and Nel are recognized as modernized versions of the mammy and jezebel stereotypes that Hazel V. Carby, in *Reconstructing Womanhood: The Emergence of the Afro-American Woman Novelist*, and Deborah Gray White, in *Ar'n't I a Woman: Female Slaves in the Plantation South*, have traced so precisely and convincingly to their racist economic and sociopolitical origins. In a chapter called "Slave and Mistress" in the above work, Carby charges that derogatory stereotypes about African American female sexual proclivities have been unquestioningly perpetuated by modern historiographies even when the presentation of other aspects of chattel enslavement have been revised.

African-descent women who split sexual and domesticated extremes, not between Euro-American wives and African sexual victims, but between two women who are both of African descent, immediately pose a situation that queries racist assumptions of "true womanhood" as being the domain of European-descent women. That is, when Pan-African women become the literary characters for whom "love of home, children and domestic duties are the only passions they feel,"[19] then the assumption that this supposedly chaste emotional makeup is available only to women of European descent is challenged. Whatever mitigating factors have contributed to the African-descent woman's sexual frigidity and domestic passion restate, at the same time, the concept of sexual frigidity or infertility, no longer as virtue or moral purity, but as handicap and domestically crippling lack. That is, in many of the literatures of women of African descent, frigidity (lack of sexual passion for one's spouse) often joins infertility as a curse upon a woman's fate, not a blessing upon her character. For example, when Nwapa's heroine, Efuru, becomes a devotee of the childless but wealthy and beautiful goddess Uhamiri, who dwells in white with her riches at the bottom of a lake, domestic tranquillity is lost with both her practice of days of sexual and culinary abstinence and her inability to bear a child who will live to adulthood.[20] This querying of a racist projection by removing it from its racialized environment serves to invalidate it by positing that the sexually neutered woman suffers and causes domestic suffering, and that the whore often intends no damage, however misguided she may be; it is beneficial, as well, to trace the mammy and jezebel stereotypes back to their European origins.

The black whore might easily have come from multiple cults of Isis which spread throughout Greco-Roman Europe, or from the cults of Libyan Aphrodite, both of whose temples often featured sacred prostitutes or hierodules, sex with whom assured the community of blessed prosperity. The mammy most resembles a bestially distorted converging of the European adoration of the Maries and Sophia, who suffered in the Egyptian desert to bring humankind wisdom and redemption, hideously mixed with the house-blessing aspects of the big-breasted holy hippo and cow of heaven, Hathor, who was brought to Europe through Greco-Roman cults of Isis.[21] Hopefully mixing the long-suffering beneficence of the Black Virgin, a potential or penitential whore who had renounced and repressed her sexuality, with the foster mothering, bovine patience of Hathor would not only provide the colonizing European-descent imagination with idealized nannies, but would set any humane consciences of colonialist beneficiaries at rest by drawing upon a European communal archetype that said housing these reformed whores, and giving them superior children to tend, would satisfy their deepest spiritual drives.

Women of African descent, finding themselves faced with these stereotypes, might respond with credulity to the erotic whore, as multiple mirror goddesses and the rites of their worshippers provide her mythatype: Oshun, Erzulie, Bast, Hathor, and Isis are probably the best known. At the same time, eroticism might never carry quite the damning connotation for these women, inheritors of opposing mythatypes, as eroticism does for those of European descent who have historically foisted these images upon Pan-African women.

Frigidity as a moral quality seems relatively absent from the literatures of women of African descent. On the other hand, eroticism represented as a woman's, goddess's, or ancestress's sexual acts motivated by preference, or at least choice, has nothing to do with being sexually victimized. African-descent women's literature often presents that there is nothing in common between being powerlessly abused (their view of their own and their ancestresses' rapes) and having inherited the status of sexually passionate goddesses (the procolonialist view that condoned the history of sexual victimization); further, Pan-African women's literature often reflects the psychomoral chasm between victimization and willing wantonness.

While older generations of women grapple with the stereotypes foisted upon them, and query those stereotypes' validity by removing their racial connotation and distributing them among women of African descent, younger generations of women in literature tend to pose more internalized questions, often responding to the spiritual vacuum one feels as an upwardly striving, least privileged member of a capitalist, racist, and sexist society. Younger pairs of women who split one whole character between two heroines often posit the development of psychospiritual qualities as opposed to the capacity to gain material benefits.

For both these kinds of split pairs, while it is true that converging their traits produces a whole woman, it is also true that blending these split personalities elevates their suffering protagonists above the psychoemotional dissection perpetrated upon their psyches by a lifetime of racist and sexist social conditioning, drawing them closer to identity with the predominant traits of most African goddesses: fecundity and ability to nurture and protect.

Tumbling (as in "Joshua fit the battle of Jericho, and the walls came a–tumbling down"[22]), by Diane McKinney-Whetstone, is a novel in which a pair of older women split into whore and mammy, and a pair of younger women split spiritually and materialistically. By the novel's close, both pairs are forced to merge and blend their characteristics to become survivors in their demanding and imperfect environments. The novel begins when Oya's wind, signaling abrupt change, drives a philandering man home to discover that a baby has been left on his and his wife's doorstep. As the wife heats milk for the baby, wishing she might breastfeed it herself, Hathor/Black Mary's sycamore outside catches her eye and serves as a sign to the reader that this woman's motherhood shall be transformative, having to do with spiritual nursing and the cyclic gaining of wisdom.

The husband's lover, an exemplary literary whore, left the baby. This woman spreads her sexuality wantonly among men because, Isis-like, she feels that she is thereby giving them life, in compensation for having unwittingly participated in her mother's stabbing of an innocent and inoffensive man. By contrast, the wife, frigid due to a childhood trauma, and the whore, wanton for an analogous reason, form a jezebel/mammy dichotomy whose extreme characters will cause them both increasing suffering until the smashing of the wife's church brings the two women together to literally walk in each other's shoes. The life-giving miraculous quality of the whore's sexual wantonness identifies her with traditional Pan-African erotic goddesses whose promiscuity is an aspect of their fecundity; what the whore misses, as long as the church walls stand, is the Pan-African goddesses' additional quality of mothering. The whore is divided against herself, unlike the mythatype of the erotic African goddess. Wanton goddesses are also mothers capable of bestowing children upon their suppliants. As soon as the church's walls fall, the whore trades shoes with the frigid mammy and walks into an adventure that will return to her the traditional role of mother, as well as erotic representative of regeneration, procreation, and rebirth. The mammy is frigid as long as the walls of her church have stood; the closest she has come to passion has been her healing experiences with her pastor and her shamed desire to nurse her first foundling. As the walls of her church blind her with their literal dust, she has been blinded previously by her participation in her church's theological construct. What she misses is the healing vision of cyclic love: the union of loving woman and man that produces more life to be nurtured and loved, as the lovemakers love each other. For the frigid mammy, the sexual act has, until the fall of her church's walls, remained inextricably identified with the violent atrocities visited upon her as a child.

The first baby, abandoned by the whore and raised by the mammy, eventually forms a dichotomous pair with the second child left on the frigid woman's doorstep: the whore's niece. The first child is psychically adept; the second is a good student and future wanton who hides a secret mania for eating wall plaster. When her cousin and foster sister eventually discovers how obsessively insane the wall-eating habit has become, the materially successful girl attacks the psychic with a hammer and initiates a further crumbling of the wall between their (foster and biological) mothers' characters and their own. For the whore must nurse her fallen daughter until help arrives, and the mammy will finally make love with her husband while that daughter convalesces. The psychic will recover from the assault, but learn that she no longer can read minds and futures; the terrified perfectionist must learn to turn purposefully inward, vulnerable before a psychiatrist, and devour self-dividing walls figuratively, not literally.

The destruction of the walls of the church has led the mammy to learn that her church, as a symbol, blinded her to the beauty of her husband's lovemaking genitals; as he bathes the dust of the fallen church's walls from the mammy's eyes, she sees for the first time how appealing he is, and he discovers that passion shared with a devoted woman can be consummately satisfying. The once frigid mammy and her philandering husband now make love all over their house as she discovers that her home is an altar in which to celebrate the divine gifts of love and well-being. The destruction of the walls of solidity that shape a home and a life can lead to the vulnerable demands for help that the psychic and the materialist were each unable to make, the former because she had extraordinary abilities and wanted no mundane ones, and the latter because she feared rejection. The blended destruction of the walls that separated (whore/mammy) and the walls that insulated (spiritualist/materialist) renders two generations of women whole and complete in themselves, more fully able to become loving and loved members of their families and communities. The women assume more fluid and osmotic identities, freed of the rigidity of their previous limited role-playing and the resultant demands placed upon them by their communities' expectations.

As the novel closes, the whore-becoming-nurturing-mother wishes to be comforted by a man who sees her as a person and cares to fulfill her needs. The mammy-becoming-sensual-lover wishes to be the passionate sharer of her husband's deepest capacities for intimate expression and feeling. The former psychic must learn to stumble through relationships whose ends she cannot foretell and make her own way in a world as closed and solid to her as it is to every other human being; she must learn to trust, hope, and have faith without assurances of fate. The materialist must learn to have her weaknesses laid bare before the eyes of others and yet believe that those others can and will care for her and help her to heal. The destruction of character-limiting walls allows each woman's identity to flow into the wholeness represented by the preancient goddesses whose signatures and signs move these stories along. The women's characters stretch and integrate with the painful relief of limbs, uncramped. Their spirits, released from damning definitions, flow as rivers undammed.

NOTES

1. Bessie Head, "The Collector of Treasures," in Bessie Head, *The Collector of Treasures and other Botswana Village Tales* (Oxford: Heinemann Educational Books, Ltd., 1992), p. 92.

2. Tsitsi Dangarembga, *Nervous Conditions* (Seattle: Seal Press, 1989), p. 106.

3. Ibid., p. 184.

4. Ibid., p. 185.

5. *Awo* Fa'lokun Fatunmbi, *Oshun: Ifa and the Spirit of the River* (Plainview, NY: Original Publications, 1993), pp. 7 and 20.

6. Dangarembga, pp. 58-59.

7. Ibid., p. 150.

8. Asphodel P. Long, *In a Chariot Drawn by Lions: The Search for the Female in*

Deity (Freedom, CA: The Crossing Press, 1993), p. 78.

9. Dangarembga, p. 98.

10. Ibid., p. 147.

11. Ibid., pp. 200-201.

12. Fatunmbi, pp. 14-15.

13. Ibid., p. 7.

14. Robert Farris Thompson, *Flash of the Spirit: African and Afro-American Art and Philosophy* (New York: Vintage Books, 1984), pp. 74-75.

15. Ibid., pp. 227, 241, and 244.

16. Ibid., p. 244.

17. These titles are gleaned from P. Amaury Talbot, "Through the Land of Witchcraft: Part 1," in *Wide World Magazine 31* (1913), pp. 428-437, and Thompson, pp. 236 and 243.

18. Octavia Butler, *Wild Seed* (New York: Warner Books, 1997), pp. 209 and 278. Compare Butler, p. 209, to Dangarembga, p. 153: "Does it matter what I want? Since when has it mattered what I want?" Tambu's mother is ostensibly talking about fate, but the incidents she names have to do with her husband's will versus her own unnamed desires. Butler's heroine is considering how her lover/nemesis's will has become fate to her and to the people for whom she cares. The powerful shapeshifter and the subsistence farmer's wife echo each other's relative hopelessness in the face of their men's desires and pursuits.

19. Barbara Berg, *The Remembered Gate: Origins of American Feminism, The Woman and the City, 1800-1860* (Oxford: Oxford University Press, 1978), p. 84.

20. Flora Nwapa, *Efuru* (Oxford: Heinemann, 1978), pp. 153-154 and 165. So distressing is the inheritance of beauty and wealth without the ability to bear children that Nwapa has left us such classic literary lines as: "'We are not going to eat happy marriage. Marriage must be fruitful,'" and, "She dreamt of the woman of the lake, her beauty, her long hair and her riches. . . . She had never experienced the joy of motherhood. Why then did the women worship her?" (pp. 137 and 221).

21. For interpretations of the spread of cults of Isis and her aspects through Europe via the Greco-Roman empires, see Ean Begg, *The Cult of the Black Virgin* (New York: Penguin Books, 1996), Sharon Kelly Heyob, *The Cult of Isis Among Women in the Graeco-Roman World, Etudes preliminaires aux religions orientales dans l'empire roman* (Leiden, Netherlands: E. J. Brill, 1975), and R. E. Witt, *Isis in the Greco-Roman World* (Ithaca: Cornell University Press, 1971).

22. Traditional spiritual song sung by enslaved Africans in North America.

9

Conclusion: This Moment of Epiphany

My study of mythatypes in the literature of women of African descent began with the realization that these works often feature heroines who have lost their mothers. This loss heightens the reader's opportunity to perceive the agency of spiritual mothers in the text interacting with the heroine and/or writer.

A classic example of this kind of loss and search is exemplified by Nella Larsen's Helga in *Quicksand*, who cannot find an acceptable identity among those offered to early twentieth-century African American women in the North, the South, or in Europe. She flings herself into loveless passion and marriage with a southern preacher named Pleasant Green (in ironic contrast to *Their Eyes Were Watching God*'s desirable and mourned "Vergible Woods"). Helga hopes by this precipitous leap to come to "belong;" she has grown up outside her society's few and rigid roles and is having trouble belatedly inserting herself into one. However, long before Helga wastes away and begins to take her unwanted children into her oblivion, the reader can see that this desperately ecstatic religious/sexual plunge was no viable choice. Helga, sinking, asks her nurse to read to her of an earlier world of African and Asian gods and whole-woman worship, where women sacrifice Isis's white doves. Helga wishes for a god who might kill Reverend Green. (See Angela of Foligno.) Instead of a god who will destroy her husband for Helga's benefit, Helga is being sacrificed so that the larger society surrounding and encompassing her can make sense of itself to itself. Otherwise, the conflation of racist and sexist persecutions, and how they mire women such as Helga, would be as horrible for that society's members to contemplate as *Quicksand* is horrible and crucial to understand.

There are rarely mothers available in these texts for these women to grow up emulating because multiple layers of colonization and the scramble for privileging hierarchies in colonized societies have historically distorted and depersonalized their mothers' roles. The resulting gendered racist hierarchies place these Pan-African heroines chronically on the bottom rung, precariously bracing the social disorder which misdefines and psychoemotionally abuses them.

The distortion of self-perception suffered in racist colonization affects men as well as women. Birago Diop introduces his collection of favorite folktales by explaining that when he left Senegal for college in France, the retelling to himself of these childhood tales grounded him and wove his tattered identity back together:

Ce retour fugitif dans le passe recent temperait l'exil, adoucissant un instant la nostalgie tenace et ramenait les heures claires et chaudes que l'on n'apprend a apprecier qu'une fois que l'on en est loin. . . . Dans la trame solide de ses contes et de ses sentences, me servant de ses lices sans bavures, j'ai voulu, tisserand malhabile, avec une navette hesitante, confectionner quelques bandes pour un pagne sur lequel grand-mere, si elle revenait, aurait retrouve le coton qu'elle fila la premiere.

(This escape to my recent past tempered my exile, sweetened for a little while the nostalgia that gripped me, and gave me back the clear bright hours that one only learns to appreciate when he is far away. . . . In the solid woof of her stories and maxims, using her flawless lines, I wanted, clumsy weaver with a hesitant shuttle, to fashion the strips to sew into a cloth where grandmother, if she could return, would have found the thread that she had first woven.)[1]

Unlike Bugul of *Le baobab fou*, Diop "in exile" immediately immerses himself in his earliest cultural memories to solidify and personally witness and take part in the making of his identity with all its ethnic markings, building a self-image that will fortify him in a foreign environment indifferent at best, hostile at worst, to his self-conception.

Eufemia Mallegui emigrated from Nigeria to Italy and suffered a spiritual and deeply personal loss of identity. She expresses her confusion and loss of self in a poem entitled <<Dimmi chi sono>> ("Tell Me Who I Am"). Her cry is addressed to a god who, she wants to believe, bridges the world, apparently known to her first in Africa and hopefully waiting for, listening to, and ready to act to save her in Europe.

Sola nel buio della notte	(Alone in the dark of night
il terrore mi avvolge nel suo manto	terror wraps around me
tenebroso.	its cloak of clouds.
Ho paura, tanta paura.	I am afraid, so afraid.
Ombre oscure mi girano intorno,	Dark clouds encircle me,
le mie mani tremano,	my hands tremble,

il mio corpo viscido	my slippery body
scivola nel nulla.	slides through nothingness.
La pioggia saltella su di me	Rain hops on me
ricordandomi che sono ancora viva.	reminding me I'm still alive.
Non ricordo chi sono.	I don't remember who I am.
Mi chiamano Lucciola.	They call me Firefly.
Sono distrutta,	I am shattered,
soffocata,	suffocated,
calpestata dalla societa.	trampled under society's foot.
Voglio respirare	I want to breathe
voglio ritornare a vivere.	I want to live again.
A te mio Dio	Toward you my God
rivolgo il mio rantoloso respiro.	I gasp.
Salvami.	Save me.
Tu lo sai chi sono.	You know who I am.
Tu conosci il mio nome.	You know my name.
Lo so, lo sento che Tu verrai nel buio	I know, I feel that You
di questa notte.	will see in this night's darkness.
Ti aspetto.	I wait for you.
Non ti lascero mai piu.	I will never leave you again.)[2]

The poet has no bearings and rejects the hopeful but feeble identity that has been given to her. She recalls that she once was fully alive and therefore is aware that her present condition and experience are, while evidently not death, a limbo of obscurity, fear, and loss. She turns to a god to whom, while she addresses him(?) familiarly, she accords the power of potentially perceiving her in the void through which she falls, restating an identity with which she will identify, and bringing her back to what she understands as life.

She promises, interestingly, never to leave this god again; but the future tense of her promise implies that this promise will be binding upon her only after s(he) has saved her. Even more significantly, the deifying capitalized pronoun is abandoned when she speaks of breathing toward this (god)dess and again when she makes her promise not to leave; the poet is promising "you," not "You." Abruptly, "my God" is humanized, hears the poet's breath as well as her words, and apparently values something that only the poet can choose to dispense as she pleases: her loyalty, allegiance, and presence. Just as the sudden image of rain on her body interrupts the highly abstracted, purgatorial description of the poet's suffering, so this abrupt offer of self to (god)dess jars the image of the poet's helplessness and invests her with the power of something valuable to offer in exchange for salvation: herself. The starkly contrasting images of abandonment and rebirth with rain recall the tragic life and representation of afterlife that are attributes of the snake orphan, Bunzi. After the birth canal images of a slippery body falling and being brought back to awareness by lively rain, the poet turns to a greater power than she to ask, like the goddess born of incest, to be reinstated into the deity's good graces.

The poet implies that she may have contributed to the onset of her suffering by leaving this deity; she thereby implies that losing her may have caused the (god)dess some suffering too, though obviously s(he) has suffered no loss of omnipotent ability to hear, perceive, name, and save the poet. The poet expresses no specific sin of her own that might have placed her at odds with her (god)dess, which enhances her interpretive similarity to Bunzi, born with the burden of her mother's incestuous act and redeemed by assuming her mother's regenerating responsibilities. Because the only agent of her suffering that the poet identifies is a nebulous trampling "society," a tenuous equation is established that suggests her place in this society is, in fact, the nothingness through which she falls and from which this familiar (god)dess will save her by seeing her and saying her name. Having finished the description of her distress, the poet proceeds to empower herself by addressing this (god)dess as ultimately concerned with her and most likely willing to do for her what she is unable to do for herself: reestablish her identity. Her statement of expectancy ("I wait for you") implies that the deity feels some sense of responsibility toward her and should respond accordingly. The beginning of her salvation lies in framing her plea for help. The demotion of her god from "You" to "you" suggests that her pursuit of this deity's humanized aspect, toward the poet and in the poet's life, will be the basis of the insulating relationship she needs to protect her from the society that treads upon and misnames her. Clearly, Mallegui's approach to her deity recalls the highly intimate relationship Angela of Foligno claimed with hers. Significant reversals are that in Mallegui's poem, it is the (god)dess who must bring life to the poet, instead of the devotee who breathes life into the deity, and Mallegui's poetic voice does not claim exclusive status with her deity. She only implies that the loss of herself is a situation the deity, too, has regretted and might be swayed by the promise of rectifying.

I finish my analysis of this poem asking myself if indeed the poet "left" her (god)dess, then how? By breaking laws, leaving Africa, making some other life change that she fears the deity saw with disapproval and as a sign of the poet's rejection? Information about the poet's implied previous abandonment of her god is not even approached in the poem. Its very cloaking is a strong indication of the self-empowering intimacy the poet seeks to reestablish in the last line. The lower case "you" the poet finally addresses knows whatever it is she did that amounted to abandonment or displeasure. The poet closes her account of lonely fear by referring to their unshared knowledge of her apparent wrongdoing and implied rectification. The poem is a vehicle through which the poet empowers herself to do what admittedly little she can, under her circumstances, to lead to the end of her own suffering. The poem's greatest contribution to the poet's revivifying reorientation is that it clearly implies she is valued, seen, heard, and known, if not by the society that treads upon her, then still by her abandoned (god)dess.

The experience of the acculturated person of African descent who relocates to a procolonialist environment for education or employment is often recounted as a pain-filled one, in which one's intimate and previously unquestioned self-concept becomes radically destabilized. In *The Souls of Black Folk*, William E. B. Du Bois used the metaphor of the Veil to describe the isolation of one's self, at once understanding how one is rigorously misperceived while striving to maintain an insular integrity in the midst of interaction with that self-alienating external identity. Each transitional survivor must discover her own avenue of self-reconstruction and healing, or she will recount not a story of survival, but one of possible self-destruction.

Anty Grah's short story, <<Cronaca di un'amicizia>> ("Chronicle of a Friendship"), tells of two young women whose Ivory Coast friendship is forever lost due to the personae they adopt while in France. The idolized older girl, Aita, leaves the Ivory Coast first, going to France for a college education. Her parents die suddenly. After their Ivory Coast funeral, she returns to France. From then on, whenever Aita visits her West African hometown, instead of coming as an impoverished orphan, she comes with incredible amounts of money for parties and gifts. Her visits are poorly timed as far as school scheduling goes. Only when the younger girl, whose narrative voice is telling this story, goes to live with an older sister in France does the reader discover why Aita has become so wealthy and mysterious. She has become a professional prostitute. When Aita's adoring younger friend discovers Aita and reminds her of her African sense of hospitality, they spend one last affectionate evening together before Aita explains that they must go their separate ways. Aita does not wish to see the people of her African childhood witnessing the self she adopted in France (or did it adopt her, an orphan?). The narrator turns to her older sister to understand this splitting:

"Sappiamo tutti che alcune cose sono vietate, condannate dalla societa africana e quindi giu ci comportiamo bene, ma ognuno ha i suoi vizi, quando arriviamo all'estero, ci sciogliamo come capelli legati, come visi nascosti dentro di noi."

("We all know that certain things are forbidden, condemned in African society, so we behave ourselves down there. But everyone has vices; when we go abroad, we come undone like bound hair, as if faces were hidden inside us.")[3]

The narrator closes her story by expressing regret that, even now that Aita has "found herself," finished her education, and returned to the Ivory Coast to practice law, they can never again be friends. Certainly, the difference here is that unlike Du Bois, this narrator speaks for a community that believes the other self found in procolonialist society is an aspect of the individual's entirety which only the pressure of an Afrocentric community represses. Rather than alienation from self, this passage argues that the loss of a censoring society simply allows previously suppressed qualities to surface. But by the narrator's choice of closing words challenges this perspective; she says her friend "has found herself." Her implication is that there was or is a true self that, reclaimed, does not want the shame of being identified with the uninhibited—and false—self that was experienced in France.

Perhaps Deborah Gray White sheds light on the apparent dichotomy between an image foisted upon one and a hidden self waiting to emerge. In "Jezebel and Mammy," White cautions against the continued use in literature and criticism of images that "have just enough grounding in reality to lend credibility to stereotypes that would profoundly affect black women."[4] Her critique implies that something about the stereotypical description, externally applied, may have just enough truth to elicit a confusion of identity in the woman of African descent who finds herself illustrated, addressed, or represented. White's call is to isolate the two historically pervasive and assaultive literary stereotypes that are applied to Pan-African women, analyze and objectify their origins, and thereby distance them, creating a space for self-definition. This feat of constructively destroying negative stereotypes and clearing space for the assertion of more realistic images is consummately executed in such works as Saundra Rice Murray's "Psychological Research Methods: Women in the African Diaspora" and Paula Giddings's *When and Where I Enter: The Impact of Black Women on Race and Sex in America.*[5]

In essence, Ama Ata Aidoo agrees with this need for self-definition and explains that "only an African knows what it is to be an African and only a woman knows what it is to be a woman and can give expression to the essence of being a woman."[6] Aidoo reinforces White's, Murray's, and Giddings's singling out of female gender as a significantly vulnerable aspect of African identity in a procolonialist environment. The unique positioning of African women in a colonized world has been identified as "a double colonization." In an anthology with that title, Lauretta Ngcobo defines African women's dilemma as the need to "integrate contradictions into a meaningful new whole."[7] Her proposal that contradictions be "integrated," rather than gleaned for unacceptable images that warrant rejection, is in full accord with the voice of the narrator's older sister in <<Cronaca di un'amicizia>>, who explains that the objectionable self that emerges is an inner aspect of self. While Ngcobo's and the older sister's explanations shed possible light upon Bugul's self-destructive sojourn in Belgium, both these viewpoints lack the apparent objectivity, of White's perspective that the "truth" in the negative image is only partial and leads to a damaging whole. The outcome of accepting the partial truth would seem to make it worthy of nothing other than wholesale rejection. This is depicted in Larsen's *Quicksand*, where a modern African American woman experiments disastrously with stereotypically dictated—and therefore seriously restricted—social life scripts available to her in European America, African America, and Europe.

This kind of uncompromised rejection of colonialist images applied to the colonized woman of African descent is expressed in the poetry of Uruguayan laborer and revolutionary Virginia Brindis de Salas. Martha K. Cobb writes of Brindis de Salas:

Hers is a militant voice. . . . She proclaims that being black is more than merely having the legacy of chattel slavery. It is also being a woman whose cultural heritage encompasses African cultural traditions which survived the ravages of slavery and provided building blocks for African-based cultures in the New World.[8]

In *Cien carceles de amor (One Hundred Prisons of Love)*, Brindis de Salas's poetry does indeed raise an insistent voice of race consciousness and racial pride that seems unprecedented in Afro-Spanish literature. Using "negra" to deny "esclava" ("I am a black woman/Not a slave woman!"),[9] Brindis de Salas calls on cross-cultural African deities with creative and avenging powers, including the snake and rainbow god, Damballah, who was also invoked in a dream in Cliff's *Free Enterprise*, where his cause and his body were trampled underfoot by suffragettes playing at revolution. In Brindis de Salas' vision, all these deities represent not a history of sporadic triumphs but a source of uncompromised power. Her poetic insistence and obvious faith recall the explosive building of revolutionary tension described in C. L. R. James's *The Black Jacobins*. Revolution in Brindis de Salas' terms cannot fail because it is waged on a spiritual level, backed by gods whose only loyalty is to their wronged revolutionary descendants. According to Brindis de Salas, right—and ultimate victory—are on the African side of the conflict. Her vision of the African woman in the Diaspora aggressively rejects, and remains undiluted by, the way in which she is perceived. Brindis de

Salas' model seems to refuse the very notion of integrating contradictory images into a meaningful whole representation of women of African descent. Instead, she reaches beyond procolonialist stereotypes to reclaim and restate herself in terms of culturally relevant, empathetic, and empowering mythatypical images.

Less self-consciously than Brindis de Salas, women who write across the African Continent and Diaspora repossess and reaffirm themselves in the context of mythatypical inheritances. Brindis de Salas's strong pro-African heritage voice becomes a broader representation of black as nurturing and white as deathly in "Lullaby," by Aquah Laluah, a pseudonym of Ghanaian Gladys May Casely-Hayford:

> Close your sleepy eyes, or the pale moonlight will steal you,
> Else in the mystic silence, the moon will turn you white.
> Then you won't see the sunshine, nor smell the open roses,
> Nor love your Mammy anymore, whose skin is dark as night.
> You will only love the shadows, and the foam upon the billows,
> The shadow of the vulture's wings, the call of mystery,
> The hooting of the night owl, and the howling of the jackal,
> The sighing of the evil winds, the call of mystery.
> Wherever moonlight stretches her arms across the heavens,
> You will follow, always follow, till you become instead,
> A shade in human draperies, with palm fronds for your pillow,
> In place of Mammy's bibini, asleep on his wee bed.[10]

Laluah's haunting imagery plays on the procolonialist equation of white as good and black as evil, pitting cross-cultural image against language as the poet subverts English to the cause of problematizing stereotypical expectations. The whiteness of the moon becomes an immediately sinister and insidiously seductive force to be resisted, as it lures the child back through the Middle Passage to his adulterated homeland and still will not let him rest or live a normal life. Clearly, safety is allegiance to the pure blackness of Mammy and resistance to the whiteness that stands out in its dangerous contrast to her. Again, as with Brindis de Salas, the figure of racial surety is the woman; it is a male child who is meant by the Fanti word "bibini." Assuming his awareness that his Mammy's love and care are good, the child or charge hearing the lullabye is being warned not to be seduced away from his rapt devotion to her, for fear that when he can no longer recognize her ("whose skin is dark as night") in himself ("the moon will turn you white"), he shall be truly lifeless and lost ("you will follow, always follow . . . a shade in human draperies.")

Cobb proposes Cuban Nancy Morejon as Brindis de Salas' poetic descendant who also embraces her African Diaspora ethnicity in her work. Yet, Morejon herself has written in unequivocal support of the Cuban nationalist goal to produce literature from which ethnicity has been expunged:

La lengua no esta ligada a la raza. . . . A veces [la cuestion tribal] logra entorpecer la urgente necesidad de afianzar la nocion de nacionalidad, tan cara a las independencias, tan indispensable en las actuales circunstancias inclinadas, en su mayor parte hacia un radical proceso revolucionario.

(The tongue is not tied to race. . . . At times it [the tribal question] manages to obstruct the urgent necessity to hold fast to the nationalist idea, so dear to independence, so indispensable to the inclination of present circumstances, for the most part toward a radical revolutionary process.)[11]

Further in her writing career, Morejon explains and displays with increasing clarity the intensity of her devotion to a Cuban nationalist ideal rather than to a racialized discovery of dynamic interaction within an ancestral community:

Los cubanos . . . nos caracterizamos por habernos propuesto la gestacion de una nacion homogenea en su misma heterogeneidad, caracterizada por un fin politico. . . mas alla de cualquier candida controversia solo cultural o racial. Somos un crisol. . . . No nos aculturamos a la espanola o a la africana. Con un espiritu altamente creador, en una busqueda constante del ser nacional y revolucionario, nos producimos como pueblo mestizo, heredero y sustentador de ambos componentes, sin ser ya mas ni africanos, ni espanoles, sino cubanos.

(Cubans . . . characterize ourselves by having propounded the gestation of a nation that is homogeneous in its very heterogeneity, characterized by a political goal . . . far beyond any naïve cultural or racial controversy. We are a melting pot. . . . We are not acculturated to the Spanish or the African. With a highly creative spirit, in a constant search for a national and revolutionary being, we produce ourselves as a mixed people, heirs and sustainers of both components, being neither African nor Spanish, but Cuban.)[12]

One wonders what is naïve: the pursuit of the right to express and explore uncompromised and possibly antinationalist aspects of racial inheritance or the willing abjuration of righting historical wrongs in one's own psyche and social milieu in the name of a nationalist ideal. Alice Walker, however, speaks spiritedly on behalf of the lack of racial consciousness evinced by young Cubans in "My Father's Country is the Poor."[13]

Yet beyond the suppression of equal rights, is not there an even more pressing need for the fullest exploration and expression of a long vilified and discounted ethnic heritage that may define otherwise inaccessible dimensions of self and lost community? Abhorred, explored, or ignored, a woman writer of African descent may always find it incumbent upon herself to define who she uniquely is and what isolating heritage it is that obtrudes itself into her works and risks value misreading in her procolonialist society.

This issue is startlingly explored in Trinidadian Marlene Nourbese Philip's short story, "Burn Sugar." "Burn Sugar" describes the gestational experience of realizing one's inescapable ties to the lives and sensate memories of ancestresses.

In the story, a woman who has moved to New York and no longer receives her mother's Christmas rum cake undertakes to painstakingly make her own. In the process of recreating the cake from memory, the protagonist revives her girlhood memories of cooking it with her mother; she also revives all the ruminations she collectively stored around the cake's creation all those years. In the shared act of reducing foodstuffs to nourishment, the protagonist undergoes the transformative experience of her symbiotic need of her mother and of becoming her mother's essence, if not image, through the pivotal rite of passage of the menstrual onset.

This linking of mother and daughter through the newly menstruating daughter's participation in food preparation is shared in Lorde's *Zami: A New Spelling of My Name*, where the grinding of pungently aromatic garlic and spices in an alembic uterine mortar with vaginal (or arguably phallic) pestle replaces Philip's aluminum (degraded to plastic in New York) bowl with whisk or spoon.[14] Both these passages demonstrate the conflated sense of self needing the nourishment of the mother in a shared act of food preparation, leading to the sensuous transition of self as mother via the menstrual allusion of passage. In the transforming, sensual experience of forcing disparate ingredients to blend, each daughter begins to perceive her own inherited transformative power through which she yearns for, fears to understand, and sees herself as becoming some timeless aspect of her mother.

Throughout "Burn Sugar"'s erratically colloquialized, immediate account, the protagonist swings between referring to her mother as "the Mother," symbolic fount of continued existence, and "Mammy," affectionate and intelligent individual who belies and defies the stereotype. Philip's use of the term "the Mother" queries D'Almeida's interpretation of that term in Bugul's *Le baobab fou (The Crazy Baobab)*. There, D'Almeida perceives the term as distancing: "[Bugul] seeks a *relationship* that would transform 'the' mother into 'her' mother."[15] In "Burn Sugar," the term "the Mother" is at once intimate and expansive, multiplying "the mother"'s significance beyond the girl's individual life and signaling her representation of lives that will plummet into the story as their cake finally clears itself of the Middle Passage.

As in devorah major's *An Open Weave*, mere contact with the memories fermenting beneath the foam of Yemaya's ocean infuses the cake—symbol and process of transition from individual through generations—with the impressions felt by the protagonist's forebears:

"Just listen—the burn sugar is something like we past, we history, and you know that smell I always tell you about?" Mammy nod her head, "I now know what it is—is the smell of loneliness and separation—exile from family and home and tribe—even from the land, and you know what else, Mammy—is the same smell of—"

"Is only a cake, child—"

"The first ones—the first ones who come here rancid and rank with the smell of fear and death. And you know what else, Mammy? is just like that funny smell of the cake when I get it—the smell never leave—it always there with us."[16]

Just as the Mother has appeared to the protagonist to supervise the making of the cake, so their ancestors have appeared and poured their lived sensations into the protagonist's life. The protagonist's identity with the nourishing mother leads to her transformative identity with the mother as ancestress and the ancestress as time-freed deity. Through this nourishing, transforming, generating, concurren, confluent identity with self, past, and myth, "Burn Sugar" dramatizes how the woman of African descent experiences and writes in dynamic communication with her own history through "this old old ritual of transformation and metamorphosis," absorbing into herself she "who was both change and constancy" in "this moment of epiphany."[17]

It is this genre-resistant insistence on a time-freed interpretation of multiple levels of community within and constantly interacting with the individual that distinguishes the writing of women of African descent. In the final analysis, when all arguments have been presented, Diaspora and Continental African women's universally repeated mythatypical symbolisms constitute their own exigent argument for unique and culturally relevant literary interpretation.

As the culture-specific analysis of Pan-African women's writings reveals both the complexity of their long-standing refusal to be a doubly colonized world community's ultimate scapegoat and the richness of their inherited and evolving self-definitions, at the same time and through the same analytic process, a wealth of literary philosophy makes itself available for the increased profundity of perception of all literatures.

Self-definition affords these writers the delicately nuanced expressions of abandonment, illusory hope, fragile variations of defeat, and the dread of finding that one has survived the unimaginable. Self-defined apprehension, the development of subject-specific tools of analysis rather than tools that render their voices perpetual objects of others' observation, magnifies and multiplies these writings' interpretive possibilities.

NOTES

1. Birago Diop, *Les contes d'Amadou-Koumba* (*The Stories of Amadou-Koumba*) (Paris: Presence Africaine, 1961), pp. 10 and 12 (my translation).

2. Eufemia Mallegui, <<Dimmi chi sono>> ("Tell Me Who I Am") in Autori Vari (Various Authors), *Mosaici d'inchiostro* (*Ink Mosaics*) (Rimini: FARA Editore, 1996), p. 41 (my translation).

3. Anty Grah, <<Cronaca di un'amicizia>> ("Chronicle of a Friendship") in Autori Vari, pp. 60-72 (my translation).

4. Deborah Gray White, "Jezebel and Mammy: The Mythology of Female Slavery," in Deborah Gray White, *Ar'n't I a Woman: Female Slaves in the Plantation South* (New York: W. W. Norton), p. 49.

5. Saundra Rice Murray, "Psychological Research Methods: Women in the African Diaspora," in Rosalyn Terborg-Penn, Sharon Harley, and Andrea Benton Rushing, Editors, *Women in Africa and the African Diaspora* (Washington, DC: Howard University Press, 1987), pp. 79-95. Paula Giddings, *When and Where I Enter: The Impact of Black Women on Race and Sex in America* (New York: Bantam Books, 1984), a psycho/socio/historical documentary whose careful reading cannot be recommended too highly.

6. Ama Ata Aidoo, quoted in Margaret Busby, Editor, *Daughters of Africa: An International Anthology of Words and Writings by Women of African Descent: From the Ancient Egyptian to the Present* (New York: Ballantine Books, 1994), p. 532.

7. Quoted in Irene Assiba D'Almeida, *Francophone African Women Writers: Destroying the Emptiness of Silence* (Gainesville: University Press of Florida, 1994), p. 43.

8. Martha K. Cobb, "Images of Black Women in New World Literature: A Comparative Approach" in Terborg-Penn, Harley, Rushing, p. 204.

9. Reprinted in Ibid., pp. 203-204 (my translation).

10. Aquah Laluah, "Lullaby" in Maureen Honey, Editor, *Shadowed Dreams: Women's Poetry of the Harlem Renaissance* (New Brunswick: Rutgers University Press, 1996), p. 114.

11. Nancy Morejon, "Poesia anonima africana" ("Anonymous African Poetry") in Nancy Morejon, *Fundacion de la imagen: ensayo (Image Foundation: Essay)* (Havana, Cuba: Editorial Letras Cubanas, 1988), p. 263 (my translation).

12. Morejon, "La cultura cubana: historia de transculturacion" ("The Cuban Culture: History of Transculturation") in Morejon, p. 190 (my translation).

13. Alice Walker, "My Father's Country is the Poor" in Alice Walker, *In Search of Our Mothers' Gardens* (New York: Harcourt Brace and Company, 1983), pp. 199-222.

14. Audre Lorde, *Zami: A New Spelling of My Name* (Freedom, CA: The Crossing Press, 1982), pp. 73-74.

15. D'Almeida, p. 48.

16. Marlene Nourbese Philip, "Burn Sugar" in Margaret Busby, p. 703.

17. Ibid.

Afterword

People's self-descriptive myths are often their most poignant, candid, and therefore vulnerable and hope-filled depictions of themselves. People claim the aspirations and the sufferings of their myths.

This work began with my realization that women writers of African descent frequently depict their heroines as motherless. Why? Does this depiction represent the lack of positive roles and, therefore, goals open to colonized women? Does it represent these women's sense of inheriting a doubly demonized womanhood, vilified and scapegoated based on both gender and race, forcing each woman to carve out an individualized niche of social well-being on her own tenuous terms?

Next came my realization that trees often fulfilled the role of the spiritual mother for these women, blatantly brought forth sometimes by conflating the absent or deceased mother or nurturing grandmother with a tree. Storms and winds often championed these women or threatened to wreak havoc on their behalf. The loss of children and the desire to be tenderly loved encircled their lives.

Literary theorists Michael duPlessis and Karla Holloway have proposed that this loss of mother and/or maternal community be examined in terms of alienation as a prerequisite condition for the epiphany of the goddess in the life of the protagonist, her community, and/or her writer. It is my sincere hope that further analysis will reveal the multiple and circular threads that bind the woman of African descent to her spiritual and material communities, weaving through the strands of her alienation to what Holloway describes as the motherless heroine's healing through learning to mother her community in turn.

Selected Bibliography

PRIMARY TEXTS

Ba, Mariama, *Une si longue lettre*. Dakar: Les Nouvelles Editions Africaines, 1987.

Bambara, Toni Cade. *The Salt Eaters*. New York: Vintage Contemporaries, 1992.

Begg, Ean. *The Cult of the Black Virgin*. London: Penguin, 1996.

Bolton, Ruthie (pseudo). *gal: a true life*. New York: Onyx, 1994.

Brent, Linda. *Incidents in the Life of a Slave Girl*. New York: Harcourt Brace Jovanovich, 1973.

Brooks De Vita, Alexis. "Wresting Order from Chaos: Reading Mythological Influences in Myriam Warner-Vieyra's *Juletane*." *The Griot*, 16.1 (Spring 1997).

Budge, E. A. Wallis. *The Gods of the Egyptians or Studies in Egyptian Mythology, Volume II*. London: Methuen and Co., 1904.

———. *From Fetish to God in Ancient Egypt*. London, 1934; reprint New York: Benjamin Blom, 1972.

Cannon, Katie G. *Black Womanist Ethics*. Atlanta: Scholars Press, American Academy of Religion, 1988.

Cliff, Michelle. *Free Enterprise*. New York: Dutton, 1993.

D'Almeida, Irene Assiba. *Francophone African Women Writers: Destroying the Emptiness of Silence*. Gainesville: University Press of Florida, 1994.

Dangarembga, Tsitsi. *Nervous Conditions*. Seattle: Seal Press, 1989.

Diallo, Nafissatou Niang. *Le fort maudit*. Paris: Hatier, 1980.

———. *Awa, la petite marchande*. Paris: EDICEF, 1981.

Fatunmbi, Awo Fa'lokun. *Ogun: Ifa and the Spirit of Iron*. New York: Original Publications, 1992.

———. *Oshun: Ifa and the Spirit of the River*. New York: Original Publications, 1993.

———. *Oya: Ifa and the Spirit of the Wind*. New York: Original Publications, 1993.

——. *Shango: Ifa and the Spirit of Lightning*. New York: Original Publications, 1993.

——. *Yemoja/Olokun: Ifa and the Spirit of the Ocean*. New York: Original Publications, 1993.

Fazel, Shirin Ramzanali. *Lontano da Mogadiscio*. Rome: DATAnews Editrice, 1994.

Gleason, Judith. *Oya: In Praise of an African Goddess*. San Francisco: Harper-Collins, 1992.

Head, Bessie. *The Collector of Treasures and Other Botswana Village Tales*. Oxford: Heinemann Educational Publishers, 1992.

Holloway, Karla. *Moorings and Metaphors: Figures of Culture and Gender in Black Women's Literature*. New Brunswick: Rutgers University Press, 1992.

Hurston, Zora Neale. *Their Eyes Were Watching God*. New York: Harper & Row, 1990.

Kafka, Phillipa. *The Great White Way: African-American Women Writers and American Success Mythologies*. New York: Garland Publishing, 1993.

Kincaid, Jamaica. *The Autobiography of My Mother*. New York: Plume, 1997.

Larsen, Nella. *Quicksand*. Deborah McDowell, ed. New Brunswick: Rutgers University Press, 1986.

——. *Passing*. Deborah McDowell, ed. New Brunswick: Rutgers University Press, 1986.

Leeming, David and Jake Page. *Goddess: Myths of the Female Divine*. New York & Oxford: Oxford University Press, 1994.

Long, Asphodel P. *In a Chariot Drawn by Lions: The Search for the Female in Deity*. Freedom, CA: The Crossing Press, 1993.

major, devorah. *An Open Weave*. New York: Berkeley Books, 1997.

McKinney-Whetstone, Diane. *Tumbling*. New York: Scribner, 1996.

Morrison, Toni. *Beloved*. New York: Plume, 1988.

Nakhjavani, Bahiyyih. "Artist, Seeker and Seer." In *Baha'i Studies/Etudes bahaies*, Volume 10. Wilmette: Baha'i Publishing Trust, 1982.

Neumann, Erich. *The Great Mother: An Analysis of the Archetype*. Trans. Ralph Manheim, Princeton: Princeton University Press, 1963.

Nwapa, Flora. *Efuru*. Oxford: Heinemann Educational Publishers International, 1978.

Perera, Sylvia Brenton. *Descent to the Goddess: A Way of Initiation for Women*. Toronto: Inner City Books, 1981.

Soyinka, Wole. *Myth, Literature, and the African World*. Cambridge, UK: Cambridge University Press, 1976; Cambridge: Canto Edition, 1992.

Steady, Filomina Chioma, ed. *The Black Woman Cross-Culturally*. Cambridge, MA: Schenkman Publishing Company, Inc., 1981.

Thompson, Robert Farris. *Flash of the Spirit: African and Afro-American Art and Philosophy*. New York: Vintage Books, 1984.

Varma, Devendra P. *The Gothic Flame*. New York: Russell & Russell, 1966.

Wahlman, Maude Southwell. *Signs and Symbols: African Images in African-American Quilts*. New York: Penguin, 1993.

Walker, Alice. *In Search of Our Mothers' Gardens: Womanist Prose*. New York: Harcourt, Brace & Company, 1983.

——. *The Color Purple.* New York: Pocket Books, 1985.

——. *Possessing the Secret of Joy.* New York: Pocket Books/Washington Square Press, 1993.

Warner-Vieyra, Myriam. *Juletane.* Paris: Presence Africaine, 1982.

——. *Femmes echouees.* Paris & Dakar: Presence Africaine, 1988.

Wilson, Harriet E. *Our Nig; or, Sketches from the Life of a Free Black.* New York: Vintage Books, 1983.

SECONDARY TEXTS

Andrews, William L., ed. *The African-American Novel in the Age of Reaction: Three Classics.* New York: Mentor, 1992.

Autori Vari. *Mosaici d'inchiostro.* Rimini: FARA Editore, 1996.

Bobo, Jacqueline. *Black Women as Cultural Readers.* New York: Columbia University Press, 1995.

Busby, Margaret, ed. *Daughters of Africa: An International Anthology of Words and Writings by Women of African Descent: From the Ancient Egyptian to the Present.* New York: Ballantine Books, 1992.

Busia, Abena. "Words Whipped Over Voids: A Context for Black Women's Rebellious Voices in the Novel of the African Diaspora." In Joe Weixlmann and Houston Baker, eds., *Studies in Black American Literature.* Greenwood, FL: Penkeville Publishers, 1988, pp. 1-43.

Butler, Octavia. *Kindred.* Boston: Beacon Press, 1988.

——. *Wild Seed.* New York: Warner Books, 1997.

Bynum, Caroline Walker. *Holy Feast and Holy Fast: The Religious Significance of Food to Medieval Women.* Berkeley: University of California Press, 1988.

Campbell, Bebe Moore. *Your Blues Ain't Like Mine.* New York: Ballantine Books, 1993.

Campbell, Joseph and Charles Muses, eds. *In All Her Names: Explorations of the Feminine in Deity.* New York: HarperCollins, 1991.

Cavendish, Richard, ed. *Man, Myth, and Magic.* New York: Michael Cavendish, 1970.

Chinweizu, Onwuchekwa Jemie, and Ihechukwu Madubuike. *Toward the Decolonization of African Literature, Volume I: African Fiction and Poetry and Their Critics.* Washington, DC: Howard University Press, 1983.

Christian, Barbara. *Black Women Novelists: The Development of a Tradition, 1892-1976.* Westport, CT: Greenwood Press, 1980.

Conde, Maryse. *Moi, Tituba, sorciere . . . noire de Salem.* Editions Mercure de France, 1986.

Connor, Kimberly Rae. *Conversions and Visions in the Writings of African-American Women.* Knoxville: The University of Tennessee Press, 1994.

Cuthbert, Margaret. *The Silent Cradle.* New York: Pocket Books, 1998.

Diop, Birago. *Les contes d'Amadou-Koumba.* Paris: Presence Africaine, 1961.

Dryden, John. *All for Love.* New York: W. W. Norton, 1993.

Ellis, Normandi, trans. *Awakening Osiris: The Egyptian Book of the Dead.* Grand Rapids: Phanes Press, 1988.

Emecheta, Buchi. *The Joys of Motherhood.* Oxford: Heinemann Educational Publishers, 1994.

Estes, Clarissa Pinkola. *Women Who Run With the Wolves: Myths and Stories of the Wild Women Archetype*. New York: Ballantine Books, 1995.

Fanon, Frantz. *Peau noire, masques blancs*. Saint Amand, France: Editions du Seuil, 1957.

Gates, Jr., Henry Louis. *Loose Canons: Notes on the Culture Wars*. New York & Oxford: Oxford University Press, 1992.

————. *The Signifying Monkey: A Theory of African-American Literary Criticism*. New York & Oxford: Oxford University Press, 1988.

Giddings, Paula. *When and Where I Enter: The Impact of Black Women on Race and Sex in America*. New York: Bantam, 1988.

Hardin, Terri, ed. *Supernatural Tales from Around the World*. New York: Barnes & Noble, 1995.

Harris, Trudier. *Exorcising Blackness: Historical and Literary Lynching and Burning Rituals*. Bloomington: Indiana University Press, 1984.

Hoch-Smith, Judith, and Anita Spring, eds. *Women in Ritual and Symbolic Roles*. New York: Plenum Press, 1978.

Honey, Maureen, ed. *Shadowed Dreams: Women's Poetry of the Harlem Renaissance*. New Brunswick: Rutgers University Press, 1996.

Hopkins, Pauline. *The Magazine Novels of Pauline Hopkins*. New York & Oxford: Oxford University Press, 1988.

James, C. L. R. *The Black Jacobins: Toussaint L'Ouverture and the San Domingo Revolution*. New York: Vintage Books, Random House, Inc., 1989.

James, Joy, and Ruth Farmer, eds. *Spirit, Space & Survival: African American Women in (White) Academe*. New York & London: Routledge, 1993.

Jones, Gayl. *Corregidora*. Boston: Beacon Press, 1986.

————. *Eva's Man*. Boston: Beacon Press, 1987.

Jordan, June. "On Richard Wright and Zora Neale Hurston: Notes Toward a Balancing of Love and Hatred." *Black World*, vol. 23 (April 1976).

Jung, Carl Gustav. W. S. Dell and Cary F. Barnes, trans., *Modern Man in Search of a Soul*. New York: Harcourt, Brace & World, 1933.

Jung, Carl Gustav, Marie-Louise von Franz, Joseph L. Henderson, Jolande Jacobi, and Aniela Jaffe. *Man and His Symbols*. New York: Doubleday and Company, Inc. 1971.

Kinsley, David. *The Goddesses' Mirror: Visions of the Divine from East and West*. Albany: State University of New York Press, 1989.

Larrington, Carolyne, ed. *The Feminist Companion to Mythology*. London: Pandora, 1992.

Lemon, Lee T., and Marion J. Reis. *Russian Formalist Criticism: Four Essays*. Lincoln & London: University of Nebraska Press, 1965.

Lorde, Audre. *The Black Unicorn: Poems by Audre Lorde*. New York: W. W. Norton & Company, Inc., 1978.

————. *Zami: A New Spelling of My Name*. Freedom, CA: The Crossing Press, 1982.

————. *Sister Outsider: Essays and Speeches by Audre Lorde*. Freedom, CA: The Crossing Press, 1984.

Mackenzie, Donald A. *Egyptian Myths and Legends*. New York: Gramercy Books,

1980.

Mauge, Conrad E. *The Yoruba World of Good and Evil.* Mount Vernon, NY: House of Providence, 1994.

McLean, Adam. *The Triple Goddess: An Exploration of the Archetypal Feminine.* Grand Rapids: Phanes Press, 1989.

Morejon, Nancy. *Fundacion de la imagen: ensayo.* Havana, Cuba: Editorial Letras Cubanas, 1988.

Morrison, Toni. *Sula,* New York: Knopf, 1973.

——. "The Site of Memory." In *Out There: Marginalization and Contemporary Cultures.* Cambridge: MIT Press, 1990.

——. *Playing in the Dark: Whiteness and the Literary Imagination.* Cambridge: Harvard University Press, 1992.

Mugo, Micere Githae. *My Mother's Poem and Other Songs.* Nairobi: East African Educational Publishers, 1994.

Naylor, Gloria. *Mama Day.* New York: Vintage Contemporaries, 1993.

Newby, Percy Howard. *The Egypt Story: Its Art, Its Monuments, Its People, Its History.* New York: Abbeville, Inc., 1978.

Petry, Ann. *The Street.* Boston: Houghton Mifflin, 1991.

Ruggiero, Guido. *Binding Passions: Tales of Magic, Marriage, and Power at the End of the Renaissance.* New York & Oxford: Oxford University Press, 1993.

Schwartz-Bart, Simone. *Pluie et vent sur Telumee Miracle.* Saint Amand, France: Editions du Seuil, 1980.

Spillers, Hortense, ed. *Comparative American Identities: Race, Sex, and Nationality in the Modern Text, Essays from the English Institute.* New York & London: Routledge, 1991.

Spivak, Gayatri Chakravorty. *In Other Worlds: Essays in Cultural Politics.* New York: Methuen, Inc., 1987.

Sweetman, David. *Women Leaders in African History.* Portsmouth, NH: Heinemann Educational Publishers International, 1984.

Terborg-Penn, Rosalyn, Sharon Harley, and Andrea Benton Rushing, eds. *Women in Africa and the African Diaspora.* Washington, DC: Howard University Press, 1987.

Walker, Barbara. *The Woman's Dictionary of Symbols and Sacred Objects.* Edison, NJ: Castle Books, 1988.

Whitmont, Edward C. *Return of the Goddess.* New York: Crossroad Publishing Company, 1990.

Wolkstein, Diane, ed. & trans. *The Magic Orange Tree and Other Haitian Folktales.* New York: Schocken Books, 1980.

Index

About the Author

ALEXIS BROOKS DE VITA is an independent scholar and researcher. In addition to her poetry and short fiction, which have appeared in numerous anthologies, Dr. Brooks De Vita has published essays in *The Griot* and *English Language Notes*, analyzing the work of writers as diverse as Morrison, Milton, and Plato.

ISBN 0-313-31068-8

90000>

EAN

9 780313 310683

HARDCOVER BAR CODE